Learn HTML5 and JavaScript for Android

Gavin Williams

Apress®

Learn HTML5 and JavaScript for Android

ISBN-13 (pbk): 978-1-4302-4347-2

ISBN-13 (electronic): 978-1-4302-4348-9

President and Publisher: Paul Manning
Lead Editor: Steve Anglin
Development Editor: Douglas Pundick
Technical Reviewer: Jim Graham
Editorial Board: Steve Anglin, Ewan Buckingham, Gary Cornell, Louise Corrigan, Morgan Ertel, Jonathan Gennick, Jonathan Hassell, Robert Hutchinson, Michelle Lowman, James Markham, Matthew Moodie, Jeff Olson, Jeffrey Pepper, Douglas Pundick, Ben Renow-Clarke, Dominic Shakeshaft, Gwenan Spearing, Matt Wade, Tom Welsh
Coordinating Editors: Corbin Collins, Christine Ricketts
Copy Editor: Vanessa Moore
Compositor: Bytheway Publishing Services
Indexer: SPi Global
Artist: SPi Global
Cover Designer: Anna Ishchenko

Distributed to the book trade worldwide by Springer Science+Business Media New York, 233 Spring Street, 6th Floor, New York, NY 10013. Phone 1-800-SPRINGER, fax (201) 348-4505, e-mail orders-ny@springer-sbm.com, or visit www.springeronline.com.

For information on translations, please e-mail rights@apress.com, or visit www.apress.com.

Apress and friends of ED books may be purchased in bulk for academic, corporate, or promotional use. eBook versions and licenses are also available for most titles. For more information, reference our Special Bulk Sales–eBook Licensing web page at www.apress.com/bulk-sales.

Any source code or other supplementary materials referenced by the author in this text is available to readers at www.apress.com. For detailed information about how to locate your book's source code, go to www.apress.com/source-code.

Dedicated to my dad, who spent hours of his retirement time reading my book and not understanding a single line of HTML/JavaScript or CSS and still finding it interesting :D.

Contents at a Glance

Contents

About the Author

 **Gavin Williams** has worked in the web industry from the age of 14, when his editor of choice was Microsoft Front Page or Notepad. Working mainly with HTML, PHP, and CSS, after finishing a computing certification, as well as several other A-levels, he took a year out before starting university to work for Agency.com as a web developer. Here, he worked with clients such as IKEA, British Airways, Channel 5, and P&G.

He then went to university to study interactive media production, where he picked up his passion for mobile and the mobile web. He won a British Interactive Media award for WiDrive, a remote control car that could be controlled over WiFi, using nothing but an iPhone. Soon after, he started Fishrod Interactive with one of his closest university friends, Siobhan Bentley, where they developed mobile web sites, apps, and interactive installations for British Sky Broadcasting, WWE, Johnson & Johnson, as well as several other smaller companies, such as Soulcialize (a cupcake company based in Crystal Palace, London) and Streetfit.tv (a street dance fitness company).

Gavin Williams is a well-rounded developer and enjoys picking up a new technology and pushing it to its extreme. Curiosity is his weakness, as he's easily distracted by new shiny things in the development world.

About the Technical Reviewer

James Graham received a Bachelor of Science in electronics with a specialty in telecommunications from Texas A&M in 1989. While still in school, he was published in the International Communications Association's 1988 issue of *ICA Communique* ("Fast Packet Switching: An Overview of Theory and Performance"). His work experience includes working as an associate network engineer in the Network Design Group at Amoco Corporation in Chicago, IL; a senior network engineer at Tybrin Corporation in Fort Walton Beach, FL; and as an intelligence systems analyst at both 16th Special Operations Wing Intelligence and HQ U.S. Air Force Special Operations Command Intelligence at Hurlburt Field, FL. He received a formal letter of commendation from the 16th Special Operations Wing Intelligence in 2001.

Introduction

Welcome to *Learn HTML5 and JavaScript for Android.* This book will provide an introduction to HTML5, JavaScript, and CSS3 for Android Browser for version 4.0 of the Android operating system (called Ice Cream Sandwich). This book will take you through how to leverage the best mobile web technologies and methodologies to develop solid mobile web sites, not just for Android but for other platforms too.

Instead of focusing on readily available frameworks and libraries, this book focuses on using vanilla JavaScript, CSS, and HTML5 in the hopes that once you complete this book, you will be competent enough to use vanilla JavaScript for mobile, as well as JavaScript mobile web frameworks.

Who This Book Is For

This book is for anybody who has some experience in web development or native mobile app development and wants to get to grips with the mobile web. You will need some knowledge of JavaScript/ActionScript or some other programming language.

How This Book Is Structured

This book is split into nine chapters.

- Chapter 1 (Getting Started): This chapter will guide you through setting up your development environment.

- Chapter 2 (An Introduction to Creating Mobile Web Apps for Android): This chapter will give you some insight into the history behind the mobile web and how it differs from desktop-based web sites. It will take you through several case studies of existing mobile web sites and explain how they could potentially be improved or changed to make them easier for the user.

- Chapter 3 (HTML5) and Chapter 4 (Starting Your Project Using HTML5): These chapters will take you through some of the new HTML5 tags, available specifically for mobile. This chapter will also show you how to encode video and audio for mobile and embed it using HTML5. After you complete the HTML5 chapter, the workshop will take you through creating the HTML foundation of your mobile web app, in the form of a movie reminder mobile web app.

- Chapter 5 (CSS3 for Mobile) and Chapter 6 (Laying the CSS3 Foundations): These chapters will show you some of the new CSS3 mobile-compatible features such as transforms, animations, shadows, and rounded corners. You will also learn how to use SASS, a CSS3 precompiler. The workshop will take you through styling your mobile web app using SASS and best practices while using the precompiler.

- Chapter 7 (JavaScript for Mobile) and Chapter 8 (JavaScript: Models, Views, and Controllers): These chapters will take you through how to use JavaScript to enhance your mobile application. There are no libraries in this chapter, such as jQuery, Sencha, or jQuery Mobile. The introductory JavaScript chapter will show you how to build a basic framework using vanilla JavaScript, and interact with canvas and audio. The workshop will take you through enhancing the mobile web app by adding paging, and communicating with a third-party API through JSONP.

- Chapter 9 (Testing and Deploying Your Mobile Web App): This chapter will show you how to test your app using QUnit and deploy it using Capistrano.

Downloading the Code

The code for the examples shown in this book is available on the Apress web site, `www.apress.com`. A link can be found on the book's information page under the Source Code/Downloads tab. This tab is located underneath the Related Titles section of the page.

Contacting the Author

Should you have any questions or comments—or even spot a mistake you think I should know about—you can contact the author at `gavin@justanotherdeveloper.co.uk`, tweet `@fishrodgavin` or visit `http://www.justanotherdeveloper.com`.

Getting Started

Prior to the launch of the first Android handset in September 2008 and the earlier release of the first iPhone handset in June 2007, there had been no immediate drive for standardization within mobile web browsers. Playing video required either Flash mobile or a low-quality 3GP version of the video. Developers avoided JavaScript, as JavaScript would have been disabled by default on the majority of mobile web browsers and others did not support JavaScript at all. One such developer, logged in at stackoverflow.com, commented that working with JavaScript was "a nightmare . . . like working with web browsers in the 90s, but with the manager expectations of tomorrow."[1]

Mobile web sites were simply Wireless Markup Language (WML) pages from the years of WAP on grayscale mobile phones, such as the Motorola V50, but with a splash of color. Not much has changed since then, and most mobile web sites still retain the same linear flow of information from top to bottom and are not very interactive. There were three reasons for this style of design.

1. WAP/GPRS and EDGE were all slow protocols that could not handle file-heavy web sites, so design and content were restricted to deliver the web site and its message quickly.

2. The resolution and aspect ratio of old handsets were terrible, such that you could barely fit any content onto the screen.

---

1 Stackoverflow.com, posted by annakata,
http://stackoverflow.com/questions/316876/using-javascript-in-mobile-web-application#316920.

3. You traditionally used a ball or keys to navigate around a mobile web site. Scrolling up and down seemed more natural than scrolling from side to side.

We are now no longer reliant on using hardware-based controls to browse content on mobile devices. The size, quality, resolution, pixel density/PPI, and color depth of screens are increasing with every new tablet and mobile phone released. We are seeing desktop browser engines, such as WebKit and Geko, being plugged into the web browsers, such as Mobile Safari, the Android Browser, and Firefox, found right on our mobile devices. This has helped developers to produce stunning mobile web sites that look and feel consistent across the now popular Android and iOS handsets and tablet devices.

In addition, the most recent mobile browsers also support GPU acceleration. This means that mobile web apps can be much more polished and interactive, as most of the rendering can now be offloaded to the graphic processor (something unheard of until a few years ago).

Given the most recent announcement of Adobe axing Flash Mobile, combined with the constant race to cram faster CPUs and RAM into mobile devices, it has never been a more exciting time to get not just into the mobile web, but also HTML5, CSS3, and JavaScript.

As a mobile web developer, you now have the chance to produce near-native applications based on existing web standards for what feels like a miniaturized laptop computer.

Don't be fooled, however; the world of the mobile web still has a long way to go in terms of standardization. So, throughout this book I will be giving you defensive programming tips to help you avoid common mistakes and misconceptions when developing for the mobile web.

Before you start, you will need a tablet and/or a mobile Android-based device to test apps with. You will also need a solid development environment to work within.

Choosing a Device to Test With

Although not essential, having a physical Android device, such as a handset and tablet, at hand will help—a lot. You can test your mobile web apps using the Android SDK or a regular web browser. There are drawbacks to this, however. The Android SDK is known for being extremely slow to start and sluggish to run; and testing on a desktop browser will not allow you to test your web app on the platform it was designed and built for.

Unlike other mobile operating systems, Android suffers from a developer's worst nightmare, known as device fragmentation. Device fragmentation can be caused by some of the following factors.

More than one device vendor produces devices for a single operating system.

Each device has varied hardware specifications and limitations.

Accelerometer

GPS

Gyroscope

Screen resolution

Pixel density (PPI)

CPU

RAM

Older devices do not support the most recent operating systems with the latest features, such as the most recent default browser with the latest APIs and rendering engines.

Because of this, it makes it extremely hard to pick a device that everybody has and to test against. To put this into perspective, see Table 1-1 for Android's device stats compared to the rest of the industry, as of December 2011.

Table 1-1. *Device Stats (As of December 2011)*

Operating System	Tablets (Including All Touch Devices)	Mobiles	Total Devices
Android	124	538	662
iOS	6	5	11
Windows Phone	0	26	26
Blackberry OS	1	90	91

Table 1-1 paints a clear picture that Android device vendors produce a wide range of devices for Android users.

In an ideal world, you should pick 12 Android devices (six mobile phones and six tablets). Also consider the following criteria.

- A high-end device ($450 or more)
    - Released within the last six months
    - Released 12–18 months ago
- A mid-range device ($150–$449)
    - Released within the last six months
    - Released 12–18 months ago
- A low-end device (less than $150)
    - Released within the last six months
    - Released 12–18 months ago

There are two main reasons why you should pick your devices in this manner.

1. Device features will vary depending on the price. For instance, more often than not, you will never see a dual core CPU in a device for under $100. You should, however, still cater to those who do not have the latest and greatest. This will allow you to test against less capable devices and make sure your mobile web app will degrade gracefully.

2. Device contracts end in cycles of 12, 18, and now 24 month. This is the ideal time for users to upgrade their handsets and for device vendors to release new hardware. Bearing this in mind, you should opt to purchase a device that users will upgrade from in 2–3 month's time. Again, this will help you test against devices and ensure that your mobile web app degrades gracefully.

If you can pick only one device, pick the latest and greatest. The device itself will last you just over a year. If you aim to upgrade your devices on a yearly cycle, you will end up with a good collection of older devices to test against and the same or similar device that your users will be using.

For the purpose of this book, I will be using an HTC Desire HD, an Asus Eee Pad, and a Samsung Galaxy smartphone.

Setting Up Your Development Environment

Now that you have chosen a device to test against, it is now time to set up your development environment.

My operating system of choice is Mac OS X Lion; however, the setup procedure for other platforms is quite similar.

I have chosen open source or free applications to develop with. All of the applications can run on Mac, Windows, or Linux.

Aptana

Aptana is an Integrated Development Environment (IDE) for web development. An IDE differs from a regular text editor, such as TextMate or BBEDIT, or web site editors such as Dreameweaver. They will provide everything you need for development out of the box and can be extended to suite your particular development style or platform.

Aptana is based on Eclipse, so can support most, if not all, Eclipse plugins; it will manage your virtual Android testing environments, perform code completion, validate your code, and deploy it for you.

To download Aptana, head over to `http://aptana.com/`. You will see the download options shown in Figure 1-1.

Figure 1-1. *Aptana download options*

Select "Standalone Version" as shown in Figure 1-1, and click the download button. Install it and proceed to installing the Android SDK.

> **NOTE:** You can alter the appearance of the editors in Aptana to suite your preference (e.g., you might want a dark or a bright theme to your IDE). To do this, simply go to Preferences. The preferences window will open. Use the filter in the top-left and type Themes. Click the themes option in the menu below the search field. The default will be Aptana Studio, but select any theme you like and click OK.

Android SDK

The Android SDK will allow you to create virtual Android environments to develop against with different hardware configurations and SDK/OS versions. There is a plugin for Eclipse that will allow you to manage, create, and configure virtual Android devices and launch them from within Aptana.

Prior to installing ADT, you will need to enable the Eclipse Helios Update Site in Aptana. This contains dependencies for the Android ADT plugin for Eclipse.

To enable the Eclipse Helios Update Site, go to Aptana Studio 3 from the Apple task bar, then choose Preferences ➤ Install/Update ➤ Available Software Sites. A screen, similar to Figure 1-2, will appear.

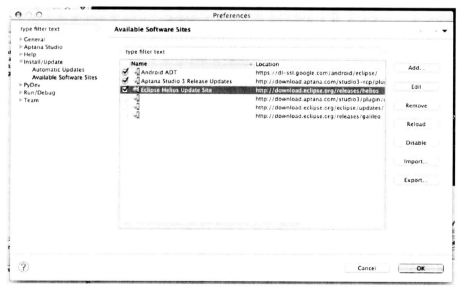

Figure 1-2. *Enabling Eclipse Helios Update Site*

To install ADT for Aptana, go to `http://developer.android.com/sdk/eclipse-adt.html#downloading`.

Follow the instructions. After you have successfully installed ADT, Aptana will restart and you will be presented with a screen similar to Figure 1-3.

Figure 1-3. *Initial ADT launch screen*

Keep all of the default options and click Next >. You can decide whether you would like to send usage data to Android, and then click Finish. Accept all of the options on the final screen and click Finish again. ADT will begin downloading the most recent SDKs, which will take a few minutes.

Now that ADT has been installed, you can install all of the SDKs to test your Android web app against. Android ADT can be found at the bottom of the Window menu, as seen in Figure 1-4.

Figure 1-4. *The new Android menus in Aptana*

Go to the Android SDK Manager. You will be presented with a list of Android SDKs to download, as shown in Figure 1-5. Expand all of the Android versions and ensure that the following options are ticked for each Android version.

- Google APIs by Google Inc.

- SDK Platform

- GALAXY Tab by Samsung Electronics

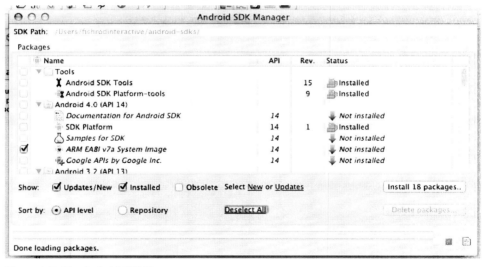

Figure 1-5. *The Android SDK Manager*

Click the install button to start the download and install process.

Select Accept All on the following screen and click Install. You should see a window similar to Figure 1-6. The process to install the SDKs can take quite a while, depending on your computer's capabilities and your Internet speed.

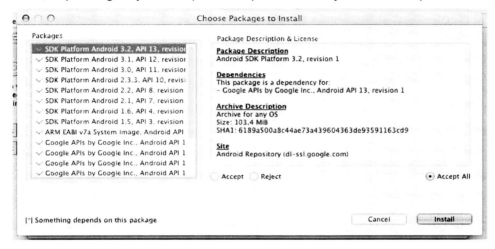

Figure 1-6. *The Android SDK Manager package installer*

After you complete these steps, you will have every version of the Android SDK to test your mobile web apps with.

SASS

SASS is a CSS preprocessor. It allows you to nest CSS rules, use variables within your CSS, reuse chunks of CSS (such as setting border radius on a group of elements with mixins), and allows CSS rules to inherit others.

SASS will be used throughout this book to write CSS. For SASS to work, the SASS Ruby gem will need to be installed.

This is reasonably simple for OS X using Terminal. Terminal can be found in Applications ➤ Utilities.

After you've opened Terminal, enter the following command:

```
sudo gem install sass
```

Enter your password and wait until the SASS gem has finished installing. To test whether SASS has successfully installed enter:

```
sass -v
```

If SASS has successfully installed, you will see SASS's version number. To install on Windows or Linux, there are installers and instructions on SASS's download page at `http://sass-lang.com/download.html`. If you do not have Ruby installed, you must install it first. Download it from `http://rubyinstaller.org/downloads/` and install. After Ruby is installed, run it from Programs ➤ Ruby [version] ➤ Start Command Prompt With Ruby. From there, run "gem install sass".

Apache

In order to test the mobile web site on Android devices outside of the development environment a web server is required. Mac OS X comes with Apache preinstalled, so it is just a case of turning it on.

In order to do this, go to System Preferences ➤ Sharing and enable Web Sharing, as shown in Figure 1-7. Click the Create Personal Website Folder button. This will create a folder for you to store your web content within your Mac account that can be viewed in a web browser. To test it, click on the link above the button. This will open your web site with a welcome page.

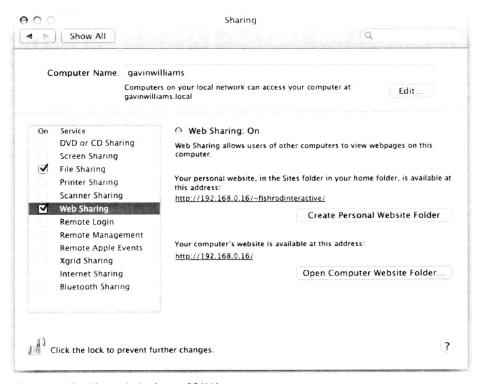

Figure 1-7. *Enabling web sharing on OS X Lion*

Summary

Now that your development environment is set up, you can start writing and testing mobile web sites for Android. This will provide you with a solid platform to develop a mobile web application on both a small and large scale.

An Introduction to Creating Mobile Web Apps for Android

Now that your development environment has been set up, you must be itching to dive into some code!

Before you begin, this chapter will take you through the basic principles of the mobile web compared to the much more traditional desktop environment.

Life would be so much simpler if you could build and deploy an application once and make it instantly available on all devices (not just Android). The mobile web aims to solve this. Native applications have their advantages, and they come into their own when they require large amounts of graphics processing, CPU, and RAM, as well as access to almost all aspects of the Android operating system.

Browser vendors such as Mozilla are attempting to change this and tip the balance in favor of web standards. By leveraging Android's native APIs, and making them available to the web developer through JavaScript APIs within the browser, we can potentially tap into the same APIs available to native application developers in the very near future. In the meantime, the introduction of HTML5 to mobile devices is helping to fill the gap while we wait, and provide a solid base to build upon. Multiple phone web-based application frameworks, such as PhoneGap, Rhomobile, and Appcelerator, will take the place of what future browsers will supply us from their draft specifications for now.

By endorsing web standards, we should be able to say that the same web application that we deploy for Android mobile handsets and tablets will also work on iOS and Windows Phone 7 handsets and tablet devices now and in the future.

This chapter will take you through a few basic principles about designing and developing for the mobile web.

> What's different about the mobile web?
>
> You will read about how the mobile web differs from desktop and ensuring that mobile users get the best experience from the controls available to them—their fingers!
>
> Catering to your audience
>
> Here you will read about how audience affects how you design and lay out your mobile web site, how to prioritize content, and deliver the best functionality for your target audience.
>
> Web vs. native apps
>
> If you are standing on the fence as to whether to develop purely native apps, hybrid apps, or pure web apps, then this will take you through the advantages and disadvantages of each solution.
>
> The first line of code: Hello World
>
> This final section will take you through the building blocks of your application, such as setting up ANT for automatic deployment, and building and compressing SASS/CSS files and JavaScript.

What's Different About the Mobile Web?

Catering to a potential audience of 365.4 million permanently connected users makes the mobile web one of the most exciting platforms to develop for. Creating web applications for the desktop environment can be satisfying. However, users are limited to a single pointing device and a keyboard to interact with your work. The mobile web brings a whole new world of possibilities. The mobile device serves as a blank canvas for interactive elements that users can simply touch to interact with. As a developer, you can create a much more intimate experience with the user by taking over the entire screen and immersing them in your mobile web application's world.

Unfortunately, for all of the real-world advantages that the mobile web brings, there are the same development and user experience stumbling blocks found in the desktop environment that you will face while the platform continues to develop.

Object/Feature Detection

The fragmentation in APIs available to developers on the mobile web can be a problem. The most common solution to fixing discrepancies in APIs across browsers has been to use JavaScript to detect browsers, or devices, and serve different stylesheets or execute certain pieces of JavaScript depending on the browser being used. This method is known as *User Agent (UA) sniffing* or *browser sniffing*. Listing 2-1 shows a common UA sniffing script.

Listing 2-1. *JavaScript Code Used for UA Sniffing*

```
// Get the user agent string
var browser = navigator.userAgent;

// Check to see whether Firefox is not in the string
if(browser.match(/Firefox/) === null){

    // If it's not Firefox, send the user to another page
    window.location.href = "sendstandardmessage.html";

} else {

    // If it is, use the Mozilla SMS API to send an SMS
    navigator.mozSms.send("01234567891", "My Message");

}
```

What could possibly be wrong with UA sniffing? While you will provide support for Firefox and a fallback for other browsers, you will fail to support browsers that might have the same APIs available as Firefox.

This particular API is also only available in Firefox 11+, so you will also need to ensure that the version is included in the UA sniffing script.

As you begin to increase the granularity of your browser detection scripts, you also decrease maintainability and increase complexity by having to constantly update your sniffing code to account for new browsers and versions. Before you know it, your JavaScript library becomes unmaintainable spaghetti code.

A better way to do this is through object detection. The revised code can be seen in Listing 2-2. First, we find out whether the SMS API exists. If it doesn't exist, we send the user to another page; if it does, then we can send our SMS.

Listing 2-2. *JavaScript Code Used for Object Detection*

```
// Check to see whether navigator.mozSms is an object (if it exists)
if (typeof navigator.mozSms === "object"){

    // If it does, send a message using the built-in SMS API
    navigator.mozSms.send("01234567891", "My Message");

} else {

    // If it doesn't, send the user to another location
    window.location.href = "sendstandardmessage.html";

}
```

The method of object detection also allows us to provide fallbacks for browser specific API's. The Firefox 11 nightlies currently only supports the SMS API, but there may be other browsers and other devices in the future that may support the same implementation through different methods or classes.

We can turn this into a feature of our application using a class. We can delegate the sending of the message within a method as seen in Listing 2-3. This should in theory allow us to use our own API's to send messages within our application. When browser vendors add the SMS API to their browser, we only need to add the method to a single location rather than find and replace it in the entire application.

Listing 2-3. *Using Delegation to Send a Message with Our Own Web Service As a Fallback*

```
var Message = function Message(message, recipient){

    this.message = message;
    this.recipient = recipient;

    this.sendSMS = function sendSMS(recipient){

        if(typeof navigator.mozSms === "object"){

            // Send SMS using the user's mobile phone
            navigator.mozSms.send(this.recipient, this.message);

        } else if (typeof navigator.otherSms === "object") {

            // Use another browser's SMS implementation
            navigator.otherSms.sendMessage(this.message, this.recipient);
```

```
        } else {

            // If sending via the user's mobile isn't possible,
            // send the message using a third-party web service
            this.ajaxSend(this.recipient, this.message);

        }

    }

    function ajaxSend(recipient, message){
        // Send the SMS using a web-based SMS gateway via Ajax
    }

}

var messageInst = new Message("my message!", "01234567891");
messageInst.sendSMS();
```

As you can see from Listing 2-3, no matter what the capability of the browser, we can use object detection to ensure the user gets the same or similar experience regardless of what the device is capable of.

Detecting these niche features using JavaScript can be quite easy. But what about testing for CSS3 or HTML5 capabilities, and providing backward compatibility for features such as CSS3 animations and 3D transforms?

A JavaScript library called Modernizr can help to facilitate this for you. It uses the same object detection methods to detect the HTML/CSS/JavaScript capabilities of the user's web browser.

It modifies the DOM (Document Object Model) by adding classes to the HTML tag in order to provide hooks for your own CSS and JavaScript feature detection. Figure 2-1 shows this in action on haz.io. This will be covered in more detail in Chapter 7.

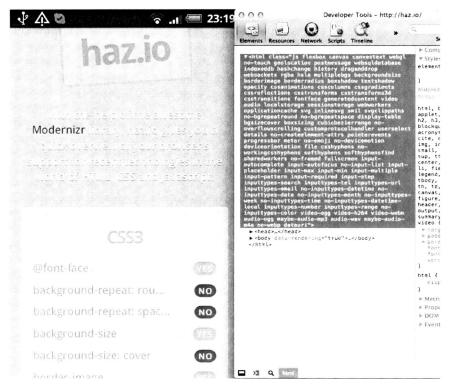

Figure 2-1. *Using Modernizr to detect features on haz.io*

Screen Sizes and Pixel Density

When developing a mobile web application, you might want to create a single application that has the same functionality for both tablet devices and mobile devices, but present a different view or layout to make use of the extra space or orientation of the device. Media queries can help to facilitate this.

Using a combination of media queries and elastic design, you can produce views that respond to the display of the user, rather than detecting the user's type of device and providing a view for it. This is known as *responsive web design*.

This method of development is much more elegant than deciding how a user should view your web site based on the *type* of device that they are using. Instead you focus on the available *space* and pixel density available.

Pixel density is a concept that allows mobile devices with the same physically sized screens, to vary in resolution due to the number of pixels available per square inch.

Android devices are divided into three categories of pixel density:

  Low

  Medium

  High

How does this affect your mobile web application? When you produce images for a normal web site, you produce a single image that will not scale and work across all screen types, as the layout will scale with the image itself to fit a fixed width or elastic layout.

For the mobile web, you will generally create a mobile application to fit the entire viewport and have the same dimensions regardless of what the device's pixel density may be.

For instance, if you make an image 500 px wide for a low pixel density screen, it will appear smaller on a high-density screen. This is because 500 px will not occupy as much space on the high-density screen as it does on the low-density screen.

The solution to this for mobile browsers is to scale images up or down, depending on the target density. For instance, if you develop your application for a medium-density screen, the browser will scale the image down for low-density screens and up for high-density screens. This causes an overhead when scaling the images either way, and pixelation when scaling the image up and potential distortion when scaling the image down.

To get around this, we can both create our applications exclusively for high-density screens, and allow the mobile to scale images down. This can be very expensive in terms of CPU/GPU and network activity. Both of these factors can have an impact on rendering time and potentially the user's pocket with unnecessary assets being downloaded. Or we can use media queries to ensure that the correct content gets delivered for the correct type of display. In order to do this, you must set the `target-densitydpi` property of the `viewport` meta tag to `device-dpi` and import pixel density–specific stylesheets using media queries, as shown in Listing 2-4.

Listing 2-4. *Using Media Queries for Pixel Density–Specific Styling*

```
// Set the viewport to match the devices pixen density and width
<meta name="viewport" content="target-densitydpi=device-dpi, width=device-width"
/>

// Pull in the main stylesheet
<link rel="stylesheet" media="screen" href="mobile.css" />

// Pull in high, medium, and low stylesheets to provide pixel density
// specific images
<link rel="stylesheet" media="screen and (-webkit-device-pixel-ratio: 1.5)"
href="hdpi.css" />
<link rel="stylesheet" media="screen and (-webkit-device-pixel-ratio: 1.0)"
href="mdpi.css" />
<link rel="stylesheet" media="screen and (-webkit-device-pixel-ratio: 0.75)"
href="ldpi.css" />
```

As you can see in Listing 2-4, the pixel ratios for each category of display are as follows.

- Low: 0.75

- Medium: 1.0

- High: 1.5

We use a generic mobile stylesheet so that we can provide fallback images just in case a device doesn't match any of the pixel ratios. We then use the stylesheets for each pixel density category to override the images.

Pixel density can be a pain, as it means that for every image that you use within your application, you must produce two more in varying sizes. It also means that even if you create graphics for the highest pixel density available today, tomorrow you will probably have to re-export everything for another display with a much higher pixel density. Be sure to bear this in mind when choosing graphics packages to create your mobile web designs.

Catering to Your Audience

It is as important to remember whom you are writing your application for just as much as what they will be using to interact with your work. The first step is ensuring that you understand what your users will be doing with your application. To do so, you must categorize it.

Categorizing your application will help you to formulate general interaction rules based on how other applications within your category are designed and what features they have. This might sound like copying, but it will help users to quickly and intuitively figure out how to use your application based on their previous experiences and, thus, get it up and running in the least amount of time.

It is important to remember that you can build on top of these rules and you do not have to stick to them. As long as you can get your users to open your mobile web application, play with it for several minutes, and immediately say "I get it," you have done your job.

There are many categories for mobile web applications, but most of them will fall under the following.

- Task based
- Social
- Entertainment

Task Based

Task-based applications are quite simple in their nature. They are built as time savers for everyday use. This can be anything from finding train times to finding out where the closest pub or bar is.

There are times when I have stood in the middle of the London Waterloo train station staring at train time boards, looking dazed and confused, only to whip out my handset to launch the Train Times app to find train times quicker.

The important thing to remember is that if a user cannot perform a task in the least amount of time with your application, they will close your browser window and find another that can perform the same task much quicker.

For task-based applications, there are two basic pieces of information you can use to help a user perform a task faster.

- Where is the user?
- What device are they using?

These two key pieces of information are readily available to your application and knowing them will make all the difference.

Finding out the physical location of the user and what they are doing will help you to preempt what the user is going to do when they go to your mobile web application.

As an example, if you are creating a journey planner, there are several things about your user that you should take into consideration.

Where is the user? Do they have limited network connectivity (e.g., 3G/EDGE or, even worse, GPRS).

Is the user on the move? Do they have time to fill out a form while walking and using their thumbs to input data?

These factors affect not just how you present interactive elements, such as input forms, but how you write code to reduce the amount of effort the user has to make to complete the task ahead.

In Figures 2-2 and 2-3, you can see how much of a difference knowing and using a user's location and understanding their situation can make when creating a location-based utility application.

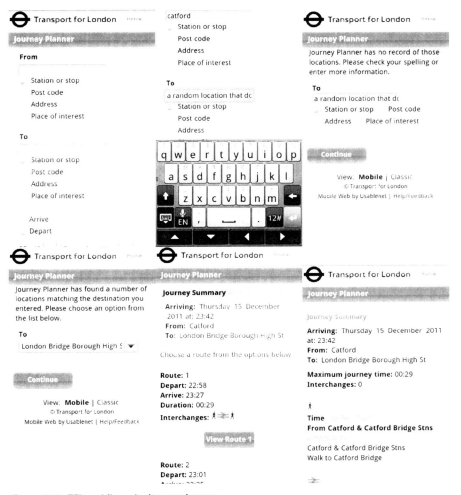

Figure 2-2. *TFL mobile web site user journey*

In Figure 2-2 you can see the TFL Journey Planner mobile web site. The user journey above depicts a worst-case scenario. This user is on the move, and is prone to making data entry mistakes. As a result of this, the user must go through two extra page loads with more form fields in order to complete the task.

What is wrong with having two extra pages to help the user with validation? Two extra pages will equate to 4+ seconds of loading time over 3G. You must also factor in the time required for a user to process the page and respond to it.

How can we improve the TFL mobile web site?

- Increase the feedback loop. We can provide suggestions to the user as they enter from/to locations using autocomplete. They can then select a suggestion that suits them to prefill the journey planner form fields.

- We can use the user's current location as a suggestion for a start/end point of their journey.

- If we use local storage, we can also suggest to the user a list of recent destinations. For example, if we know that they have just planned a journey to get to somewhere, there's a big chance that they will want to know how to get back when they reopen the mobile web application.

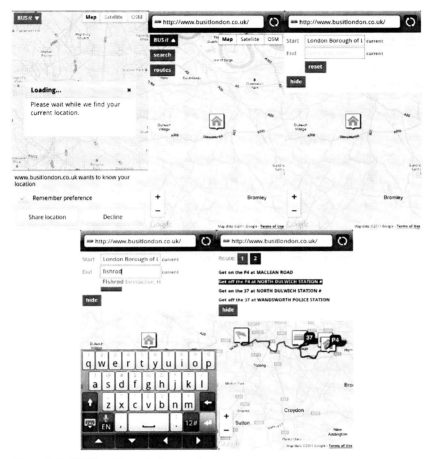

Figure 2-3. *BUSit mobile web site user journey*

Figure 2-3 shows a good example from busitlondon.co.uk. Upon first launching the mobile web application, it will attempt to find your current location for you. As users type Start and End locations, it will suggest options for the user to select using the Google Maps API and autocomplete. You also always have the option available to select the user's current location.

After you have planned your destination, it will then suggest routes to you. All of this information is contained on a single page with no page reloads. A user can easily change or modify the view without having to wait for graphics (apart from map tiles) to load. This offers more of a "native application" look and feel.

Social

A social application's primary goal is to facilitate the ability to connect and communicate with friends or other people of interest. The time spent interacting with social mobile web applications is usually significantly higher than time spent using utility-based applications.

The primary goals for social media applications are usually threefold.

> Users visit to consume content.

> Users visit to contribute content.

> Users visit to participate.

These three fundamental rules underpin nearly every social mobile application available today. If users do not contribute content, there will be no content for other users to consume and participate with.

Just because users spend more time on social mobile web applications does not mean that the path to complete a task, such as sharing content, should be any more different than that of a task-based application. The same considerations for the user's situation should be accounted for. It should be both easy to share content and easy to consume content.

As an example, Twitter and Facebook are poles apart in terms of feature set, but the primary goal for both applications on the mobile web is to make it easy for users to consume, contribute, and participate.

Figure 2-4 shows three screens from the Facebook touch-based mobile web site (to the left). Upon login, you are presented with the Facebook news feed, so you can immediately consume content. You are also presented with three clear and distinct buttons to share content such as your status, photos, and current location (check-in). You also have a toolbar at the top to provide you with content and updates related specifically to you (Friend Requests, Messages, and Notifications) in the form of modal menus or pop-outs. Further features are in the hidden menu, which leaves scope to add more secondary features and actions without cluttering the rest of the application.

Figure 2-4. *Facebook Touch and Twitter mobile web sites make it easy to share and consume content.*

Twitter's core functionality can be found in its top toolbar. A clear action button to share content is highlighted in blue with a distinctive icon. Upon logging in, the user knows that this is a button to share content if they have used the twitter web site. This same design pattern now resonates through the desktop, mobile, and web versions of Twitter.

Entertainment

Entertainment-based applications are primarily created to satisfy a need to overcome some form of boredom. The solution to this comes in many forms, from the obvious games to delivering music and video content. Entertainment applications are usually designed to immerse the user within the application's environment. This can be achieved even with the most basic HTML5 games available on the mobile web today.

Web Apps vs. Native Apps

A cause for great debate and discussion during the past few years has been whether to build a project as a native app or a mobile web app. There are advantages and disadvantages to both. However, it is important to remember that the solution you choose should be picked based on the requirements for your specific project and your own capabilities as a developer. Most importantly, pick the solution that will get your project finished the quickest!

There are a few factors that will help you make the decision as to whether to create a mobile web app or a native application.

- Whether you already know how to develop for the target platform

- Whether your application relies on network connectivity or some form of dynamic data stored online

- What type of device features your application relies on (e.g., GPS, Accelerometer, Gyroscope, Address Book, Calendar, intensive CPU/GPU operations)

- Whether there is scope within your project to port functionality to other platforms now or in the future (e.g., iOS, Blackberry, Windows Phone, desktop)

- How frequently you will be releasing the application, and how you will handle users not updating your application on their devices

- Time and budget

If you know how to develop using web standards already, then a mobile web app might be the best solution. However, if you can develop for the target platform already, it might be advantageous to make a native application. This will, however, ever so slightly close the door to making an application that will work on other platforms, as the same app will need to be re-created for all platforms unless you use a cross-platform application framework such as Marmalade.

Making a mobile web app can be a cost effective way to test or prototype your application across all platforms before turning it native. By using analytics, you can see which platforms you should target with a native app. By doing user research, you can see whether creating a native application with platform-specific features will be advantageous to your users.

If your application relies on APIs that cannot be accessed through the web browser, such as the Phone Book, Calendar, Gyroscope, or Accelerometer, then a mobile web application might be out of the question, as these APIs are not currently available through most mobile web browsers.

If your application relies on dynamic data, it might be a sensible choice to develop an application using web standards, as you can use Ajax to quickly deliver content to your application over the network. You can also cache and store files with a mobile web application, so your application can still be used offline when there is no network connectivity.

If you frequently provide updates to your mobile application, you might experience issues with users not updating to the latest version as often as you would like. By creating a mobile web application, you can simply push updates to your web server, and all of your users will instantly have the latest version of your application.

In Figure 2-5 you can see how the Twitter native application (left) and mobile web application (right) show the difference between a social application as a native application and as a mobile web application. As you can see, there is no real difference. The main feature to be dropped in the mobile web application is the ability to share content using third-party native applications. Twitter has also removed the ability to share photos on the mobile web application. Object/feature detection could provide the ability to upload photos on certain devices.

Figure 2-5. *Twitter native application (left) and Twitter mobile web application (right)*

The information gathered so far in this section should help you decide whether to go native or mobile web.

There is, however, a third option. Multiple phone web-based application frameworks, such as PhoneGap, Appcelerator, and Rhomobile, will allow you to build your applications in XHTML/JavaScript and CSS, but leverage some of the APIs that might only be available to native web apps.

These frameworks provide a web view for you to develop your app within, and provide a proxy to the mobile's APIs by using JavaScript as a bridge between the two. Figure 2-6 shows the structure of multiple phone web-based application frameworks.

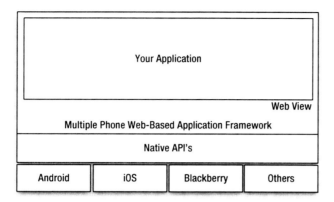

Figure 2-6. *The structure of a multiple phone web-based application framework*

Deploying your mobile web application this way leads you to new opportunities. We know that at some point, mobile web browsers will provide APIs to interact with third-party applications and take advantage of the mobile device's hardware such as CPU/GPU and camera. So it makes sense to continue development for the browser. However, multiple phone web-based application frameworks help to bring the APIs and services that are available to native applications to web applications as well.

By building your application in this manner, you can build once and deploy a mobile web application that has limited functionality. You can then progressively enhance that same application using object/feature detection within a multiple phone web-based application framework as a native application. This gives you the best of both worlds.

The First Line of Code: Hello World

It's now time for you to write your first line of code. In this Hello World application, you will simply create an HTML web page with "Hello World!" and display it on the Android Virtual Device.

Setting Up

Start by opening Aptana Studio. You will need to create a new project, so go to File ➤ New ➤ Web Project.

You will be presented with a screen similar to the one in Figure 2-7. Enter a project name and click Finish. I have chosen Chapter-2 as mine.

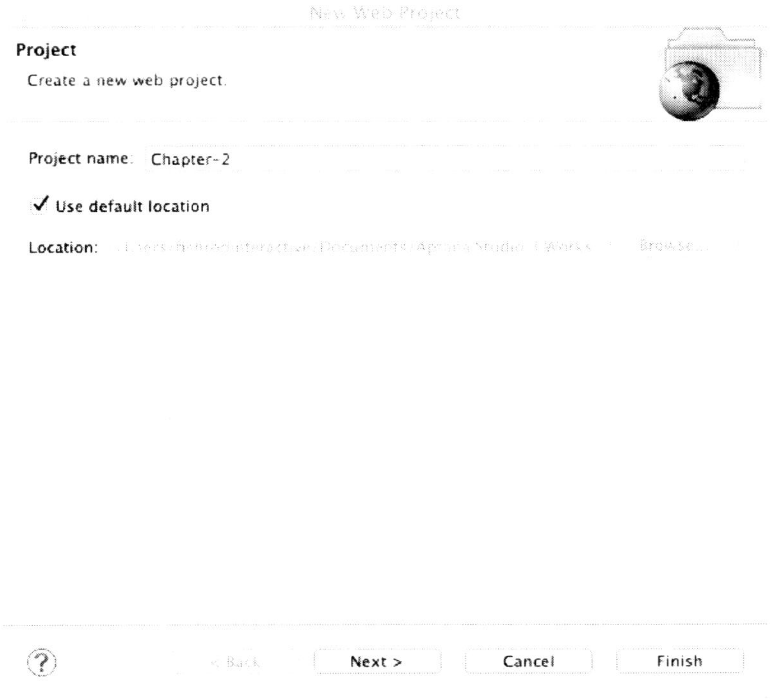

Figure 2-7. *Aptana's New Web Project wizard*

This will create a new empty project in Aptana. The new project will appear in the App Explorer panel on the left-hand side.

HTML

Writing for the mobile web is not dissimilar to writing for desktop web applications. We'll start by creating a basic HTML5 document.

Create a new file in much the same way as creating a new folder, except select File instead of Folder. Name this file index.html. It's important to make sure that this file exists in the root of your project. The following code will form the basis of our HTML file.

Listing 2-5. *HTML Source Code for Hello World!*

```
<!DOCTYPE html>
<html lang="en-GB" dir="ltr">

    <head>

        <meta charset="UTF-8" />
        <meta name="viewport" content="width=device-width; initial-scale=1.0;
        maximum-scale=1.0; user-scalable=0; target-densitydpi=device-dpi;"/>
        <title>My First Mobile Web App</title>

    </head>

    <body>

        <h1>Hello World!</h1>

    </body>

</html>
```

If you are not familiar with some of the HTML elements shown in Listing 2-5, the first line is the new HTML5 doctype. In HTML5, you do not need to specify a DTD, which can usually be found in XHTML 1.1 pages. Listing 2-6 shows the difference between an XHTML 1.1 doctype declaration and an HTML5 doctype declaration.

Listing 2-6. *The Difference Between an XHTML 1.1 Doctype Declaration and an HTML5 Doctype Declaration*

```
<!-- HTML4 Doctype Decleration -->
<!DOCTYPE html PUBLIC "-//W3C//DTD XHTML 1.1//EN"
"http://www.w3.org/TR/xhtml11/DTD/xhtml11.dtd">

<!-- HTML5 Doctype Decleration -->
<!DOCTYPE html>
```

As you can see, there is now no need to Google or memorize the location of the DTD path or specify the HTML version.

In the HTML tag, I have added two attributes: `<html lang="en-GB" dir="ltr">`. lang will specify the language used within the document, and `dir` dictates the reading direction. `dir` has been set to `ltr` for left to right, and lang has been set to en-GB for English - Great Britian.

Proceeding to the head element, there are two meta tags, as shown in Listing 2-7.

Listing 2-7. *Meta Elements from the Source Code*

```
<meta charset="UTF-8" />
<meta name="viewport" content="width=device-width; initial-scale=1.0; maximum-
scale=1.0; user-scalable=no; target-densitydpi=device-dpi;"/>
```

The first meta tag specifies the character set used within the document. This should usually be UTF-8, which will cover the majority of language characters.

The second meta tag is specifically used to control the layout or viewport on mobile web sites. With this meta tag, we can set the width of the page to be the same, smaller, or bigger than the viewport (visible area of the browser screen) using the width property.

You can also use this tag to control how much a user can zoom into your web application with the initial-scale and maximum-scale properties.

The user-scalable property is a flag used to enable or disable users from pinching or tapping to zoom into or out of your mobile web application.

Finally, the target-densitydpi property is used to dictate how the web page should scale based on the pixel density of the user's screen. Setting this property to device-dpi will prevent images from automatically scaling up for devices with a high pixel density or down for devices with a low pixel density. This helps to prevent pixilation in images commonly found when images are scaled by the device. In Chapter 3, you will discover how to use media queries to prevent images from becoming pixelated on high/medium and low-density devices. Listing 2-8 shows the full definition for the viewport meta tag.

Listing 2-8. *Full Viewport Meta Tag Definition*

```
<meta name="viewport"
   content="
     height = [pixel_value | device-height] ,
     width = [pixel_value | device-width ] ,
     initial-scale = float_value ,
     minimum-scale = float_value ,
     maximum-scale = float_value ,
     user-scalable = [yes | no] ,
     target-densitydpi = [dpi_value | device-dpi |
                         high-dpi | medium-dpi | low-dpi]
   " />
```

Listing 2-9 shows the `<title />` tag, which contains the title of the page.

Listing 2-9. *Title Tag*

```
<title>My First Mobile Web App</title>
```

Finally, as shown in Listing 2-10, within the body, there is an `<h1 />` tag containing the text "Hello World!".

Listing 2-10. *Title and Link Tags*

```
<body>

    <h1>Hello World!</h1>

</body>
```

Testing

Before continuing, you should create an Android Virtual Device (AVD) using the Android SDK in Aptana to test your web site and to see its progress. For the purpose of this chapter, you will create a simple AVD with minimal functionality.

Start by going to Window ➤ AVD Manager, as shown in Figure 2-8.

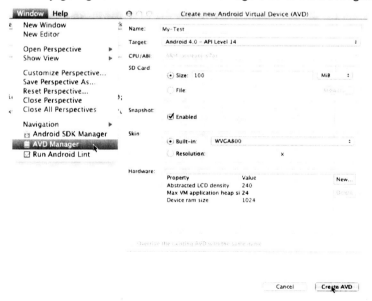

Figure 2-8. *Creating a new Android Virtual Device*

When the AVD dialog window appears, click new, which can be found on the right-hand side of the window.

In the Create new Android Virtual Device (AVD) dialog box, use the following parameters.

- Name: My-Test

- Target: Android 4.0 – API Level 14

- SD Card: Size: 100 MiB

- Snapshot: Enabled

- Skin: Built-in: WVGA800

- Hardware:

    - Abstracted LCD density: 240

    - Max VM application heap size: 24

    - Device ram size: 1024

After all options have been set, click the Create AVD button. Your new AVD will appear in the Android Virtual Device Manager. Select it and click Start. A new dialog will appear, in which you should accept the defaults and click Launch. The AVDs are known to be extremely slow to start and run. There are alternatives, but they will not be covered in this book.

After several minutes, you should have a virtual Android device up and running. Click the Internet icon to launch the browser.

You now need to deploy your application to your web server. In the Chapter 3, you will find out more about automatically deploying your application, but for now you can use Aptana to export the project to the appropriate folder. Go to File ➤ Export. In the Export dialog, select General ➤ File System and click Next. Select Chapter-2 and select Browse in the "To directory". Browse to your Sites folder within your home directory and select Open. Click Finish and Aptana will begin to publish documents to that directory.

You can now visit the web site using the AVD's built-in browser and the URL you took a note of in Chapter 1 (`http://your-ip-address/~username/Chapter-2/`). If everything is working, as it should, you should see what is shown in Figure 2-9 inside the AVD's screen.

Hello World!

Figure 2-9. *Hello World!*

Summary

In this chapter, you should have learned about the three different types of web applications: task based, social, and entertainment.

You should have an understanding as to how users may interact with your application. You should have an understanding of how to take a user's potential situation into consideration when developing mobile web applications beyond this book, and how this can impact your features, design, and user experience.

This chapter should have given you an insight into best practices in JavaScript development, as well as scratching the surface of responsive design.

Finally, this chapter should have given you some bearings on whether to start your project as a native, web, or multiple phone web-based application framework project.

HTML5

With the demand to produce cross-platform mobile applications, HTML5 has never been so important to the mobile industry. It is one of the best candidates for creating simple, yet feature rich applications that can be built and deployed once to support every major smartphone handset and tablet device available today.

The common misconception for HTML5-based applications is that they can be slow, unresponsive, and do not live up to the speed and quality that users have come to expect of native mobile applications. This is only half true, as you might have seen from the previous chapter; it depends on the type of application being built. For example, the Financial Times app available on the App Store appears to be a native application. However, if you look closely, you will see that the Financial Times app is simply the Financial Times mobile web app (app.ft.com) wrapped in a WebView within the native app.

As you can see from Figure 3-1, both apps for the iPhone and Android look similar. Putting aside several platform-specific enhancements brought out by the UI, they are in fact the same application.

> **NOTE:** There is nothing wrong with building a web app and exposing it to the various app markets using multiple phone web-based application frameworks such as PhoneGap. It increases exposure for your application and makes it more accessible to your users. Making your applications in this way can also provide you with an immediate solution should the App Store's terms and conditions change to not be in your favor.

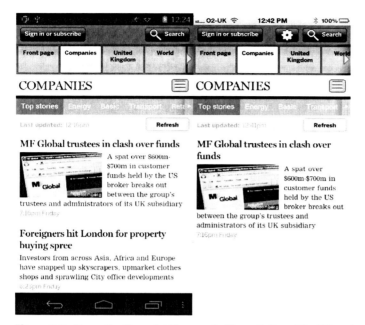

Figure 3-1. *The native Financial Times android app (left) and the iOS web app (right)*

In this chapter, you will learn the key fundamentals of HTML5 and how to leverage it for the mobile web.

You will also learn how to encode video and audio content for mobile and the types of services that are available to facilitate the delivery of that content to your users.

The chapter will go into more depth on how to use media queries to style your content based on screen attributes.

Finally, you will learn about the new form elements and how to hint at certain types of input data to affect the keyboard in the browser.

What's New?

HTML5 has made a significant leap from HTML4/XHTML1.1. It provides new HTML tags such as header, footer, hgroup, nav, section, and article in a step to improve the way we mark up documents. This has allowed us to produce more meaningful and machine-readable content. For example, we can now use <. Along with this, HTML5 also brings the standardization of access to APIs, such as geolocation, canvas, web sockets, and web storage.

There are many new changes to the HTML5 spec, but for this chapter, we will focus on the changes that are applicable to mobile.

The changes in the HTML5 spec will be apparent in code examples provided. But you may ask yourself, what's the point? Your users will see the same thing regardless of whether you use the new HTML5 elements. There are several reasons why making this change will have an impact on your users.

You can produce cleaner code that is easier to maintain.

Machine consumers will have an easier time reading and understanding your code. Machines include search engine bots, browser plugins, and features that rely on understanding how your document's content is structured.

You don't have to define as many classes and IDs within your document. You can rely more on the cascade to do much of the work for you.

NOTE: Although the examples do not show `<body />`, `<html />`, or `<head />` tags, all elements can be placed within the body of the document unless otherwise specified.

`<article />`

The `<article />` element is used to represent independent content on a page, such as a blog post, news article, or comment. In principle, an article should contain its own header, content, and footer. You may also nest information about the article's author within the element. You can also nest article elements within another article element to help further structure content such as article comments.

Figure 3-2 shows where an `<article />` element may be placed in relation to an HTML5 document. Listing 3-1 shows the structure of some basic HTML5 elements, and where the `<article />` element fits into this hierarchy.

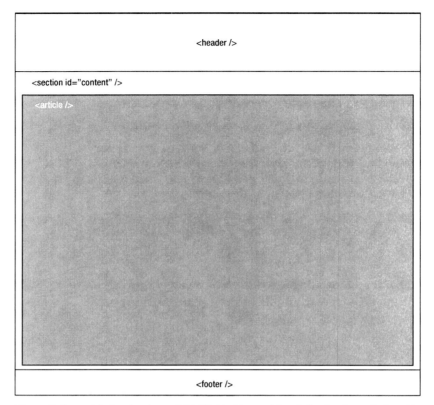

Figure 3-2. *⟨article /⟩ element (highlighted in gray) in relation to elements found in a mobile web site document*

Listing 3-1. *Proposed Structure of an Article in HTML5*

```
<article>

    <header>

        <h1>Article Title</h1>

        <p>

            Created by Daniel Carpenter on
            <time pubdate="2012-03-15">March 15<sup>th</sup> 2012</time>

        </p>

    </header>
```

```
<p>Article Content</p>

<footer>

    <address>

        <p>

            Written by
            <a rel="author" href="mailto:daniel.carpenter@somewhere.com">
                Daniel Carpenter
            </a>

            <br />

            Follow him on
            <a rel="author" href="http://www.twitter.com/mrdanc">Twitter</a>

        </p>

    </address>

</footer>

</article>
```

The elements shown in Listing 3-1 appear to have meaning. The <header /> element contains all of the header information related to the article, such as the title, author, and the time of publishing. Notice that the content within the article does not need to be wrapped in another element. Finally, the <footer /> contains information about the author, which is nested within an <address /> element.

Compare this to Listing 3-2, which shows how you might have written this in previous versions of HTML.

Listing 3-2. *Proposed Structure of an Article in HTML4 and Prior*

```
<div class="article">

    <div class="header">

        <h1>Article Title</h1>

        <p>

            Created by Daniel Carpenter on
            <span class="published">March 15<sup>th</sup> 2012</span>

        </p>

    </div>

    <p>Article Content</p>

    <div class="footer">

        <div class="author-details">

            <p>

                Written by
                <a rel="author" href="mailto:daniel.carpenter@somewhere.com">
                    Daniel Carpenter
                </a>

                <br />

                Follow him on
                <a rel="author" href="http://www.twitter.com/mrdanc">Twitter</a>

            </p>

        </div>

    </div>

</div>
```

As you can see from Listing 3-2, there is no real apparent structure to the markup. There are a lot of divs with classes associated with them; however, there is no real standard for creating a document like this.

<aside />

The `<aside />` element can be used to represent content unrelated to the main content of the web site, such as tweets, related links, tags, and navigation elements. These normally appear to the left or right side of the document, as shown in Figure 3-3.

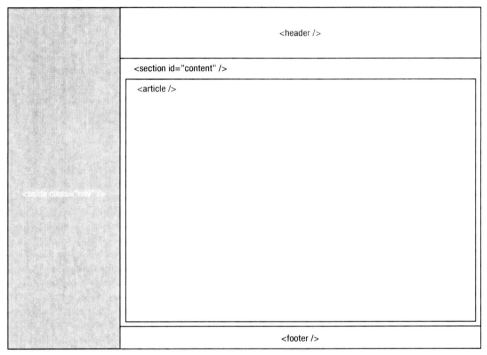

Figure 3-3. *Structure of a document with the `<aside />` element (highlighted in gray)*

We can make use of the aside element for mobile by hiding it based on the screen size, and revealing it when a user clicks a button to show it. This design pattern can be found on the facebook mobile web app, and will be explored in more depth with the workshop in Chapter 4.

Listing 3-3 shows how the aside element should be used, and Listing 3-4 shows how you might have written the same code in HTML4.

Listing 3-3. *Proposed Structure of Aside in HTML5*

```
<aside>

    <nav>

        <h2>Places To Go</h2>

        <ul>

            <li><a href="somewhere">Somewhere</a></li>

            <li><a href="somewhere-else">Somewhere Else</a></li>

        </ul>

    </nav>

</aside>

<section class="content">

    <!-- Your Content Goes Here -->

</section>
```

As you can see from Listing 3-3, we use the `<aside />` element to house navigation for the web site, as it exists outside of the content section defined by the `<section class="content" />` element. The `<aside />` element would be floated to the left of the content.

The same markup written for HTML4 would look like Listing 3-4.

Listing 3-4. *Proposed Structure of Aside in HTML4*

```
<div class="sidebar">

    <div class="navigation">

        <ul>

            <li><a href="somewhere">Somewhere</a></li>

            <li><a href="somewhere-else">Somewhere Else</a></li>

        </ul>

    </div class="navigation">

</div>
```

```
<div class="content">

    <!-- Your Content Goes Here -->

</div>
```

As you can see, using divs instead of meaningful markup makes it harder to understand the content at first glance.

<audio />

The `<audio />` element is used to embed audio content within a web page. This is new to HTML5 and is not available in HTML4. For browsers not supporting HTML5 audio, you can provide a link to a 3gp version of the audio file within the `<audio />` tag. Listing 3-5 shows how to embed an audio file.

Listing 3-5. *How to Use the Audio Tag in HTML5*

```
<audio controls="controls">

    <source src="media/audio.oga" type="application/ogg">

    <source src="media/audio.mp3" type="audio/mpeg">

    <p>

        Your browser does not support HTML5 Audio,
        <a href="media/audio.3gp">click here to download</a>

    </p>

</audio>
```

This will render the native audio player for the handset. Within the `<audio />` tag, you will see several `<source />` elements. These are used to provide different audio formats for the browser, such as MP3, OGG, or WAV. You should specify the mime type of the audio file in order for the browser to pick the correct audio file.

Figure 3-4 shows what an `<audio />` element looks like in Android 4.

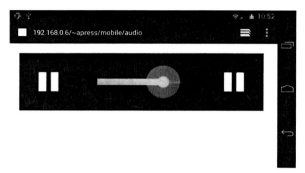

Figure 3-4. *<audio /> element in Android 4 Ice Cream Sandwich*

The <audio /> tag also supports several additional media-based attributes. Table 3-1 shows these attributes and their descriptions.

Table 3-1. *HTML5 Audio Attributes*

Attribute	Value	Description
src	—	Used to specify a single audio file instead of using the <source /> tags.
preload	none | metadata | auto	Used to specify whether to preload the audio file. It's advisable to set this to either none or metadata. This will prevent the browser from downloading the entire audio file without the user's knowledge.
autoplay	autoplay	Used to tell the browser to automatically play the audio file. If you do not want the audio to play automatically, do not add this element.
loop	loop	Used to specify whether the audio should continuously loop. This attribute will not accept a number. If you would like your audio to loop for a specific number of times, you can do this using the JavaScript audio API.
muted	muted	This will mute the audio. Note that this does not appear to be supported in Android Browser.
controls	controls	Used to tell the browser whether to render the default controls. If you produce your own UI for your audio player, this can be handy.

Supported Media Formats

Not all media formats will work on Android. Table 3-2 shows the formats that should work with most, if not all, Android handsets.

Table 3-2. *Supported HTML5 Audio Formats*

Format	Mime Type	File Name Extension
OGG Vorbis Audio	application/ogg	.ogg
MP4 Audio	audio/mp4	.m4a, .mp4, .3gp, .aac
WMA Audio	audio/x-ms-wma	.wma
MP3 Audio	audio/mpeg	.mp3

\<canvas />

The \<canvas /> element provides a context/stage in HTML for you to draw shapes within. You will learn how to draw with the canvas JavaScript API in Chapter 7.

The canvas API will give you an alternative to using DOM elements for graphic-intensive animation or drawing. The \<canvas /> element supports width and height attributes. Any text within the \<canvas /> element will be shown to browsers that do not support it.

Listing 3-6 shows how to draw a simple semitransparent square using canvas.

Listing 3-6. *Drawing a Simple Square in HTML5 Canvas*

```
<canvas id="test-canvas" width="400" height="400">
    <p>Your browser does not support HTML5 Canvas :(</p>
</canvas>

<script type="text/javascript">

    var canvas = document.getElementById("test-canvas");
    var context = canvas.getContext("2d");

    context.fillStyle = "rgba(0, 0, 0, 0.5)"
    context.fillRect(0, 0, 400, 400);

</script>
```

As you can see, you define the canvas in HTML using the `<canvas />` element. Any text within the `<canvas />` element will be visible to browsers that do not support canvas. You then use JavaScript to draw paths onto the canvas. Figure 3-5 shows the result.

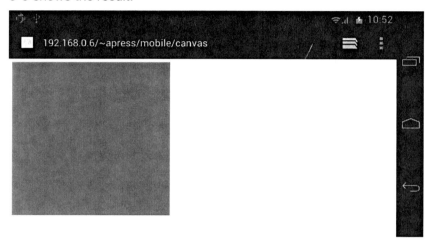

Figure 3-5. *Rendered rectangle on the `<canvas />` element*

`<figure />` and `<figcaption />`

The `<figure />` and `<figcaption />` elements are used to mark up figures on a web page, such as a code sample, image, or diagram. Listing 3-7 shows how a figcaption should be written in HTML5.

Listing 3-7. *Creating a Figure and Caption*

```
<figure id="figure-1">

    <img src="amazing-graph.jpg" alt="Amazing Graph" />

    <figcaption>Figure 1. Graph showing how amazing and awesome something
is</figcaption>

</figure>
```

As you can see in Listing 3-7, the `id` attribute has been used. This will allow you to use URL hashes to jump directly to a figure from a link. For example, `<a href="#figure-1">Jump to Figure 1</a>` can be used to link directly to a figure within a page.

Notice that `<figcaption />` has been nested within the `<figure />` element. This allows you to provide a caption for the item being used as the figure. If you are referencing text, you can also use the `<cite />` element to reference the source of the text. Listing 3-8 shows how you can use this.

Listing 3-8. *Citing a Source*

```
<figure id="figure-2">

    <img src="what-mother-says.jpg" alt="Scan from my mothers notebook" />

    <figcaption>
        Figure 2. A scan from my mothers magazine <cite>The Notebook</cite>
    </figcaption>

</figure>
```

`<footer />`

The `<footer />` element can be used to replace a `<div />` element, and is commonly used to create a footer within a document. The `<footer />` element will usually be used to contain contact and copyright information and links to privacy policies or terms and conditions. Listing 3-9 shows how to create a `<footer />`. You can also use more than a single footer within a document, such as within a section or article.

Listing 3-9. *Creating a Footer in HTML5*

```
<footer>

    <p class="copyright">&copy; 2012 My Company</p>

</footer>
```

Listing 3-10 shows how you would achieve the same thing in HTML4.

Listing 3-10. *Creating a Footer in HTML4*

```
<div id="footer">

    <p class="copyright">&copy; 2012 My Company</p>

</div>
```

Figure 3-6 shows where the `<footer />` would normally be rendered within the DOM.

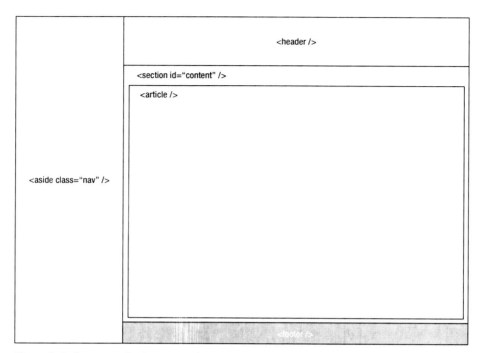

Figure 3-6. *Structure of a document with the* `<footer />` *element*

`<header />`

The `<header />` element can be used to create a header within the document. The `<header />` tag can be used more than once within a document. It will usually contain a logo and/or a group of header elements. The most common use for a `<header />` element would be to add a logo and navigation at the top of a page. Listing 3-11 shows how to do this.

Although not required, you can wrap the `<ul />` commonly used for navigation with a `<nav />` element. This makes it clear to consumers reading your code that it is a navigation element.

Listing 3-11. *Creating a Header Within an HTML5 Document*

```
<header>

    <img src="logo.png" alt="My Company's Logo" />

    <nav>
```

```
    <ul>

        <li><a href="/home.html">Home</a></li>

        <li><a href="/about.html">About</a></li>

        <li><a href="/contact.html">Contact Us</a></li>

    </ul>

  </nav>

</header>
```

You can achieve the same result in HTML4 using the code in Listing 3-12.

Listing 3-12. *Creating a Header in HTML4*

```
<div id="header ">

    <img src="logo.png" alt="My Company's Logo" />

    <ul class="navigation">

        <li><a href="/home.html">Home</a></li>

        <li><a href="/about.html">About</a></li>

        <li><a href="/contact.html">Contact Us</a></li>

    </ul>

</div>
```

\<hgroup />

The \<hgroup /> element can be used to group together related headings, such as an \<h1 /> element for a title, and an \<h2 /> element for a subtitle. \<hgroup /> elements should not contain any elements other than header elements (i.e., \<h1 />, \<h2 />, \<h3 />, \<h4 />, etc.).

The rank of an \<hgroup /> within a document is defined by the highest ranked header element within that \<hgroup />.

Listing 3-13 shows how to use an \<hgroup /> in HTML5, and Listing 3-14 shows how you may have grouped headings in HTML4.

Listing 3-13. *Defining Headers in HTML5 Using Hgroup*

```
<hgroup>

    <h1>My Header</h1>

    <h2>My Subheader</h2>

</hgroup>
```

Listing 3-14. *Defining a Group of Headers in HTML4*

```
<div class="header-grouping">

    <h1>My Header</h1>

    <h2>My Subheader</h2>

</div>
```

<mark />

The <mark /> element can be used to highlight text within a document. Listing 3-15 shows how this can be used in HTML5, and Listing 3-16 shows how this would have been achieved in HTML4 using a combination of CSS and HTML.

Listing 3-15. *Using the Mark Tag in HTML5*

```
<p>This is an <mark>important</mark> reminder for Inga Lyon</p>
```

Listing 3-16. *Highlighting Text in HTML4*

```
<p>This is an <em class="highlight">important</em> reminger for Inga Lyon</p>

<style type="text/css">

  em.highlight {
     background: yellow;
  }

</style>
```

<nav />

The <nav /> element can be used to define navigation links within a page. The <nav /> element should only be used to define major navigation elements within a page, such as the primary navigation or side/sub navigation. You can add any content within the <nav /> element, as long as it contains links to content within the web site. Listing 3-17 shows how to use the <nav /> element in HTML5, and Listing 3-18 shows how you may have defined a navigation in HTML4.

Listing 3-17. *Creating a Nav in HTML5*

```
<nav>

    <ul>

        <li><a href="/home.html">Home</a></li>

        <li><a href="/about.html">About</a></li>

        <li><a href="/contact.html">Contact Us</a></li>

    </ul>

</nav>
```

Listing 3-18. *Creating a Navigation in HTML4*

```
<ul class="navigation">

    <li><a href="/home.html">Home</a></li>

    <li><a href="/about.html">About</a></li>

    <li><a href="/contact.html">Contact Us</a></li>

</ul>
```

<output />

The <output /> element can be used to show the results of a calculation. The <output /> element can come in handy when displaying the result of a dynamic/AJAX form. Rather than showing the results by modifying the inner HTML of a <span /> element, you can set the value in much the same way as any other HTML form-based input element.

> **NOTE:** Submitting a form with the <output /> tag will not send the value of the output. If you wish to do this, you must set the value of a hidden field to be the result of the calculation.

Listing 3-19 shows how to implement this in HTML5, and Listing 3-20 shows how you might have done this in HTML4. The `for` attribute can be used to specify the related inputs used for the calculation.

Listing 3-19. *Using the Output Element in HTML5*

```
<form action="calculate.php" name="calculate">

    <input type="number" name="a" value="0" /> +
    <input type="number" name="b" value="0" /> =
    <output name="c" for="a b" />

</form>

<script type="text/javascript" charset="utf-8">

    function calculate(){
        var form = document.calculate;
        form.c.value = form.a.valueAsNumber + form.b.valueAsNumber;
    }

    document.calculate.addEventListener("input", calculate);

</script>
```

Listing 3-20. *Creating Something Similar to Output in HTML4*

```
<form action="calculate.php" name="calculate">

    <input type="number" name="a" value="0" /> +
    <input type="number" name="b" value="0" /> =
    <span id="c" />

</form>

<script type="text/javascript" charset="utf-8">

    function calculate(){
        var form = document.calculate;
        document.getElementById('c').innerText = form.a.valueAsNumber +
form.b.valueAsNumber;
    }

    document.calculate.addEventListener("input", calculate);

</script>
```

<section />

The <section /> element can be used to define a section within an HTML5 document. You can use the <section /> tag to group together common elements, such as chapters for a blog post or product information for an ecommerce web site. A common misconception is to replace all <div /> elements with <section /> elements. If you are using <section /> elements to help with styling or scripting and not for creating a semantic document, you should probably use a <div /> with a class.

Listing 3-21 shows how to use a <section /> element to group together comments on a blog post.

Listing 3-21. *Using a Section Element in HTML5*

```
<article>

    <header>

        <h1>Article Title</h1>

        <p>

            Created by Daniel Carpenter on
            <time pubdate="2012-03-15">March 15<sup>th</sup> 2012</time>

        </p>

    </header>

    <p>Article Content</p>
    <section class="comments">

        <article id="comment-1">

        <header>
            <p>
                From Becci Buckley on
                <time pubdate="2012-03-15">March 20<sup>th</sup> 2012</time>
            </p>
        </header>

        <p>This is a great article Dan, it might need some work :D</p>

        </article>

    </section>
```

```
<footer>

    <address>

        <p>

            Written by
            <a rel="author" href="mailto:daniel.carpenter@somewhere.com">
              Daniel Carpenter
            </a>

            <br />

            Follow him on
            <a rel="author" href="http://www.twitter.com/mrdanc">Twitter</a>

        </p>

    </address>

</footer>

</article>
```

As you can see from Listing 3-21, you can nest `<article />` elements within a `<section />` element. In fact, you can add any HTML element you like within a `<section />` tag.

<time />

The `<time />` element can be used to specify time within a document. It does not appear to do much at the moment other than provide semantic markup for time-based elements. The `<time />` element supports a `datetime` attribute that can be used to give the date or time in a machine-readable format. It also supports the `pubdate` attribute that will relate to the closest parent `<article />` element. Listing 3-22 shows how to use the `<time />` element.

Listing 3-22. *Using the Time Element to Show the Publish Time for an Article*

```
<article>

    <header>

        <h1>Article Title</h1>

        <p>
```

```
      Created by Daniel Carpenter on
      <time pubdate="2012-03-15">March 15<sup>th</sup> 2012</time>

    </p>

  </header>

</article>
```

<video />

The `<video />` element can be used to embed video within a page. I cover this in the section "Embedding Video with HTML5" later in this chapter.

The `<video />` element provides an alternative to using Flash to embed video within an HTML document. It also has several JavaScript APIs to control the playback of the video.

The video being played will automatically enter full screen in Android Browser on versions lower than Android 4 Ice Cream Sandwich, but will remain in place in Android 4 and above.

Table 3-3 shows the attributes available for the `<video />` element.

Table 3-3. *HTML5 Video Attributes*

Attribute	Value	Description
src	—	Used to specify a single video file instead of using the `<source />` tags.
preload	none | metadata | auto	Used to specify whether to preload the video file. It's advisable to set this to either none or metadata. This will prevent the browser from downloading the entire video file without the user's knowledge.
autoplay	autoplay	Used to tell the browser to automatically play the video file. If you do not want the video to play automatically, do not add this element.
loop	loop	Used to specify whether the video should continuously loop. This attribute will not accept a number. If you would like your audio to loop for a specific number of times, you can do this using the JavaScript video API.

Attribute	Value	Description
muted	muted	This will mute the audio. Note that this does not appear to be supported in Android Browser.
controls	controls	Used to tell the browser whether to render the default controls. If you produce your own UI for your video player, this can be handy.
height	height in pixels	Specifies the initial height of the video element.
width	width in pixels	Specifies the initial width of the video element.
poster	url to poster image	This is the path to the image used within the video tag prior to the video playing.

The `<video />` element also currently supports most popular video containers and codecs.

Table 3-4 shows the formats and mime types that are currently supported by Android Browser. How to encode for these formats will be covered later in this chapter.

Table 3-4. *HTML5 Video Supported Formats*

Container	Extensions	Mime	Notes
MPEG-1	.mpg, .mpeg, .mpv	video/mpeg	—
MP4	.mp4	video/mp4	—
OGG	.ogv, .ogg	application/ogg	—
WebM	.webm	video/webm	Supported only in Android 4 (Ice Cream Sandwich)
MKV	.mkv	video/x-matroska	—
Windows Media Video	.wmv	video/x-ms-wmv	—

Handling Multimedia in HTML5

With the ever-increasing speeds available on mobile devices, and mobile web browsers supporting more and more video and audio containers and codecs, there has never been a better time to explore adding video to a mobile web application.

There are several things you need to think about when adding video to a mobile web site. It's unfortunately not as simple as encoding video and audio for a certain file extension or format.

When encoding video and audio for HTML5, there are four things you should take into consideration.

The supported containers for the device

The supported codecs and decoders on the device

The quality of the final video and audio

The file size of the final video and audio

In order to play back video, you will need to encode the video and audio using a codec that the target device can understand and play back.

> **NOTE:** A codec comes in two parts: an encoder and a decoder. When you compress a video using a specific codec, that same codec is required to decompress the video ready for playback. The different codecs are capable of different types and qualities of compression (e.g., H.264 will encode video differently to VP8). The different codecs have an effect on file size and quality due to how they compress video.

The quality of the encoded video depends on the bitrate you set; this also has an immediate impact on the file size. If you have a target file size in mind, you can calculate what the bitrate for the video should be and work from there. The following formula should help you work this out.

((video bitrate [kb/sec] + audio bitrate [kb /sec]) * length [seconds]) * 0.125) = file size [Kb]

There are various bitrate calculators available online that will help you to calculate what bitrate a video or audio file should be, based on a number of other factors. This can be useful when using command-line encoding tools such as FFMPEG or Mencoder.

Surrounding the compressed/uncompressed video and audio is a container. The container will usually provide details on the multiple tracks for video. One track will be used for the video itself, and the second track will be used for the video's audio. A container will not necessarily describe how a video or audio file has been encoded, but may define a certain standard as to how a video should be encoded for that specific container.

When picking a container, it's important to pick one that supports a limited number of codecs. This will make encoding much simpler, as you will not have to research which codecs are supported on current and newer devices. For example, the Matroska (MKV) container supports almost any video and audio codec available today, so it's a much bigger task to choose which codecs to use within the container; whereas WebM will only support the VP8 video codec and Vorbis audio codec. This makes it a simpler task when encoding for a device that supports the WebM container.

To avoid confusion, Table 3-5 shows the most popular codecs and containers that you should provide support for when embedding video for mobile.

Table 3-5. *HTML5 Video Suggested Containers and Codec Combinations*

Container	Video Codec	Audio Codec	Mime
MP4	H.264 AVC (Baseline)AAC		video/mp4
WebM	VP8	Vorbis	video/webm

The Android documentation also suggests the following resolutions, shown in Table 3-6, based on quality.

Table 3-6. *HTML5 Video Suggested Resolutions*

Quality	Resolution	Frames Per Second (FPS)
SD (low quality)	176 × 144px	12
SD (high quality)	480 × 360px	30
HD (not for all devices)	1280 × 720px	30

Table 3-7 shows the recommended supported containers and codecs for audio on Android.

Table 3-7. *HTML5 Audio Suggested Containers and Codec Combinations*

Container	Audio Codec	Mime
MP3	MP3	audio/mpeg
OGG	Vorbis	application/ogg

Supporting these two containers and codecs should provide enough support for all Android devices without requiring you to do mass amounts of batch encoding and testing.

Optimizing Video for the Mobile Web

You should now have an understanding of the complexities of encoding video for the mobile web. There are dozens of applications that will allow you to encode video for the web. Some of these are free and open source desktop applications (such as Easy HTML5 Video for Mac/Windows, and the new Miro Video Encoder for Mac/Windows), and others are hosted, web-based solutions that also provide support to host your videos online (such as bitsontherun.com, zencoder.com, or encoding.com).

You should use the best encoding solution to suit your needs.

Hosted Solutions

Hosted solutions are perfect for on-demand encoding, and if you wish to offload a lot of your site traffic to another server. Most of the hosting solutions provide APIs that allow you to push videos to their service over the web. After the video has finished encoding, you will be given a URL, which can be used to embed your video. They will usually consume a video encoded in any format, and encoding usually takes minutes. The hosted solutions will also provide a list of common encoding options based on device or format.

The simplest to use of these hosted solutions is bitsontherun.com, though encoding.com and zencoder.com offer more control over how you encode your videos, as shown in Figure 3-7.

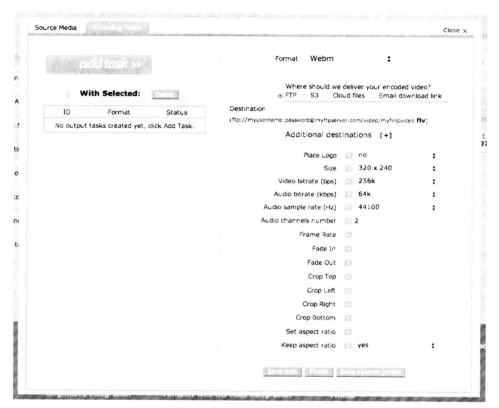

Figure 3-7. *Encoding options on encoding.com*

As you can see, bitsontherun.com is much more simplistic when creating encoding settings by providing basic options, as shown in Figure 3-8. If you want to have more control over the compression options for your video, then encoding.com and zencoder.com will provide the best options. If you simply want to encode video and not worry about the various compression options, then bitsontherun.com is the best option. Hosted encoding solutions provide the best solution if you do not have a very powerful machine and want to encode video quickly, or if you have a mass amount of video to encode. The presets available on the hosted solutions are also constantly refined and tuned.

The downside to using a hosted solution is that you pay based on how much you upload and download, and in the case of zencoder.com, you pay based on how many hours of video you encode.

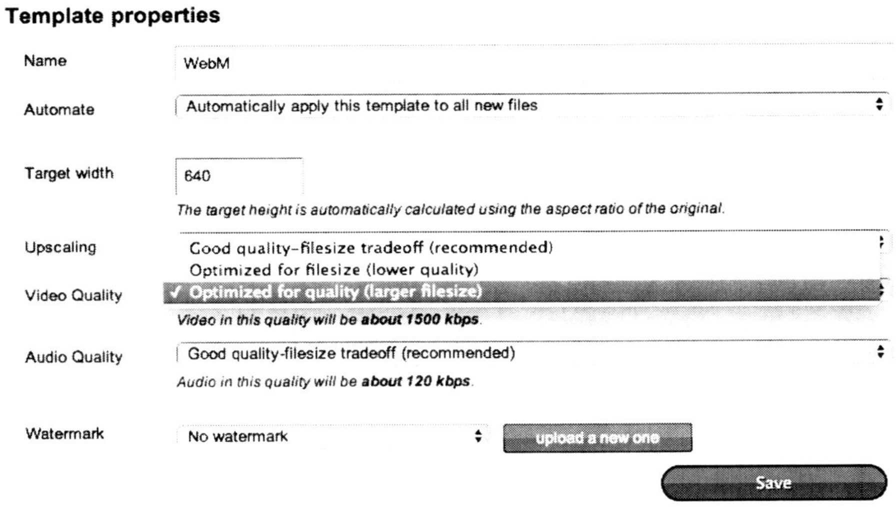

Template properties

Name	WebM
Automate	Automatically apply this template to all new files ⬍
Target width	640

The target height is automatically calculated using the aspect ratio of the original.

Upscaling	Good quality–filesize tradeoff (recommended) ⬍
Video Quality	Optimized for filesize (lower quality) ✓ Optimized for quality (larger filesize) ⬍

*Video in this quality will be **about 1500 kbps**.*

Audio Quality	Good quality–filesize tradeoff (recommended) ⬍

*Audio in this quality will be **about 120 kbps**.*

Watermark	No watermark ⬍	upload a new one

Save

Figure 3-8. *Encoding options on bitsontherun.com*

Desktop Solutions

Desktop encoding solutions are perfect for small encoding runs. If you have a low-spec computer, be prepared to head to the closest pub for a beer or two while you leave a fan on next to your computer to stop it from overheating! Encoding videos requires large amounts of processing power and can take several seconds to render a single frame. This process can be time consuming. The better the processor in your computer, the shorter the encoding time will be.

Using the command-line tools, such as FFMPEG and Mencoder, instead of the GUIs that provide an interface for them, can have its advantages. For instance, it gives you the ability to trigger encoding jobs from a server-side script written in Python, PHP, or Ruby. You can also wrap the various encoding parameters in a bash script. This allows you to potentially batch encode a folder full of videos, all at once.

The simplest free desktop solution for Windows and Mac is Miro Video Converter, shown in Figure 3-9.

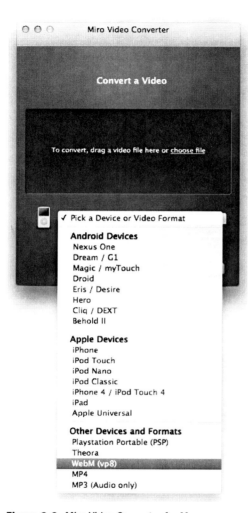

Figure 3-9. *Miro Video Converter for Mac*

As you can see, it has a simple drag-and-drop UI, and can convert to a number of different formats. When encoding video for desktop-based HTML5 web sites, Miro is perfect; however, you will want to squeeze as much as you can out of the videos for the mobile web without compromising on quality. Miro, at the moment, doesn't allow you to adjust any of the settings for output.

Because of this, the best option for now is to use bitsontherun.com to encode video for the mobile web.

Encoding Videos with Bits on the Run

The first thing to do is to head over to `www.bitsontherun.com` and create a free account. A free account will give you up to one hour of video storage and 20 hours of streaming time per month. This should be just enough for this book. If you require more, you can always upgrade to a pro account.

After you have created your account, you will want to create templates for your encoding jobs.

Templates allow you to create custom encoding templates for your videos and audio. You can create a template once, and use it for all of your video and audio files.

> **NOTE:** Unfortunately, if you create a template, you must manually re-encode any videos with the new template. There is a way around this by using the Bits on the Run API.

Log in and go to the account page, as shown in Figure 3-10.

Figure 3-10. *Account options on bitsontherun.com*

Click the properties tab on the account page (also shown in Figure 3-10). Under account properties, click the Templates tab.

From here, you will create two templates. One will be for MP4 (H.264) and the other will be for WebM (VP8).

Click on the "Add new template" button, which you can find toward the bottom of the page, as shown in Figure 3-11.

Templates define a format, quality and watermark for encoding your original video.
You can create templates for audio (AAC, MP3, Vorbis) and video (MP4, FLV, WebM).

Figure 3-11. *"Add new template" button*

You should then be presented with a "Create new template" dialog similar to that shown in Figure 3-12. Ensure the following settings have been set:

     Name: HTML5 MP4

     Format: MP4 Video (H.264/AAC)

Click Create.

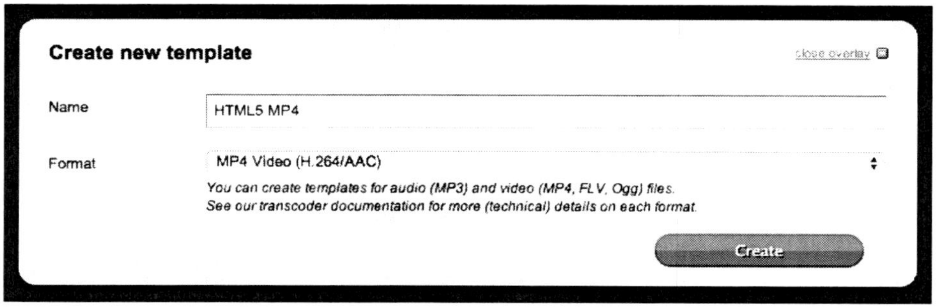

Figure 3-12. *"Create new template" dialog*

The "Template properties" page, similar to Figure 3-13, will then be presented to you. Ensure the following options are set.

     Automate: Automatically apply this template to new videos

     Target Width: 480

     Upscaling: Always build this template, even if the original is smaller

     Video Quality: Good quality-filesize tradeoff (recommended)

     Audio Quality: Good quality-filesize tradeoff (recommended)

     Watermark: No Watermark

Click Save.

You will need to repeat the process again for WebM. Except enter the following information on the "Create new template" dialog.

     Name: HTML5 WebM

     Format: WebM Video (VP8/Vorbis)

Enter the following information on the "Template properties" page.

     Automate: Automatically apply this template to new videos

     Target Width: 480

Upscaling: Always build this template, even if the original is smaller

Video Quality: Good quality-filesize tradeoff (recommended)

Audio Quality: Good quality-filesize tradeoff (recommended)

Watermark: No watermark

Template properties

Name	HTML5 MP4
Automate	Automatically apply this template to new videos
Target width	480
	The target height is automatically calculated using the aspect ratio of the original.
Upscaling	Always build this template, even if the original is smaller
Video Quality	Good quality-filesize tradeoff (recommended)
	Video in this quality will be about 900 kbps.
Audio Quality	Good quality-filesize tradeoff (recommended)
	Audio in this quality will be about 120 kbps.
Watermark	No watermark upload a new one

Save

Figure 3-13. *Template properties*

You should now be ready to begin uploading videos to your Bits on the Run account. In order to do this, go to the videos tab, and click "Upload new video" from the right sidebar, as shown in Figure 3-14.

Upload new video

Filter by tag

all videos   0

FTP Uploads

Figure 3-14. *"Upload new video" button*

You will be presented with the "Upload new video: Step 1" dialog box, similar to that shown in Figure 3-15.

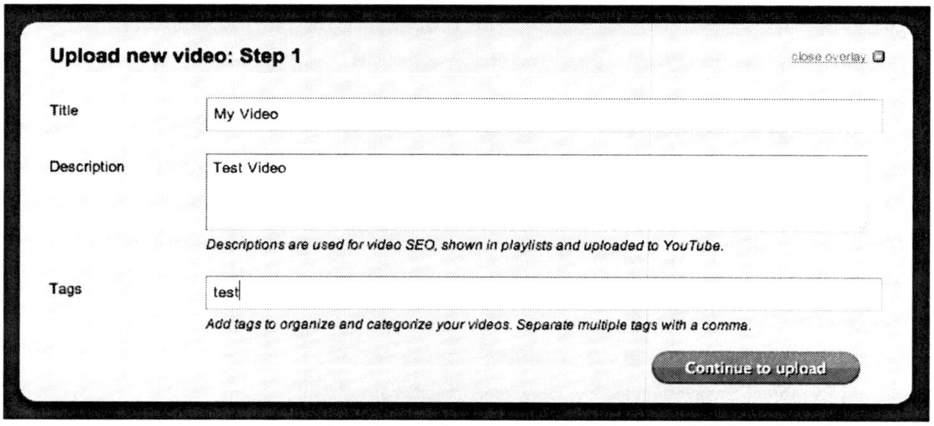

Figure 3-15. *"Upload new video: Step 1" dialog*

Enter the appropriate information into the fields. As this is a test video, you can choose anything you like. From here on, "My Video" will refer to the video that you have just uploaded. Click the "Continue to upload" button.

You should now be in Step 2 of the "Upload new video" dialog. Click the Browse button, as shown in Figure 3-16, and select any video you wish to use as a sample video. Ensure you select a video that is less than 100 MB; otherwise, you might have to wait quite a while for the test video to upload.

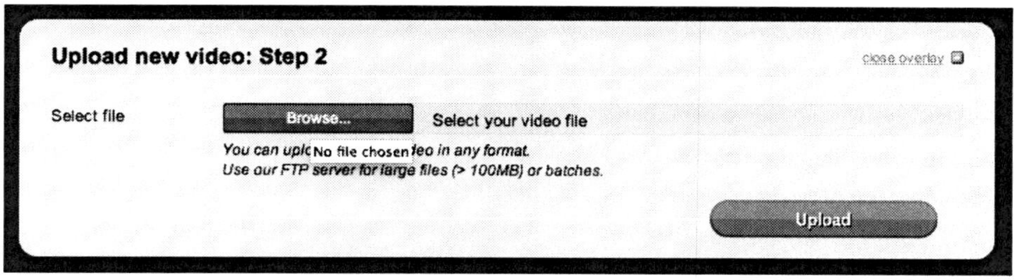

Figure 3-16. *"Upload new video: Step 2" dialog*

After the upload completes, Bits on the Run will begin the encoding process. Your video will now be ready for embedding. You can both download the video and copy it to your mobile web project or link directly to it using the `src` attribute in the `<video />` element. The advantage of downloading it is that you do not have to worry about your data allowance with Bits on the Run cutting out when you reach your limit.

Embedding Video with HTML5

Embedding video on the web used to be a very long-winded process. Before Flash became popular, all of the browsers, computers, and even the same version of the same operating system had varying support for codecs and containers. There was no real common format, and you could not simply embed several formats of the same video so that the browser could choose the correct video for the user.

Flash came along and fixed most of those problems. By requiring only one plugin to play all formats, it was the "knight in shining armor" for video on the web. So much so that almost every web site used it to deliver videos to their users.

Then smartphones came about and Flash for mobile became a nightmare. It required high amounts of CPU, which would drain the mobile phone's battery like a vampire. The same could be said for Flash on almost any portable device, racking up large amounts of CPU power, which had an effect on not just the performance of the machine but the battery draw from cooling the CPU and powering it. To this day, Flash still consumes large amounts of CPU on Macs.

In addition to this, developers often didn't produce Flash-based content with mobile phone handsets in mind. So when watching a video on a mobile that was targeted for desktop, you would usually get a 500 MB HD video that wasn't really optimized for your handset. This also has an effect on user's pockets, as that 500 MB per month data plan would be consumed by a single video in minutes.

Along came HTML5. Finally, the focus was on the browser, standards, and hardware acceleration without the need for third-party plugins.

HTML5 brought about HTML5 video. HTML5 video provides a way for browsers to support decoding video within the browser regardless of the codecs supported on the platform. This now means that if a user is using Android Browser, they will definitely have support for WebM or MP4; and if they are using Safari browser, they will definitely support MP4 but not WebM. Not only this, but HTML5 video also supports multiple video sources of different types. This means that you can provide video files that are optimized for each codec and container. The browser will pick the best codec and container from the list of sources, sudo-stream it, and deliver it to the user's browser.

New to the HTML5 spec is also the support of media queries within video sources. This can ensure that if you are using a tablet device, you can get a much higher resolution video delivered to you without having to choose the quality of the media you wish to view. If you are on a mobile handset, you will get video that is optimized for your handset with a smaller file size so that it doesn't consume all of your data allowance.

> **NOTE:** Video media queries exists within the HTML5 spec, but it doesn't seem to be supported by any browsers yet.

Embedding your video in HTML5 is relatively simple. You use the `video` tag and specify the `width` and `height` attributes of the video. You can then specify the poster frame for the video. The poster frame is a single still from the video that you can use to display to the user prior to them clicking on the play button.

Create a new folder called tutorials in Aptana, and within that create a folder called video. This folder will be used for this exercise. Within the video folder, create a folder called media. Copy the video and poster image files you have encoded and downloaded from Bits on the Run to the media folder and rename them as follows.

- video.webm
- video.mp4
- poster.jpg

Create a new file in the video folder called `index.html`. Your folder structure should look similar to the following:

- tutorials
    - video
    - media
        - video.webm
        - video.mp4
        - poster.jpg
    - index.html

Open `index.html` in Aptana and enter the HTML from Listing 3-23.

Listing 3-23. *Embedding a Video in HTML5*

```
<!DOCTYPE html>
<html>

    <head>
        <meta charset="utf-8">
        <meta name="viewport" content="width=device-width, initial-scale=1,
maximum-scale=1">
        <title>Exercise Video</title>
    </head>

    <body>

        <video controls width="480" height="270" poster="media/poster.jpg">
            <source src="media/video.mp4" type="video/mp4">
            <source src="media/video.webm" type="video/webm">

            <p>
                Your browser does not support HTML5 Video, <a
href="media/video.mkv">click here
                to download</a>
            </p>

        </video>

    </body>

</html>
```

Save and export your video. Go to the file in your Android browser. The URL should be http://<your computer ip address>/tutorials/video/media/. You should be presented with a screen similar to Figure 3-17.

Figure 3-17. *HTML5 video inline with the content*

Tap the play button and the video will begin to buffer and play. As of Android 4+, Android Browser will play video inline with content instead of automatically going to full screen. This poses a small problem, as it presents inconsistencies between how video is handled with newer and legacy devices. The solution to this is to automatically enlarge video using the JavaScript video API to full screen. This will be covered in Chapter 7.

Optimizing Audio for the Mobile Web

Fortunately, Bits on the Run also supports audio encoding and hosting for the web. However, as encoding audio is significantly less CPU intensive than encoding video, you can use desktop software to do this. The most popular free, cross-platform audio application is Audacity. You can download and install the current stable beta version from the Audacity web site at `http://audacity.sourceforge.net/download/`.

The same rules apply when encoding audio for the mobile web.

- Ensure the file size is small.

- Ensure the quality of the final audio is good enough to be heard through headphones and small speakers.

As with video encoding, you will need to find a happy medium between quality and file size. Unlike video, where the user must focus on both the audio and video, with just audio, the user will primarily be focused on listening to your audio, so the quality of the audio is of the utmost importance. This means that more care must be taken to ensure that each track is transcoded and compressed in the right way.

A lot of trial and error will be required, but depending on the type of audio you wish to transcode, you can begin to build presets within Audacity. For instance, you will use different settings for audio content only containing voice, such as an audiobook, as compared to audio content containing a music track. The number of frequencies that you hear from a human voice is much narrower than what you might hear from a rock band, for example. This means that the file size for an audiobook may potentially be smaller than that of a music track using lossy compression.

> **NOTE:** There are two types of compression types: lossless and lossy. Lossless compression tries to encode the audio in such a way that it has a smaller file size when encoded, but when it is decoded it will still be the same as it was prior to compression. Lossy compression will analyze the audio content and remove parts of it that might not be audible. This means that with lossy compression, you will lose information regardless of the decompression technique.

Encoding Audio with Audacity

Encoding audio with Audacity can be a simple process. For the sake of this example, you will need to download an uncompressed audio file, so head over to SoundCloud (`www.soundcloud.com`). Using SoundCloud, perform a search for any music track you like and ensure that the following options are selected, as shown in Figure 3-18.

- An uncompressed file
- Track should be: Downloadable
- Search only for Creative Commons licensed tracks
- They should be: Free to use commercially

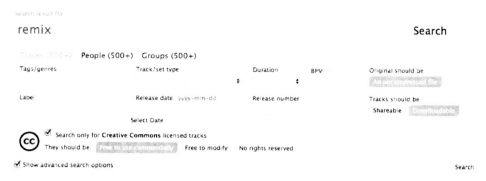

Figure 3-18. *soundcloud.com search options*

Pick any song that has a high frequency range (something from the dub step genre would be a good choice) and download it. This should give you an uncompressed WAV or AIFF file to experiment with.

Our aim for this music track is to get the file size to between 0.5 and 1 MB for every minute of audio. This should equate to taking 4–8 seconds to load 1 minute of audio on HSDPA or 1–2 seconds on 3G. Table 3-8 should be used when trying to calculate how long it may take to download 1 MB of data on mobile data networks.

Table 3-8. *Average Download Times for Audio*

Connection Type	Average Download Speed	Average Download Time (per MB)
3G	4 Mbps	2 seconds
HSDPA	1 Mbps	8 seconds

The sample track for this book is a WAV file with these settings: 86.1 MB, 4:59 in time size, averaging at 18.75 MB per minute. The target file size for this track for each format will be between 4 and 5 MB.

Encoding OGG

You will encode the audio file in the OGG format first. It's the simpler of the two, as Audacity provides a single option to configure. Open Audacity and open your file by going to File ➤ Open, and select the file you have just downloaded. If you are presented with the warning shown in Figure 3-19, ensure that "Make a copy of the files before editing (safer)" and "Don't warn again and always use my choice above" are both checked.

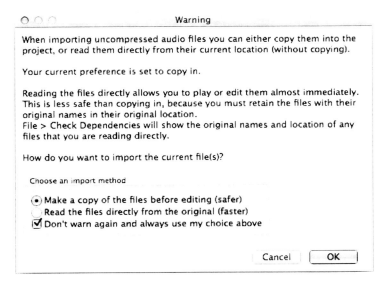

Figure 3-19. *Warning dialog from Audacity*

When the file has finished processing, you should be presented with a waveform for the file, similar to Figure 3-20.

You can now export the audio file as an OGG Vorbis audio file. Go to File ➤ Export. Under format, select "Ogg Vorbis Files" and click the "Options…" button to the right of the selection.

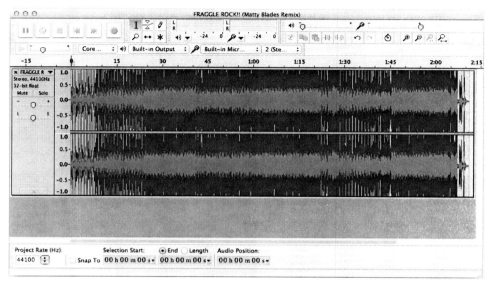

Figure 3-20. *Waveform of the track*

You will be presented with an options dialog similar to Figure 3-21. Select the lowest quality and click OK. Vorbis is a form of Variable Bit Rate (VBR) encoding. VBR will use different bit rates throughout the track, depending on the complexity of the audio for each segment. This can potentially produce a very small file with reasonable quality as compared to a file encoded at a constant bitrate with the same or less quality but a much bigger file size due to the complexity of the audio.

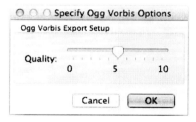

Figure 3-21. *Ogg Vorbis export options*

The result of this encoding should be an audio track that should sound similar to the original WAV file but with a file size less than 3 MB. The result from the test track used for this book when encoding in OGG's lowest quality setting is a file size of 2.5 MB with no noticeable difference in sound quality.

Encoding MP3

The process for encoding MP3 audio is similar to exporting audio for Vorbis. Follow the same steps to open the original WAV file, and go to File ➤ Export. Select MP3 Files from the Format drop-down (instead of Ogg Vorbis Files). Click the Options… button.

You will be presented with an export dialog similar to that shown in Figure 3-22. MP3 VBR encoding doesn't appear to perform as well as OGG Vorbis. Even at its highest compression setting, the audio file size is still double that of the output of the OGG Vorbis compression. Using the average bit rate mode at 128 kbps will give you the same or similar quality as the lowest OGG Vorbis compression option, but with a file size that's larger and still within the acceptable file size of 0.5 to 1 MB per minute of audio.

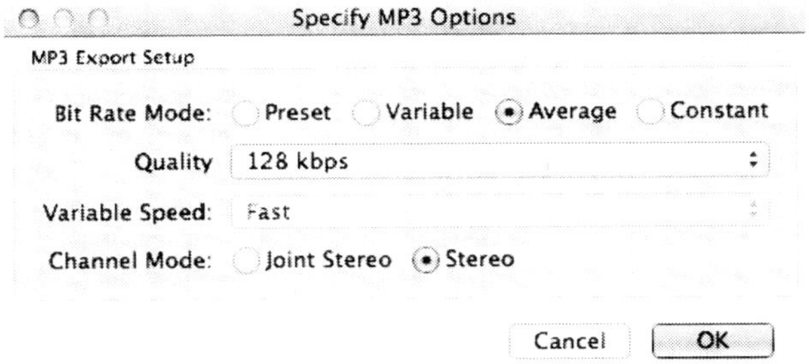

Figure 3-22. *MP3 export options*

Click OK and save. If you wish to enter metadata on the next screen, go ahead and enter it; otherwise, click OK once more and the audio file will begin to export.

Embedding Audio with HTML5

Embedding audio with HTML5 is quite simple. Prior to HTML5, there was no real standard way to embed audio with different codecs, especially in mobile. With mobile, the preferred way was to either use Flash or provide a link to a 3GP file, a format that is widely supported by mobile devices. As the ability to deliver and play high-quality music on mobile devices becomes more popular, the audio tag will begin to be widely used.

The process to embed audio in HTML5 is similar to embedding video. You use the audio tag and specify several sources for the browser to pick the correct one.

Create a new folder in the tutorials folder called audio, then create a new folder within the audio folder called media, and create a new file called `index.html`. Copy your converted audio files to the media folder and rename them to `audio.ogg` and `audio.mpg`.

Your folder structure should look similar to this.

> tutorials
>> audio
>> media
>>> audio.mp3
>>> audio.ogg
>> index.html

Open the `index.html` file and use the code from Listing 3-24.

Listing 3-24. *Embedding Audio in HTML5*

```
<!DOCTYPE html>
<html>

    <head>

        <meta charset="utf-8">
        <meta name="viewport" content="width=device-width, initial-scale=1,
maximum-scale=1">
        <title>Testing Audio</title>

    </head>

    <body>

        <audio controls>

            <source src="media/audio.ogg" type="application/ogg">

            <source src="media/audio.mp3" type="audio/mpeg">

            <p>
                Your browser does not support HTML5 Audio, <a
href="media/audio.mp3">click
                here to download</a>
            </p>

        </audio>
```

```
    </body>
```

```
</html>
```

Open the page in your device's browser; you will see something similar to Figure 3-23.

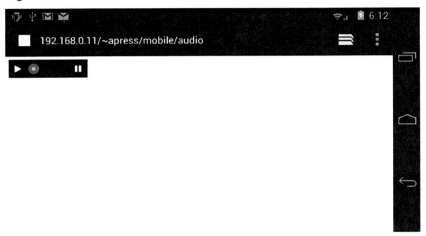

Figure 3-23. *Audio in HTML5*

Click the play button and you will hear audio through your device's speakers or headphones. You can create a custom player with your own UI using the HTML5 audio tag. This will be covered in Chapter 7.

HTML5 Mobile Forms

Forms can be a dull and boring subject, both for the user filling them out and the developer creating them. Remember how irritating it was the last time you filled out a registration form on a computer, and now imagine how irritating filling out that same form would be if you were on a device with a small screen and without a mouse and keyboard.

Working with forms for mobile is no different than working with forms for the general web. Consideration must be taken for the layout of the form due to the restricted screen size and how much information you really need to collect from your users. Figure 3-24 shows the difference between confused.com's car insurance quote forms for mobile and desktop.

Figure 3-24. *Car insurance quote form for mobile (left) and desktop (right)*

As you can see, the same questions are asked, but consideration is taken for the screen size by repositioning the field labels and fields themselves to take advantage of the narrow but long screen.

Fields for Different Data Types

Depending on the type of field and data required, you can use different types of input fields for Android browsers. Table 3-9 shows which HTML5 field types are currently supported on Android Browser.

Table 3-9. *Supported Field Types on Android Browser*

Field Type	Support
color	no
datalist	no
date	no
datetime	no

week	no
time	no
email	yes
number	yes
range	no
search	no
tel	yes
url	no

As you can see, the only field types currently supported by Android Browser are email, number, and tel. The other field types should be implemented at some point in the future. You can choose to implement them now and work around the lack of support, but you could experience issues after support finally arrives.

You can test this out on your device by creating a new folder for this exercise within your project called forms. Create a new file within that called index.html.

Listing 3-25 shows the code that will produce the three different input form types.

Listing 3-25. *Input Type Code*

```
<!DOCTYPE html>
<html>

    <head>
        <meta charset="utf-8">
        <title>Form Fields</title>
        <meta name="viewport" content="width=device-width, initial-scale=1,
maximum-scale=1">
    </head>
    <body>

        <form>

            <fieldset>

                <legend>HTML5 Input Types</legend>
```

```
        <p>
            <label for="email">Email</label>
            <input type="email" name="email"
placeholder="someone@somewhere.com">
        </p>

        <p>
            <label for="number">Number</label>
            <input type="number" name="number">
        </p>

        <p>
            <label for="telephone">Telephone</label>
            <input type="tel" name="telephone" placeholder="+44
012345678901">
        </p>

    </fieldset>

</form>

</body>

</html>
```

This is just a standard HTML5 form. You might notice that there is an attribute on some of the fields called placeholder. The placeholder attribute allows you to display useful example text for a form input to help the user figure out what they need to put in the form field. When a user taps to fill the form field out, the placeholder text will disappear.

Depending on the input type, you will be presented with different keyboards to help the user input their information much faster. Figure 3-25 shows the different keyboard layouts used for the three supported input types.

Figure 3-25. *Keyboard layouts for number (left), tel (center), and email (right)*

Load the new web page in your mobile phone's browser to test it out.

Summary

This concludes HTML5 for Android. From this chapter, you should have gained a large amount of knowledge related to encoding video and audio for the web and mobile web. You should also now have a basic understanding about the different ways you can encode media, and that you don't need a powerful machine just to encode media, but simply a fast Internet connection.

This chapter has taken you through all of the new HTML5 elements that are currently supported by Android Browser and how to use them effectively.

Hopefully, this chapter will prepare you for the rest of the book as we begin to explore interactivity in a little more detail. HTML itself provides the foundation that we build upon using CSS for presentation, and JavaScript for interaction, further into this book.

In the next chapter, you will focus on the beginnings of your mobile web application by creating the HTML framework. Throughout this book, you will learn about a particular aspect of mobile web development and then use that knowledge to build and enhance your application. This is known as *progressive enhancement*, and is a practice adopted for the web to ensure that your applications work across all platforms regardless of their capabilities.

You will also learn the three different types of presentation solutions for the mobile web, including using standard HTML pages for each page of your application, using a card-based system where all pages are located in a single HTML file, and loading each page using Ajax.

The next chapter is very practical, so load up Aptana Studio and get ready to code!

Chapter

4

Starting Your Project Using HTML5

HTML provides a good starting point for any web project. It essentially gives you a skeleton for you to work with when enhancing the web page with CSS (visual style) and JavaScript (interactivity). For the three workshops in this book (HTML5, CSS, and JavaScript), you will progressively enhance a mobile web application called MoMemo. MoMemo will take advantage of the following HTML/HTML5 features.

- Canvas
- JavaScript APIs
- CSS3 transitions
- Media queries
- HTML5 video/audio
- Offline storage

In this chapter, you will learn three different methods to lay out your web pages, depending on the type of mobile web application you are making.

You will also begin to create the framework for the MoMemo application in HTML. Before this, you will learn how to take a mobile application from an idea, to requirements gathering, to IA, and finally coding it in HTML5. You will also briefly touch upon application caching, a feature that allows you to dictate what elements get cached on the user's mobile device and how to fall back onto files that shouldn't be cached when there is no network connection.

Paging Strategies

There are three main ways to create pages in HTML.

Standard HTML: Creating standard HTML pages and linking to them

Single-page Ajax: Using a single page and loading subsequent pages using AJAX

Single-page container: Using a single page as a container with multiple pages being held within a container `<div />` and moving between them using JavaScript

Each method has its advantages and disadvantages. For example, a mobile web application that has many pages and resources (images, CSS, JavaScript) could have performance issues when using the single-page container method, as all resources and pages will be loaded upon the first page load. Therefore, the Ajax or standard HTML method might offer better performance and load times.

For small applications and for prototyping, the single-page container method might be preferred. CSS3/JavaScript can handle animated transitions between pages and, as the number of resources may be minimal, it will not have a large impact on page loading. This might be preferred, as the end user does not have to wait for pages to load through Ajax or the standard HTML methods. This creates a much more app-like experience.

For simpler applications, the standard HTML method might be preferred. However, animation between pages could become impractical and there will be a slight wait time while pages and resources load when navigating through pages.

> **NOTE:** To work with the exercises in this chapter, create a new folder within your Aptana project called `exercises` and one within that called `chapter4`. We will refer to this as the "chapter folder" in the examples.

Paging with Standard HTML

The method to create standard HTML paging is simple. To start with, create a new folder in chapter folder in your project called `standard` and create two basic mobile-friendly web pages called `index.html` and `index2.html`, as shown in Listing 4-1.

Listing 4-1. *Basic HTML Mobile Web Page*

```
<!DOCTYPE html>
<html lang="en-GB" dir="ltr">

    <head>

        <meta charset="UTF-8" />
        <meta name="viewport" content="width=device-width; initial-scale=1.0;
maximum-scale=1.0; user-scalable=0; target-densitydpi=device-dpi;"/>
        <title>Standard Paging</title>

    </head>

    <body>


    </body>

</html>
```

There is nothing special here, as explained in Chapter 1 we set the `charset` and `viewport` meta tags to ensure that the page scales accordingly and to prevent the user from zooming in with their fingers. We also set the page title for good measure. Within the body of `index.html`, create a link and header, as shown in Listing 4-2.

Listing 4-2. *Creating a Link in index.html*

```
<h1>Page 1</h1>
<a href="./index2.html">Page 2</a>
```

In `index2.html`, create another link in the body linking back to the previous page, as shown in Listing 4-3.

Listing 4-3. *Creating a Link Back to index.html in index2.html*

```
<h1>Page 2</h1>
<a href="./index.html">Page 1</a>
```

Load it up in your mobile browser and test it out. It's as simple as that. There's nothing special about creating links to other standard HTML pages for mobile.

Paging with Single-Page Ajax

Creating a mobile application with single-page Ajax requires a little bit more thought and effort. Ajax allows content to be dynamically pulled in from a file or page outside of the current web page that the user is on. This can make an application a little bit more scalable, as you do not have to house several pages on a single page. Instead, you pull them in as and when you need them. The benefit of this is that you can use CSS3 to apply animations as the user moves between pages. Listing 4-4 shows the very basics of what is required to load an HTML page via Ajax.

Listing 4-4. *Loading HTML Using Ajax*

```
<div id="container">
   <div id="card">
      <h1>Page 1</h1>
      <a href="index2.html" data-method="xhr">Page 2</a>
   </div>
</div>

<script>

   /**
    * This method will bind find all links within the div with the ID of
    * container. The query will also only match those links with the data-method
    * attribute with a value of xhr.
    * i.e., <a href="index2.html" data-method="xhr">Page 2</a>
    */
   function bindLinks(){

      /**
       * This will call forEach within the context of the query
       * selector. If you're familiar with jQuery, it's the equivelant to
       * $('#container a[data-method="xhr"]).each(...);
       */
      [].forEach.call(document.querySelectorAll('#container a[data-method="
xhr"]'), function(el){
         /**
          * For every matched element, this anonymous method will be
          * called. The forEach method callback accepts the returned
          * object as a parameter. In this case, it will be the
          * matched element now set to el.
          */

         /**
          * Here you add an event listener to the object. There are
          * several touch event listeners such as touchend, touchcancel,
```

```
       * and touchstart, all of which are explained in Chapter 5.
       */
      el.addEventListener("touchend", function requestCard(event){
         /**
          * This will call the loadCard method with the target
          * link location as the parameter (index2.html).
          */
         loadCard(event.target.href);

         /**
          * This prevents the original path of the link from
          * being handled by the browser.
          */
         event.preventDefault();
      });
   });

}

/**
 * This method will dynamically load a card from the deck based on the path
 * that is passed to it through the path parameter.
 */
function loadCard(path){

   /**
    * This creates a new XMLHttpRequest object request. This will be
    * used to pull the html page in dynamically using JavaScript.
    */
   var xhr = new XMLHttpRequest();

   /**
    * Creates a GET request (this can either be POST or GET). A POST
    * request is useful for sending large amounts of data; a GET request
    * should be used to get information from a server using a parameter-
    * based URI. The third parameter sets the request to be asyncronous.
    * Setting this as false or not including it will block the UI and
    * prevent the user from interacting with the application. This will
    * not send the request straight away. You must call xhr.send();
    */
   xhr.open("GET", path, true);

   /**
    * This sets callbacks for when the state of the request has changed.
    * The state can be determined by the this.readyState. In
    * this instance, it is event. The different states are:
    *
    *  DONE - Request complete
    *  LOADING - Request loading
    *  HEADERS_RECIEVED - Headers have loaded but the request body hasn't
```

```
 *   OPENED - The open method has been called
 *   UNSENT - The XMLHttpRequest object has been instantiated
 *
 * You can create conditions for each readyState using a switch
 * statement.
 */

xhr.onreadystatechange = function contentLoaded(){
  /** Here you check the request state **/
  if (this.readyState === this.DONE) {

    /**
     * Here you select the container element that will be
     * populated with the new content.
     */
    var container = document.querySelector("#container");

    /**
     * This will check the response status, 200 is OK.
     * You can find the various HTTP status codes at
     * http://www.w3.org/Protocols/HTTP/HTRESP.html
     */
    if (this.status === 200) {

      /**
       * Here you create a DOMParser object that will
       * parse the returned HTML so that is can be
       * traversed.
       */
      var domParser = new DOMParser(),
      /**
       * For now, HTML retrieved by XMHHttpRequest is
       * returned as a string. To convert it to a
       * traversible DOM document, it needs to be
       * converted.
       */
      externalDocument = domParser.parseFromString(this.responseText,
'text/html'),

      /**
       * The next thing to do is select the card from
       * the DOM Document returned by parseFromString.
       * DOMParser allows you to use DOM methods to
       * traverse any HTML returned by an
       * XMLHttpRequest.
       */
      card = externalDocument.querySelector("#card").outerHTML;

      /**
       * Next you simply call the setCardContent
```

```
             * method, which is defined below passing in the
             * HTML as a string from the card.
             */
            setCardContent(card);

            /**
             * Finally, you rebind all of the links, so that
             * any new content links are bound to
             * XMLHttpRequest calls.
             */
            bindLinks();

        } else {

            /**
             * If the request fails, you simply set the
             * contents of the div to show an error message.
             */
            setCardContent('<div id="card"><h1>Oops</h1><p>Something went
wrong!</p></div>');

        }
    }

}

    /**
     * Finally, send the request. As the request's state changes, the
     * callback method will be called.
     */
    xhr.send();
}

/**
 * This will set the content of the container to be the card from the
requested
 * HTML file. POSH is simply an acronym for Plain Old Semantic HTML.
 */
function setCardContent(posh){
    container.innerHTML = posh;
}

/**
 * Finally, you call bindLinks(), which bind the links currently
displayed
 * on the page.
 */
bindLinks();

    /**
```

```
  * Unfortunately, some Android browsers do not support DOMParser's text/html
  * type. The method below from Eli Grey will allow browsers that do not
support
  * the text/html type to support it via prototype.
  */

/*
 * DOMParser HTML extension
 * 2012-02-02
 *
 * By Eli Grey, http://eligrey.com
 * Public domain.
 * NO WARRANTY EXPRESSED OR IMPLIED. USE AT YOUR OWN RISK.
 */

/*! @source https://gist.github.com/1129031 */
/*global document, DOMParser*/

(function(DOMParser) {
   "use strict";
   var DOMParser_proto = DOMParser.prototype
   ,real_parseFromString = DOMParser_proto.parseFromString;

   // Firefox/Opera/IE throw errors on unsupported types
   try {
      // WebKit returns null on unsupported types
      if ((new DOMParser).parseFromString("", "text/html")) {
         // text/html parsing is natively supported
         return;
      }
   } catch (ex) {}

   DOMParser_proto.parseFromString = function(markup, type) {
      if (/^\s*text\/html\s*(?:;|$)/i.test(type)) {
         var doc = document.implementation.createHTMLDocument("")
            ,doc_elt = doc.documentElement
            ,first_elt;

         doc_elt.innerHTML = markup;
         first_elt = doc_elt.firstElementChild;

         // are we dealing with an entire document or a fragment?
         if (doc_elt.childElementCount === 1 &&
first_elt.localName.toLowerCase() === "html") {
            doc.replaceChild(first_elt, doc_elt);
         }

         return doc;
      } else {
         return real_parseFromString.apply(this, arguments);
```

```
        }
    };
}(DOMParser));
```

```
</script>
```

The code in Listing 4-4 might look slightly confusing and long-winded, but it will allow you to load external HTML documents and traverse its DOM like a regular HTML document and pick out elements from it. It also binds any links with the `data-method` attribute set to xhr.

The benefit to doing it this way, compared to using XML or JSON, is that if you want to degrade the web application to work on devices without JavaScript support, you don't have to do as—you do not need to make a different view, you can simply remove the JavaScript code to move between pages.

To do this, the first thing we do is set up the page as shown in the following snippet.

```
<div id="container">
    <div id="card">
        <h1>Page 1</h1>
        <a href="index2.html" data-method="xhr">Page 2</a>
    </div>
</div>
```

This creates a container to house the cards. Within the container, there is a basic card with a header and link. HTML5 allows us to set custom attributes in the markup using data attributes.

Next, you must bind all of the links to a JavaScript method using the following code snippet.

```
function bindLinks(){

    [].forEach.call(document.querySelectorAll("#container a[data-method]"),
function(el){

        if(el.getAttribute("data-method") == "xhr"){
            el.addEventListener("click", function requestCard(event){
                loadCard(this.href);
                event.preventDefault();
            });
        }
    });

}
```

This functionality is contained within a function called `bindLinks` so that it can be used a little latter. The second line in this method iterates through the list of

HTML elements or the NodeList returned from the query selector. The method of doing this looks slightly complicated. You first begin by creating a new empty array object using []. From here, you use the `call` method to run the `Array` object's `forEach` method within the context of the NodeList returned from the query. The `forEach` method accepts a callback function as the first parameter. The callback function also accepts the following three arguments:

- The current element being iterated

- The current element's index within the array

- The actual array

You will only need the current element so that you can use it within your callback function; this is called `el`.

The third line within this method checks to see whether the attribute `data-method` exists and that the value is `xhr`. If this is true, it adds an event listener to the link. This allows you to manually specify which links should be pulled in via Ajax.

The fourth line adds an event listener to the click event. The click event acts in much the same way as it does on the desktop, with the exception that if a user drags his finger away from the link, it will cancel the event. You use a named function for this so that it can be tracked in a call stack when debugging in Android Browser or Chrome for Android.

Within the event listener function, when the user taps the link, the method `loadCard` is called with a parameter containing the link's intended path `event.target.getAttribute("href")`. This is taken from the link's `href` attribute. `event.preventDefault();` stops the link from being followed through in the browser, and the next page from loading in the usual way.

The `loadCard` function shown in the next code snippet will load the html from the path parameter using an `XMLHttpRequest`, fetch the card within the page, and replace the card on the current page with the new content using the `setCardContent` method. After that is complete, the method will rebind the links with the event handlers so that all further pages are loaded in the same way, as any new links in the new content will not have event handlers attached to them.

```
function loadCard(path){

    var xhr = new XMLHttpRequest();
    xhr.open("GET", path, true);
    xhr.onreadystatechange = function contentLoaded(){

        if (this.readyState === this.DONE) {
```

```
        var container = document.querySelector("#container");

        if (this.status === 200) {

            var domParser = new DOMParser(),
            externalDocument = domParser.parseFromString(this.responseText,
'text/html'),
            card = externalDocument.querySelector("#card").outerHTML;

            setCardContent(card);
            bindLinks();

        } else {

            setCardContent('<div id="card"><h1>Oops</h1><p>Something went
wrong!</p></div>');

        }

    }

  }

  xhr.send();

}
```

The first line in this function instantiates a new XMLHttpRequest (xhr) object. The second line sets up the xhr request. The open method accepts the following five parameters:

- Method—GET, POST
- URL
- Async—true, false (defaults to true and will continue to run JavaScript after the send method is called. If set to false, it will freeze the browser until the request is complete after running the send method)
- User (if the request is protected by an HTTP username and password, you can enter the username here)
- Password (if the request is protected by an HTTP username and password, you can enter the password here)

Calling open does not make the Ajax request. The fourth line sets the handler for the onreadystatechange event.

Paging with a Single-Page Container

Paging with a single-page container allows you to create a set of cards within a deck in a single HTML page and navigate between them using JavaScript. As your application grows, this could produce potential problems with trying to manage numerous sections/features containing several cards. The solution to this would be to split each deck or set of features into several HTML pages. Within each HTML page, would be a deck of cards related to that particular feature. To navigate between the different decks, you could either pull them in via Ajax, or use standard HTML to navigate to and from them without animation.

Creating a single-page container mobile web application is simple, and works in much the same way as the Ajax method.

First, create a folder within the exercise folder called `container`. Within this folder, create a folder called `css`. Create a new CSS file called `mobile.css` and add the CSS from Listing 4-5.

Listing 4-5. *CSS for Single-Page Container*

```
/**
 * Sets the body, html, and deck element styles
 */
body, html, #deck {
   height: 100%; /** Sets the height of the document to 100% of the viewport **/
   overflow: hidden; /** Set so that all content that flows outside is hidden **/
   margin: 0; /** The body's margin is usually never 0, so this removed any margin **/
   position: realtive; /** The card will be positioned relative to the deck **/
}

/**
 * The card within the deck's styles
 */
#deck .card {
   overflow: auto; /** If there is too much content, this lets the user scroll **/
   height: 100%; /** Sets the height of the card to be 100% **/
   position: absolute; /** Allows the card to be absolutely positioned **/
   left: -100%; /** Sets the default position to be off the screen (hidden) **/
   width: 100%; /** Sets the width of the card to be the width of the deck **/
}

/**
 * Sets the active card style so that it is visible when the class is added to it
 */
```

```
#deck .card.active {
    left: 0; /** moves the card back into view **/
}
```

The first rule in this CSS will set the body, html, and deck to a height of 100%. This will fill the web browser's viewport with the deck and cards. From here, you set the overflow to hidden so that any content outside of these elements will be cut off and not display scroll bars. You also set the margin to 0; this will apply only to the body, but this saves having to write a new CSS rule specifically for the body.

The second rule sets the style for the cards themselves. Every card has the overflow set to auto. This will allow users to scroll with their fingers for more content within the card when the content flows beyond the visible height of the screen. Each card has a position of absolute so that its position can be placed anywhere within the deck itself. Doing this allows cards to be placed off screen when they are not needed. Setting the left CSS rule to -100% will push all non-active cards within the deck to the width of the viewport to the left so that it isn't visible to the user.

The third rule sets the CSS rule to active cards. This will set the card's left position to 0, which will bring the card back in view for the user. Showing the card is as simple as adding and removing the active class for the card you want to present to the user using JavaScript. Listing 4-6 shows how to do this.

Listing 4-6. *JavaScript to Show and Hide a Card*

```
function goToCard(to) {
    /**
     * Gets all cards with the active class and removes it. This hides the card
     * from view.
     */
    document.querySelectorAll('.card.active')[0].classList.remove('active');

    /**
     * Adds the active CSS class to the target card and brings it into view.
     */
    document.querySelectorAll(to)[0].classList.add('active');
}
```

From the goToCard method, you can see that it takes a to parameter. The to parameter is a hash taken from the URL in a link from the HTML shown in Listing 4-7

Listing 4-7. *HTML for a Link to Load a Card from the Deck*

```
<a data-method="push" href="#card-index">Page 1</a>
```

From this, you can see that the data attribute is used to identify links to be used to push content to the top of the deck. In this instance, push is used; however, any other attribute can be used to your requirements. The href attribute is associated with the ID of the card, as shown in Listing 4-8.

Listing 4-8. *HTML for a Deck*

```
<section class="card" id="card-index">
    <h1>Page 1</h1>
    <a data-method="push" href="#card-second-page">Page 2</a>
</section>
```

As you can see from this section of code, the id of the card is set to card-index. You use card as a prefix to help namespace the deck cards. This will prevent you from inadvertently using index for instance on another HTML element, causing issues with paging. Listing 4-9 shows how to use JavaScript to activate the pages.

Listing 4-9. *Activating Cards within a Deck*

```
/**
 * Works in much the same way as the previous method. It will iterate over all
matched
 * elements and call the callback method.
 */
[].forEach.call(document.querySelectorAll('.card a[data-method="push"]'),
function(el){
    /**
     * As you can see, the callback method is named. Instead of function(event){
     * function pushCard(event) is used. This can help with debugging; e.g., in
     * the JavaScript stack trace you can see the function's name rather than
     * anonymous.
     */
    el.addEventListener("click", function pushCard(event){
        /**
         * This gets the hash (#card-second-page) element of the href in
         * the link and assigns it to pageid. The href object has various
         * properties, all of which can be found at
         * http://www.w3.org/TR/html5-author/urls.html#url-decomposition-idl-
         * attributes.
         */
        var pageid = this.href.hash;
        /**
         * This calls the goToCard method that will load the content with the
         * specified pageID.
         */
        goToCard(pageid);
```

```
    /**
     * This will prevent the browser from following the URL.
     */
    event.preventDefault();
  });
});
```

You use the same style of JavaScript as the Ajax method to bind events to links with the push data attribute. Within the event listener, you get the hash from the link using `this.href.hash`. This is passed to the `goToCard` method from Listing 4-5, which removed the `active` class from the visible card and adds it to the card to be shown to the user. The complete code example can be seen in Listing 4-10.

Listing 4-10. *Complete Single-Page Container Example*

```html
<!DOCTYPE html>
<html lang="en-GB" dir="ltr">

<head>
    <meta charset="UTF-8" />
    <meta name="viewport" content="width=device-width; initial-scale=1.0;
maximum-scale=1.0; user-scalable=0; target-densitydpi=device-dpi;"/>
    <title>Single Page Container</title>
    <link rel="stylesheet" type="text/css" href="css/mobile.css" />
</head>

<body>
    <div id="deck">
        <section class="card active" id="card-index">
            <h1>Page 1</h1>
            <a data-method="push" href="#card-second-page">Page 2</a>
        </section>

        <section class="card" id="card-second-page">
            <h1>Page 2</h1>
            <a data-method="push" href="#card-third-page">Page 3</a>
        </section>

        <section class="card" id="card-third-page">
            <h1>Page 3</h1>
            <a data-method="push" href="#card-index">Page 1</a>
        </section>

    </div>

    <script>
        [].forEach.call(document.querySelectorAll('.card a[data-method="push"]'),
function(el){
```

```
        el.addEventListener("click", function pushCard(event){
            var pageid = this.href.hash;
            goToCard(pageid);
            event.preventDefault();
        });
    });

    function goToCard(to){

document.querySelectorAll('.card.active')[0].classList.remove('active');
        document.querySelectorAll(to)[0].classList.add('active');
    }

  </script>

</body>

</html>
```

As you can see, there are several useful methods for paging for mobile. Although the examples are presented as separate, you can combine them. For instance, you can combine the container and Ajax methods to separate the different sections and functionality of your application. You can also use Ajax to load content and data dynamically using JSON/XML with any of the methods mentioned within this chapter to generate new dynamic views.

The next section will take you through the first stages of creating the MoMemo application.

Creating the App

The key to creating a usable mobile web application is in the planning. Deciding what key functionality your mobile web application has, and how users will get to the important features and data, will help you to decide how to implement the application itself, using paging techniques, design, and UI. If you do not like planning, this can be a laborious and boring task, but it will help you iron out problems before you start development and design.

Planning MoMemo

The first step in this process is to define the application in a single sentence. When defining an application in a single sentence, you should try to avoid including features or technical details. The sentence should simply describe the app and its goal. For MoMemo, the application definition would be as follows:

MoMemo is an application that allows users to quickly note down movie trailers that they see in the cinema and be reminded when the movie is released.

The next step is to define the must-have features that will help to satisfy the primary goal for the application. MoSCoW (Must have, Should have, Could have, Won't have) can be a good method to define the core features and functionality of the application. It will allow you to define the core features (must have), the features that provide added value (should have), the features that would be nice to implement if there is time left over at the end of the project (could have), and the features that you can't afford to implement due to time or funding restrictions but could implement in the very near future (won't have). This will help to prevent scope creep and the "never-ending project" syndrome, where developers constantly talk about an app and its extremely long list of impossible features, but never actually create it.

For MoMemo to be successful, the application must:

- Allow users to quickly add and remove movies to and from a personal list
- Allow users to view movies in the list

It should:

- Provide a list of movie suggestions while the user types
- Show information about the movie including
    - Synopsis
    - Release date
    - Cast list

It could:

- Allow users to view the movie trailer
- Allow users to play sound clips from the movie
- Allow users to share items added to their list on social networks
- Display a map of the closest cinemas to the user when viewing a movie memo

It won't:

> Send notifications to users when movies are released
>
> Allow users to rate movies after they have been seen
>
> Allow users to invite other users to the cinema to see movies

Now that the core features and functionality have been defined, we can start to create a user journey based on the must-have, should-have, and could-have feature set.

To begin with, we should build upon our core feature set from the must-have category. Figure 4-1 shows how the core functionality of the application should function. The user should launch the app and be presented with a list of movies that they have added. From here, they can add to the list or delete from it. They will then be taken back to the Movie List.

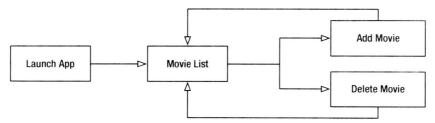

Figure 4-1. *Primary features of the application*

Now you can build upon this and start adding the should-have features. In Figure 4-2, you can see that only the Movie Info feature has been added. We still need to provide a list of movie suggestions while the user is typing, but this list of movie suggestions will be a feature of the Add Movie feature, rather than the Movie Info feature.

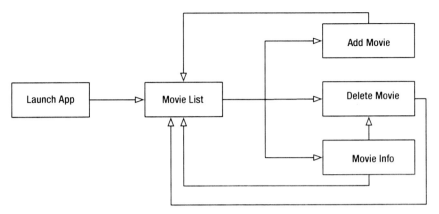

Figure 4-2. *Secondary features of the application*

Finally, you can add the could-have or value add features, as shown in Figure 4-3.

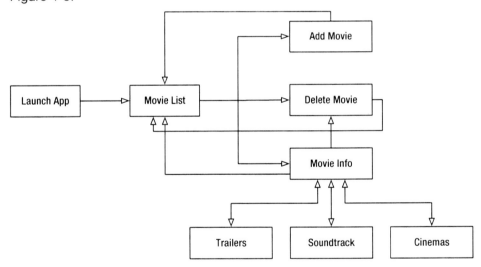

Figure 4-3. *Value add features*

As you can see from Figure 4-3, the Movie Info feature has three subfeatures that will allow you to navigate to and from the main Movie Info feature. This adds complexity to your application and suggests that the Movie Info should potentially be broken out into its own page or deck.

Now that we have a clear insight as to how the application should currently function, we can begin to create the UI.

Creating the UI and HTML

If you have ever developed an app (native or web) for Android specifically, you will know that some design principles differ from what you may expect from other mobile operating systems such as iOS or Windows Mobile. For instance, on the Google Galaxy Nexus and Samsung Galaxy Tab, the system bars (Navigation Bar and Combined Bar) are found at the bottom of the screen and are always active or visible when using Android Browser. A good design principle is not to stack toolbars on top of the system bar; this will prevent users from inadvertently tapping on system buttons when they actually meant to interact with your application.

In order to make it easy for the user to use this application, it makes sense to present a clear way for users to add and view their movies while also providing the ability for you to add new features in the future.

LinkedIn provides a good and clear example of this. As you can see from Figure 4-4, it is clear that the primary use for the mobile web application is to search for people and see the most recent updates. If you want to access more functionality, there is a toolbar hidden under the "in" icon next to the search bar. If you want to update your LinkedIn status, you click on the message balloon icon at the top right.

Figure 4-4. *LinkedIn's solution for an uncluttered landing/home page*

This top bar is visible on every page within the application. When designing any mobile-based web site, you should keep in mind that it will be viewed on a variety of screen sizes in either landscape or portrait mode.

> **NOTE:** To date, there is no known way to lock the web browser's orientation to landscape or portrait. So when you design a mobile web application, you should take into consideration that the orientation will change.

Creating the Movie List

The UI for the MoMemo application revolves around the search bar at the top of the screen. Figure 4-5 and Figure 4-6 show the Movie List section of the application, including the taskbar for both tablet and mobile devices.

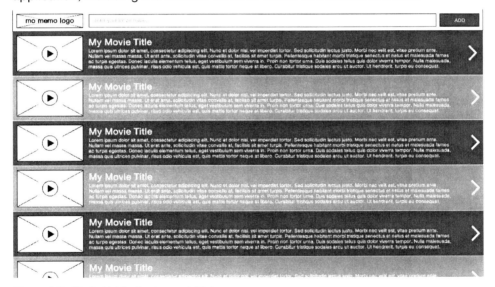

Figure 4-5. *Movie List for landscape tablet*

As you can see from Figure 4-5, the ability to search for and add movies can be accessed while browsing through movies previously added to the list. It is also clear to the user that this will add items to the list rather than search through the existing list, as the button to submit the form is marked as ADD rather than search.

Figure 4-6 presents the information in the same way, but for a smaller screen; however, the list items are slightly larger to accommodate for the user's situation in which finger-tapping accuracy might be low. Although the list items are bunched together, the target that the user has to tap to view more information about a movie is reasonably large. Placing the taskbar at the top also allows a user to thumb through their list of saved movies naturally and with ease, and not worry so much about accidentally activating another part of the application. Both UI mock-ups for the application are the same in terms of HTML; however, we can use CSS media queries to target specific display sizes and orientations. You can also utilize a fluid layout to ensure the application reacts correctly to changes in orientation and screen size.

Figure 4-6. *Movie List for portrait mobile*

Marking this up in HTML is quite simple. First, create a folder in the root of your project called `application`. Within that folder, create three more called `css`, `img`, and `js`. The `css` folder will store your CSS/SASS, `img` will store all of your images and sprites, and `js` will store all of your library and application JavaScript.

You will also need to create two folders called `lib` and `app` within `js`, a file in the `js/app/` folder called `bootstrap.js`, and a file in the `css` folder called `mobile.scss`.

Create a new file called `index.html` within the `application` folder; the code in Listing 4-11 will help to bootstrap the application.

Listing 4-11. *Initial Bootstrap HTML*

```
<!DOCTYPE html>
<html lang="en-GB" dir="ltr">

    <head>

        <meta charset="UTF-8" />
        <meta name="viewport" content="width=device-width; initial-scale=1.0;
maximum-scale=1.0; user-scalable=0; target-densitydpi=device-dpi;"/>
        <title>Mo Memo</title>
        <link rel="stylesheet" type="text/css" href="css/mobile.css" />
        <link rel="apple-touch-icon-precomposed" href="img/home-screen-icon.png">
    </head>

    <body>

        <div id="shoe">

            <div id="deck">


            </div>

        </div>

        <!-- This script will instantiate any JavaScript necessary -->
        <script src="js/app/bootstrap.js"></script>

    </body>

</html>
```

As you can see, there is a `div` that surrounds the deck called shoe. This will help to contain the global elements that appear on every page, such as the top taskbar, and it will hold multiple decks should the application need to expand in the future. You can use any hierarchical naming convention other than that related to casinos and playing cards.

> **NOTE:** This is simply a naming convention that I have adopted to make it easier for me and other developers to understand the structure of my applications. This also makes it semantically clear when writing CSS and JavaScript to hook into the functionality of the mobile web application. You can use any IDs or classes you wish, or you can follow suite and use mine. Just make sure that they are meaningful.

You will notice that the CSS doesn't link to `mobile.scss`. This is because the SCSS file will need to be compiled and converted to CSS by SASS. Once the compilation is complete, the `mobile.css` file will appear. Open the `mobile.scss` file and press Shift + CMD + R and then press 1. This will compile the SASS file into a CSS file. (SASS will be covered in Chapter 5.)

It's time to create the header for the application. The code shown in Listing 4-12 should be added just inside the `<div id="shoe">` element but just before the `<div id="deck">` element.

Listing 4-12. *Header Code*

```
<header id="taskbar">

    <h1 class="branding">Mo Memo</h1>

    <form method="post">
      <input type="text" name="query" placeholder="enter your movie
name&hellip;" />
      <input type="submit" value="ADD" />
    </form>

</header>
```

This will simply create a title and form for the user to search, as shown in Figure 4-7. Using CSS, this will be placed at the top of the screen.

Figure 4-7. *Taskbar with no styling*

Now it's time to add the first card to the deck, the Movie List card. This is simple and is done by creating an unordered list of data, as shown in the code in Listing 4-13.

Listing 4-13. *List of Saved Movies*

```
<ul class="list alternating medium">
   <li>
      <a href="path/to/movie/">
         <video poster="img/video.jpg" title="Movie Title">
            <source type="video/webm" src="path/to/video.webm" />
         </video>
         <h2>My Movie Title</h2>
         <p>My Movie Description</p>
      </a>
   </li>
   <li>
      <a href="path/to/movie/">
         <video poster="img/video.jpg" title="Movie Title">
            <source type="video/webm" src="path/to/video.webm" />
         </video>
         <h2>My Movie Title</h2>
         <p>My Movie Description</p>
      </a>
   </li>
</ul>
```

In HTML5, you can surround block-level elements with the href tag. This makes it easier to make the entire content of a list item a link to another resource.

As you can see from Figure 4-8, the page looks pretty boring. The next workshop will cover using CSS to style the application.

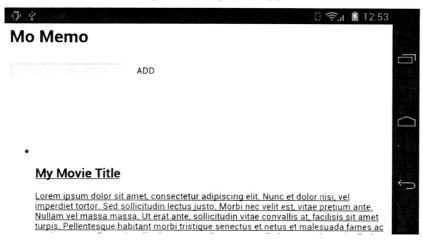

Figure 4-8. *Full movie listing page*

Movie Search and Add

With the Movie List feature in place, it's now time to cover the task of searching and adding movies. This can be performed in one of two ways.

- The user searches for a movie and is presented with a list. From this list, the user taps the movie, which then brings them to the Movie Info screen. From this screen, the user can then add the movie to the list and return to the Movie List.

- The second option is to present the user with suggestions, allow them to tap the suggestion that suites them, and click on the add button. The user can then view the Movie Info at a later date.

There is nothing wrong with either option, but the most optimal one lies again in the situation the user is in when searching for movies. To answer this, you need to refer back to the MoSCoW requirements for the project. One of the must-have requirements is to "Allow users to **quickly** add and remove movies to and from a personal list". Chances are that the user will open the application, search for the movie, add it, close the application, and look at the list of movies in more detail at a later date. Figures 4-9 and 4-10 show what the search functionality will look like for tablet and mobile, based on this.

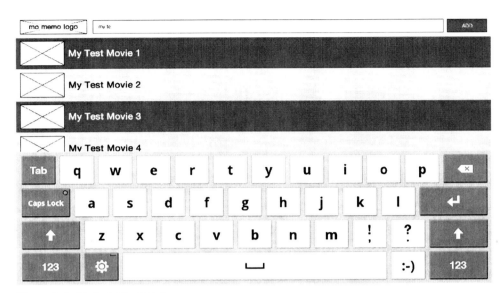

Figure 4-9. *Movie list for tablet*

Searching and showing the search results will be a task for JavaScript (covered in Chapter 8).

Figure 4-10. *Movie list for mobile*

Movie Info

The final part of the MoMemo application is the Movie Info section. It has several subfeatures including the movie synopsis, clips, cast, soundtrack, and closest cinema. You could present this information on separate cards, however you will end up with lots of empty space when viewing small sections (such as the synopsis) on a device with a large screen (such as a tablet). To get around this, you can place all of the content within the same view, but allow users to side scroll to content on portrait-orientated devices to make use of the vertical space, and scroll normally in landscape mode. Figures 4-11 and 4-12 show how this should be presented.

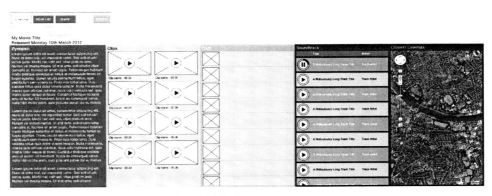

Figure 4-11. *Movie info on a portrait mobile device*

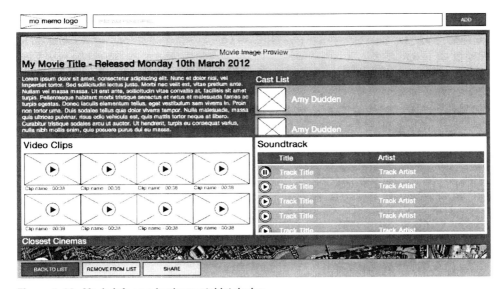

Figure 4-12. *Movie info on a landscape tablet device*

Although both views are presented slightly differently, the content is the same and can be repositioned using CSS media queries to suit the orientation of the device. Create a new card with an `id` of `card-movie_info` and add the HTML from Listing 4-14.

Listing 4-14. *Movie Info Header*

```
<header>

    <img src="path/to/movie/photo.jpg" alt="Movie Title" />
    <hgroup>
       <h2>My Movie Title</h2>
       <p>Released: Monday 10th March 2012</p>
    </hgroup>

</header>
```

This will create the markup for a header that can be presented differently using CSS, depending on the orientation of the device. You use the hgroup to group the release date info, which shouldn't be contained in the h2 element.

Listing 4-15 shows the synopsis block, which will simply contain text. There is a div with a class of content surrounding the content within a block but excluding the main header. This is so that the content can scroll, but the header remains in view at all times.

Listing 4-15. *Synopsis Block*

```
<section class="block" id="block-synopsis">
    <div class="content">
       <p>Hello world, this is my synopsis</p>
    </div>
</section>
```

Listing 4-16 shows the cast block. From the designs, the cast list should be scrollable within its block; however, the header should remain at the top at all times. This block also shows that the lists will be standardized to reduce the amount of bloat in the CSS.

Listing 4-16. *Cast Block*

```
<section class="block" id="block-cast">
    <h3>Cast List</h3>
    <div class="content">
       <ul class="list scrolling medium">
          <li>
             <img src="path/to/actor/photo.jpg" alt="Actor Name" />
             <p>Actor Name</p>
          </li>
       </ul>
    </div>
</section>
```

You then move on to the video block, as shown in Listing 4-17. In both wireframes the videos are displayed in a grid format, but they are flexible in that a row may contain two or four videos, which makes using a table inflexible. For this, you would opt to use a regular list and format it using CSS, depending on the device's orientation.

Listing 4-17. *Video Block*

```
<section class="block" id="block-video">

    <h3>Video Clips</h3>

    <div class="content">
        <ul class="list grid">

            <li>
                <video poster="path/to/posterframe.jpg" title="Clip Title">
                    <source type="video/webm" src="path/to/video.webm" />
                </video>
                <p>Clip name - 00:38</p>
            </li>

        </ul>
    </div>

</section>
```

The soundtrack block is quite simple, as it's similar in both orientations, and on both tablet and mobile. This is shown in Listing 4-18.

Listing 4-18. *The Soundtrack Block*

```
<section class="block" id="block-soundtrack">

    <h3>Soundtrack</h3>

    <div class="content">

        <table class="alternating">

            <thead>
                <tr>
                    <th> </th>
                    <th>Title</th>
                    <th>Artist</th>
                </tr>
            </thead>
```

```
            <tbody>
              <tr>
                <td>
                  <canvas class="audio"></canvas>
                </td>
                <td>
                  A Ridiculously Long Track Title
                </td>
                <td>
                  Track Artist
                </td>
              </tr>
              <tr>
                <td>
                  <canvas class="audio"></canvas>
                </td>
                <td>
                  A Ridiculously Long Track Title
                </td>
                <td>
                  Track Artist
                </td>
              </tr>
            </tbody>

        </table>

    </div>

</section>
```

As you can see, there is a canvas element in the first column of each row. We will be using HTML canvas to generate the play button and animate the progress bar.

Finally, Listing 4-19 shows the closest cinemas block. This consists of a div with a class of map. The Google Maps API will be used for this task.

Listing 4-19. *The Closest Cinemas Block*

```
<section class="block" id="block-closest_cinemas">

    <h3>Closest Cinemas</h3>

    <div class="content">
      <div class="map"></div>
    </div>

</section>
```

This concludes creating the markup for MoMemo. How the taskbars react to the application will be covered in Chapter 8 on JavaScript.

Do not be alarmed if you see something similar to what is shown in Figure 4-13. You will learn how to use SASS to generate modular CSS in Chapter 5.

Figure 4-13. *The complete markup on the Samsung Galaxy Tab*

The last and final thing that you might wish to do is start to implement the offline caching capabilities of the application. This will allow users to browse their movie list while they have no reception.

The first step is to add the `manifest` attribute to the `html` tag, as shown in Listing 4-20.

Listing 4-20. *Application manifest Attribute*

```
<!DOCTYPE html>
<html lang="en-GB" dir="ltr" manifest="momemo.cache">
```

Now create a file in the root of the application directory called `momemo.cache`. Within this file, add the code from Listing 4-21.

Listing 4-21. *Cache Manifest File*

```
CACHE MANIFEST
index.html
js/app/bootstrap.js
css/mobile.css
```

This will ensure that the `index.html`, `bootstrap.js`, and `mobile.css` files are cached for offline viewing. As you build the application, more files and rules will be added to the cache manifest file.

Summary

From this chapter, you should have gained an understanding of how to manage paging in mobile web applications, and how to pick the appropriate paging strategy, depending on the requirements of the project. You should also have an understanding of how to begin building an application—from an idea through to requirements, from IA/wireframes through to coding the foundation in HTML, and how the device's orientation and screen size will affect how you design your application.

In Chapter 5, you will next learn how CSS can change the way you style, animate, and increase the performance of your mobile web application, as well as how SASS can help to organize your CSS rules and produce a structured set of CSS files.

CSS3 for Mobile

One of the most exciting aspects of developing for mobile is the support for CSS3 through browsers on the latest smartphones. Prior to CSS3, we relied upon using JavaScript to provide eye-popping animations and transitions, simply applying styles to DOM elements such as the last element within a parent element or alternating table rows.

In this chapter, you will learn some of the new CSS3 features, such as animations and transitions. You will learn how CSS3 can provide similar features to the most basic of animation concepts, called *keyframing*.

You will learn how to import new font faces within your mobile web application, which will provide a much broader set of typefaces for your audience. You will also take a look at some of the key CSS3 features, such as text shadows, selectors, gradients, and new border properties. In addition, you will briefly touch upon CSS media queries that will help you apply styles based on screen resolution and pixel density.

Finally, you will see the power of CSS precompilers in the form of Syntactically Awesome Stylesheets (SASS), with which you will learn how to streamline your CSS workflow and reduce time coding.

Vendor-Specific Properties

At the time of this writing, many CSS3 properties, such as `border-radius` and `opacity`, have been standardized. However, browser manufacturers can develop their own implementations of new CSS properties. To avoid conflicts caused by differences in syntax, new CSS properties that have not been standardized will usually be preceded by a vendor prefix. For instance, prior to the standardization of `border-radius`, there were several possible ways to declare it in CSS3.

- `-moz-border-radius`
- `-o-border-radius`
- `-webkit-border-radius`
- `border-radius`

As you can see, the last declaration in this list is the now-standardized version, and the vendor-specific implementations are prefixed with `-moz-` for Gecko-based browsers (Firefox), `-o-` for Opera, and `-webkit-` for Webkit-based browsers (Chrome, Android Browser, Dolphin).

There are more vendor-specific prefixes, but in general, for Android, `-moz-`, `-o-`, and `-webkit-` should suffice. It's important to always include the standard implementation.

There are ways to overcome having to declare all four CSS properties when you need them, which I explain in the section "CSS Precompilers (SASS)," later in this chapter.

CSS Animations and Transitions

CSS3 introduces CSS transitions and transforms for DOM elements. You can use these to replace the traditional method of animating DOM elements by manipulating their CSS properties using timers in JavaScript. You may be asking yourself, why should I use CSS for animation instead of JavaScript? Surely, CSS should be used for styling, and JavaScript for interaction. The truth is that by using CSS3 for animations, you can offload a lot of the heavy lifting often passed onto the device's CPU using JavaScript, to the device's GPU if it has one. This can make for much smoother animations.

Transitions

CSS transitions allow you to create transitions between two CSS styles. You invoke the transition by creating a CSS style and adding another to it. The CSS transition will handle the changes between the two states.

Creating a transition in CSS3 is quite simple. First you create your `div` element.

```
<div class="test"></div>
```

Next, create a style for the CSS element. Within this style, you set the `width` and the `height` to 100px, and set the `position` to `absolute`, as you will be moving the element to different positions on the page. You can also make the square into a circle by setting the `border-radius` to 50px. You also explicitly set the `top` and `left` positions to `0px`, and the `background-color` to blue.

```
.test {
    width: 100px;
    height: 100px;
    position: absolute;
    top: 0px;
    left: 0px;
    border-radius: 50px;
    background-color: blue;
}
```

This will render something similar to the image shown in Figure 5-1.

Figure 5-1. *Rendering of a CSS circle*

Now you need to set the next state for the ball. This is as simple as creating a new style with different properties.

```
.second-position {
    left: 50%;
    background-color: yellow;
}
```

As you can see, the new properties set the circle to be positioned in the middle of the screen with a `background-color` of `yellow`. Add this CSS class to the test div.

```
<div class="test second-position"></div>
```

Now you will see a screen similar to the one shown in Figure 5-2.

Figure 5-2. *Final position for the test div*

The final thing to do is to add a transition to the `.test` class. This will dictate how and what properties should be transitioned, as well as the timings for the transition.

The transition property is currently vendor specific and, as always, it is good practice to include all of the vendor properties. The following code will create a transition for all properties of the `test` element.

```
.test {
    width: 100px;
    height: 100px;
    position: absolute;
    top: 0px;
    left: 0px;
    border-radius: 50px;
    background-color: blue;
    transition: all 2s;
    -moz-transition: all 2s;
    -webkit-transition: all 2s;
    -o-transition: all 2s;
}
```

In order for the transition to work, you need to dynamically add the `second-position` class to the element. You can do this using JavaScript. The following script will search for the first element with a class name of `test` and append the `second-position` class to it. You should place it underneath the test element, as shown.

```
<div class="test"> </div>

<script>
   document.getElementsByClassName('test')[0].classList.add('second-position');
</script>
```

When you load the page on your mobile device, the circle should animate to the center of the screen and gradually change color to yellow.

You can also control which properties should be transitioned by specifying the property, the duration, timing function, and delay, as shown in the following example.

```
[-moz-|-o-|-webkit-]transition: property transition-duration transition-timing-
function transition-delay [, property duration timing-function delay]
```

You can specify as many properties as you wish to animate using this shorthand method. Table 5-1 lists the possible values.

Table 5-1. *CSS Transition Properties*

Property	Description	Values/Options
[-moz-|-webkit-|-o-]transition-property	The CSS property to animate	all, width, height, opacity, etc.
[-moz-|-webkit-|-o-]transition-duration	The duration of the transition in seconds; the default is 0	*X*s
[-moz-|-webkit-|-o-]transition-timing-function	The timing function to use; the default is ease	linear, ease, ease-in, ease-out, ease-in-out, cubic-bezier
[-moz-|-webkit-|-o-]transition-delay	The number of seconds to delay the transition by	*X*s

For example, you might want to begin transitioning the left position five seconds after the color transition begins and ease the left position out. In that case you would use the following code.

```
.test {
   width: 100px;
   height: 100px;
   position: absolute;
   top: 0px;
   left: 0px;
   border-radius: 50px;
   background-color: blue;
   transition: left 5s ease-out 5s, background-color 5s ease 0s;
```

```
    -moz-transition: left 5s ease-out 5s, background-color 5s ease 0s;
    -webkit-transition: left 5s ease-out 5s, background-color 5s ease 0s;
    -o-transition: left 5s ease-out 5s, background-color 5s ease 0s;
}
```

Animations

At times, you might want more control over your animations. For instance, wouldn't it be nice if you could animate from one position to another while altering certain CSS properties at certain points in your animation? This is better known as *keyframing*. If you have experience in Flash animation, you will know it better as creating significant alterations to an object in the flash timeline and creating tweens between them. Keyframes are now available in CSS. As always, this is vendor specific at the time of writing, so use all of the available vendors for compatibility. For this demo, you will animate a circle on the screen and make it bounce.

Before diving into creating the bouncing ball animation, look at the intended animation shown in Figure 5-3.

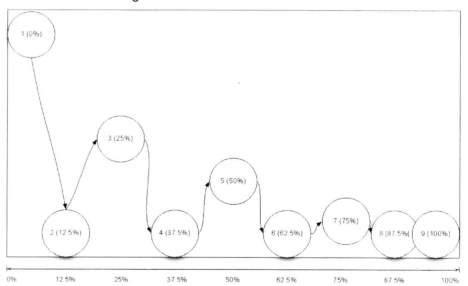

Figure 5-3. *Desired animation sequence*

As you can see from the animation sequence in Figure 5-3, the intention is to mimic a bouncing ball. The CSS keyframes feature allows you to specify the

CSS styles that you would like to animate at percentage increments. We can use the information shown in Figure 5-3 to create the keyframe rule.

You begin by creating a new keyframe definition using the `@keyframes` rule and a name for the keyframe as shown in the following code.

```
@keyframes bouncyball {
}
```

Next, you specify where you would like the animation's attached element to start using the percentage marker and CSS styles.

```
@keyframes bouncyball {
    0% { top: 0px; left: 0px; }
}
```

Here, you have specified that the associated element should start from the top left.

Next, you specify the individual segments within the animation. Using Figure 5-3 as a guide, there are CSS rules for 0%, 12.5%, 25%, 37.5%, 50%, 62.5%, 75%, 87.5%, and 100%.

```
@keyframes bouncyball {
    0% { bottom: 100%; left: 0px; }
    12.5% { bottom: 0px; left: 12.5%; }
    25% { bottom: 50%; left: 25%; }
    37.5% { bottom: 0px; left: 37.5%; }
    50% { bottom: 25%; left: 50%; }
    62.5% { bottom: 0px; left: 62.5% }
    75% { bottom: 12.5%; left: 75% }
    87.5% { bottom: 0px; left: 87.5% }
    100% { bottom: 0px; left: 100% }
}
```

Now it's time to create a new CSS rule for your ball. The following code will create a circle from a square, and apply the animation to the element.

```
.ball {
    background: black;
    width: 100px;
    height: 100px;
    position: absolute;
    border-radius: 50px;
    animation: bouncyball 2s ease-in-out;
    -moz-animation: bouncyball 2s ease-in-out;
    -webkit-animation: bouncyball 2s ease-in-out;
}
```

The animation CSS property in this example is written in shorthand and is, once again, vendor specific. Table 5-2 lists the parameters that the animation property takes in order.

Table 5-2. *CSS Animation Properties*

Property	Description	Values/Options
`[-moz-|-webkit-]animation-name`	The name of the animation to apply to the element	—
`[-moz-|-webkit-]animation-duration`	The duration of the animation in seconds	Xs
`[-moz-|-webkit-]animation-timing-function`	The timing function to use; the default is ease	`linear, ease, ease-in, ease-out, ease-in-out, cubic-bezier`
`[-moz-|-webkit-]animation-delay`	The number of seconds to delay the transition by	Xs
`[-moz-|-webkit-]animation-iteration-count`	The number of times to repeat the animation; the default is 1	Integer
`[-moz-|-webkit-]animation-direction`	Tells the animation whether or not to play the animation back in reverse on alternate cycles; e.g., if you specify 2 as the `animation-iteration-count`, the animation will play backward on the second iteration	`normal, alternate`
`[-moz-|-webkit-]animation-play-state`	Specifies whether the animation is playing or not; this can be modified using JavaScript	`running, paused`

When you load the animation on your device, it should automatically play. It's not a very smooth bouncing ball, but this is just to prove that CSS can be a very powerful tool for animations, with little effort. You can also use JavaScript to dynamically script CSS animations. For more intensive animations there is also HTML5 Canvas.

New CSS3 Features

Along with animations, transforms, and transitions, there are several new noteworthy features to the CSS3 spec. In this section, you will learn how to use @font-face to introduce new typefaces to your mobile web application by importing the font files.

You will also learn how to use several new border styling elements, such as border-radius (which will allow you to create rounded borders on elements without requiring extra markup or JavaScript), box-shadow, and border-image. You will also learn how to create CSS3 gradients that will scale, depending on the size of the document, without requiring repeating background images and saving on bandwidth.

This section also covers several of the new CSS3 selectors that make it easier to style DOM elements based on state and hierarchy.

@font-face

@font-face is a new, standardized feature of CSS3 that allows you to use fonts outside of the web-safe font list (fonts such as Arial and Times New Roman, which are typically found on most devices). This gives you the freedom to become much more creative with your typefaces. Prior to @font-face, nonstandardized methods of using fonts that were not web safe included cufon (a technique taking advantage of Canvas and SVG), sIFR (although now no longer being maintained, sIFR made use of Flash), and standard CSS image replacement (a method that makes use of prerendered images of text as a background image for the text that should be displayed on the screen).

It's important to remember that although you have complete freedom over the typefaces that you use, you must make sure that the typeface really relates to your content and audience. It's also important to remember that some typefaces are suitable for headings, but not suitable for body text as it becomes unreadable at smaller font sizes (see Figure 5-4). For instance, Comic Sans is a bad font choice for body text.

> *"Comic Sans is unique: used the world over, it's a typeface that doesn't really want to be type. It looks homely and handwritten, something perfect for things we deem to be fun and liberating. Great for the awnings of toyshops, less good on news websites or on gravestones and the sides of ambulances."*

> www.bbc.co.uk/news/magazine-11582548

Figure 5-4. *Hello World with a web font*

There are several caveats to using @font-face for the Web. The biggest one is regarding licensing. In order to render fonts in the browser, the font has to be downloadable. This poses potential problems when using purchased fonts that could have a license attached. Before using a web font for your project, you should check to see whether the license allows for the font to be downloaded or delivered using @font-face. If you can't use the font you want, you may use the Google font directory and use any font from its growing collection of open source web fonts (see Figure 5-5). Google also provides a handy way to embed web fonts that are hosted on its server.

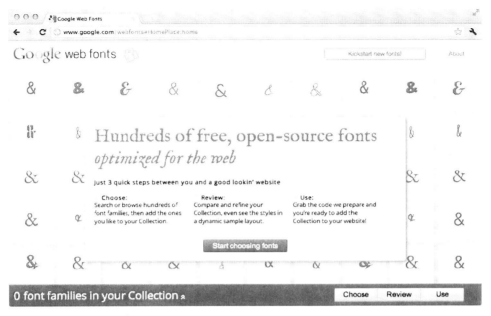

Figure 5-5. *Google web fonts*

The second caveat with web fonts is their file size. Using a single web font won't have too much of an impact on loading time, but should you use several active web fonts or a web font with lots of font styles, you could run into issues with slow page loading times. It is, therefore, important to only include the character set and font style that you require for your web application, so as to reduce the font payload.

Android Browser is smart enough to only load a font family when it is actually used on the page. For example, if you define an h4 element to use a web font, the web font will not download unless that element exists on the page, even if there is a definition for that font in a CSS class.

Android Browser, at the time of this writing, supports only TTF and SVG fonts, two of the biggest and uncompressed font formats available. Other formats include EOT and WOFF. It is important to include all font formats when declaring @font-face to support other browsers and, so that as Android Browser begins to support other formats, they can be loaded without requiring a change in your code. The order should be in size preference (with the smallest first), as Android Browser will select the first usable format to use. On the off chance that Android might have included the font that you would like to use on the device, you can also specify the local name of the font first. If the font is found, the font will not need to be loaded and downloaded from the Web.

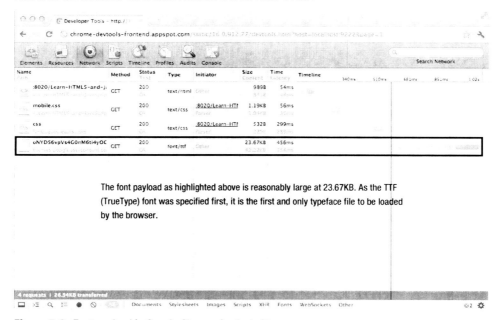

The font payload as highlighted above is reasonably large at 23.67KB. As the TTF (TrueType) font was specified first, it is the first and only typeface file to be loaded by the browser.

Figure 5-6. *Font payload in Google Chrome for Android*

The `@font-face` declaration is used to declare a new font. You use `@font-face {}` for every new font declaration in your CSS document.

```
@font-face {
    font-family: "MyFont";
    src: url('/path/to/my/font.otf');
}
```

From here, you then define the `font-family` that will be used to to reference the font in your CSS. Finally, you declare the source of the font. This can either be a path on the server or a font hosted on a remote server.

You are then free to use the font family anywhere in your CSS using the traditional method.

```
h1 {
    font-family: "MyFont";
}
```

The following code example shows a full declaration of how to use @font-face.

```
@font-face {
    font-family: "My Font With Spaces";
    src: local("My Font With Spaces"),
        url("/path/to/fonts/my-font-with-spaces.woff") format("woff"),
        url("/path/to/fonts/my-font-with-spaces.eot") format("embedded-opentype"),
        url("/path/to/fonts/my-font-with-spaces.svg") format("svg"),
        url("/path/to/fonts/my-font-with-spaces.ttf") format("truetype");
    font-style: normal;
    font-weight: normal;
}
```

text-shadow and text-stroke

text-shadow allows you to create varying amounts of shadow behind text using CSS. text-stroke allows you to draw an outline on the inside edge of text. text-shadow and text-stroke can also be used on @font-face typefaces.

To create a basic shadow around text, you simply need to add the text-shadow property to your CSS. The property accepts the following values and format.

```
text-shadow: horizontal-offset vertical-offset blur color;
```

For instance, the following CSS style will produce results similar to that shown in Figure 5-7.

```
h1 {
    text-shadow: 10px 10px 10px #000000;
}
```

You can also use negative numbers for the shadow's position. This will offset the shadow to the left for the horizontal offset, and toward the top for the vertical offset.

You define the text-stroke property by specifying the stroke width in pixels and its color. The text-stroke property accepts the following values with the following format.

```
text-stroke: width color;
```

It is used in much the same way as text-shadow, as shown in the next code snippet.

```
h1 {
    text-stroke: 1px #000000;
}
```

Figure 5-7. *Text shadow effect (left) and stroke effect (right)*

Selectors

Selectors allow you to apply styles to DOM elements using CSS. There are usually two types of selectors: regular CSS class and element and ID selectors, such as .elementclass, #elementid, and element. There are also pseudoselectors, such as :link, :visited, :hover, and :active.

CSS3 introduces several new selectors that allow you to select elements based on attribute values, input state, and an element's position within the DOM.

Useful Form Selectors

Form selectors will enable you to style form inputs based on their state or type. Prior to CSS3, you needed to manually assign classes to text, checkbox, radio, and submit fields and buttons, as there was no clear way to apply styles to those fields. This is because they are all <input /> elements, so any attempt to create a global style for an input element would style all field types exactly the same.

With CSS3, you can now apply styles to specific input types using the new attribute selectors. Table 5-3 gives the attribute selector formats.

Table 5-3. *Attribute Selectors*

Selector	Description
`element[attribute="value"]`	This will match all elements with attributes that exactly match the specified value.
`element[attribute*="value"]`	This will match and apply a style to all attributes that contain the specified value. * acts as a wildcard attribute selector.
`element[attribute^="value"]`	This will match and apply a style to all attributes that begin with the specified value. ^ acts as a starting indicator for the selector.
`element[attribute$="value"]`	This will match and apply a style to all elements with attributes that end with the specified value. $ acts as an end flag for the element's attribute value.

You can change the attribute and value to match any element. For instance, to select all text fields in a form you would use the following CSS.

```
input[type="text"] {
    border: 1px solid #000000;
}
```

This will create a one-pixel border around all text elements.

You can also select all elements that are checked, enabled, or disabled using the pseudoselectors given in Table 5-4.

Table 5-4. *Pseudoselectors*

Selector	Description
`:enabled`	Selects all form elements that are enabled
`:disabled`	Selects all form elements that are disabled
`:checked`	Selects all form elements that are checked

You can combine and and chain CSS selectors. For instance, if you wanted to select all text form fields that were disabled, you could use the following CSS.

```
input[type="text"]:disabled {
    opacity: 0.5;
}
```

Useful Selectors to Replace JavaScript

It was commonplace to select the last child element of another element using JavaScript, and apply a class to it to remove margin or padding to floated elements. If you had a three-column layout with multiple rows, you could have also selected every third child within an element using JavaScript and applying classes to it. With CSS3, you no longer need to do this.

You can select the last child of an element using the :last-child pseudoclass. For instance, if you wanted to select the last li within a ul, you would use the following CSS.

```
ul li:last-child {
    margin-right: 0px;
}
```

You can also do the same to select the nth child of any element. Using the :nth-child, :nth-last-child, :nth-of-type, and :nth-last-of-type, you can make selections based on child index and child type and index, as shown in Table 5-5.

Table 5-5. *nth Selectors*

Selector	Description
:nth-child(index)	Selects elements that are at the specified index of its parent
:nth-last-child(index)	Selects elements that are at the specified index, starting from the end of its parent
:nth-of-type(index)	Selects elements that are at the specified index of its parent, while only including elements of the same type when comparing indexes
:nth-last-of-type(index)	Selects elements that are at the specified index of its parent, starting from the end, while only including elements of the same type when comparing indexes

For example, if you wanted to select every third li in a ul and make the text gray, you would use the following CSS style.

```
ul li:nth-child(3) {
    color: #CCCCCC;
}
```

As you can see, there are many new CSS selectors available to make styling your mobile web app easier. There are much more advanced selectors to choose from.

Gradients

CSS3 gradients allow you to add background gradients to elements without needing to use repeating images. This can save bandwidth and allow you to create gradient backgrounds that scale, depending on screen size and orientation. CSS3 gradients are vendor specific for now. Each vendor appears to have their own way to produce CSS3 gradients. This section will focus on the WebKit implementation.

There are two types of gradients that you may use in CSS3: linear and radial. Linear gradients will flow from one side of the screen to the other, and radial gradients will emanate from a central point outward, as shown in Figure 5-8.

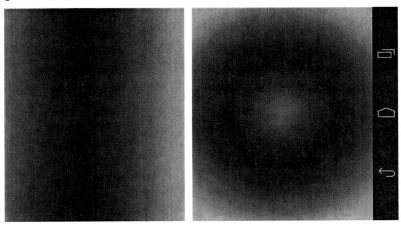

Figure 5-8. *Linear (left) and radial (right) gradients*

Linear Gradients

A linear gradient has the following syntax and must be applied as a background using the `background` property.

```
.box {
    background: -webkit-linear-gradient(start, start-color, end-color);
}
```

You may specify the start position as either a single position (left, top, right, bottom) or a combination of these positions. For instance, to start a linear gradient from the bottom-left corner, you can use the following code.

```
.box {
    background: -webkit-linear-gradient(bottom left, green, red);
}
```

Figure 5-9 shows the result of this snippet.

Figure 5-9. *Linear gradient with a bottom-left starting point*

You can also specify the gradient's start point in degrees. For instance, setting the start point to be 45deg will have the same results as setting the start point as bottom left.

```
.box {
    background: -webkit-linear-gradient(45deg, green, red);
}
```

Along with standard two-color gradients, you can also use several colors within a gradient background. You simply specify more colors after the position. For instance, the following code will create an Irish flag using a linear gradient, as shown in Figure 5-10.

```
.box {
    background: -webkit-linear-gradient(left, green, white, orange);
}
```

Figure 5-10. *Creating an Irish flag using CSS3 gradients*

CSS3 gradients also support color stops. Color stops allow you to specify where the gradient should stop along the gradient line. For instance, you can create a true Irish flag in CSS3 without any gradient, using stops. In order to do this, you would specify that the green color would stop at 33% (one-third) of the element, a white color would then start at 33% and stop at 33%. This would create an immediate line of color between green and white, instead of a gradient. From here, you would then use another white color and specify the stop at 66% of the screen; and finally orange, which will stop at 66%, creating another line of color.

The code would look similar to the following, and you can see the result in Figure 5-11.

```
.box {
   background: -webkit-linear-gradient(left, green 33.3%, white 33.3%, white
66.6%, orange 66.6%);
}
```

Figure 5-11. *Creating an Irish flag using CSS3 gradient color stops*

Radial Gradients

Radial gradients are slightly more complex than linear gradients. You can specify where the gradient's position should start from and its shape. Radial gradients have the following syntax.

```
.box {
    background: -webkit-radial-gradient(center, [circle|elipse]
    [closest-side|closest-corner|farthest-side|farthest-corner|contain|cover],
    start-color, stop-color);
}
```

You can specify the center position in pixels, or percentage left and top positions. The second argument accepts a shape keyword, and this can be either a circle or an ellipse. The second argument also accepts a size keyword, these are `closest-side`, `closest-corner`, `farthest-side`, `farthest-corner`, `contain`, and `cover`. Finally, the gradient also accepts a start and stop color as hex, keyword, RGB, or RGBA colors.

For instance, you can make a Japanese flag using CSS3 using the following code, the result of which can be seen in Figure 5-12.

```
.box {
    background: -webkit-radial-gradient(center, circle contain, red, white);
}
```

Figure 5-12. *Japanese flag with a radial gradient*

You can use the same color stop technique as found in the linear gradient example to remove the gradient on the radial gradient and create a full circle. You can use the following code to achieve this, and Figure 5-13 shows the result.

```
.box {
    background: -webkit-radial-gradient(center, circle contain, #C00C00 70%,
white 70%);
}
```

Figure 5-13. *Japanese flag with radial gradient removed*

Borders

With CSS3, you can now apply new border styles, such as `border-radius` and `box-shadow`.

border-radius

The `border-radius` property allows you to create rounded corners on elements. Prior to having the ability to do this, in order to make flexible elements with rounded corners, you would either use several images to simulate rounded corners, or use a JavaScript helper, such as Curvy Corners, which would generate lots of `div` elements and position them to simulate a rounded corner.

`border-radius` allows you to generate rounded corners using CSS3 without any additional help from images or JavaScript. It is now part of the CSS3 spec, and using the following CSS can create a rounded border.

```
.box {
    border-radius: 10px;
}
```

This will create a border with a radius of 10 pixels. You can also specify the radius for each corner of your element using the following syntax, the result of which you can see in Figure 5-14.

```
.box {
    border: 1px solid #000000;
    border-top-left-radius: 5px;
    border-top-right-radius: 10px;
    border-bottom-left-radius: 15px;
    border-bottom-right-radius: 20px;
    width: 100px;
    height: 100px;
}
```

Figure 5-14. *Border radius*

box-shadow

The `box-shadow` property allows you to create shadows on block-level elements. This can be handy when designs call for drop shadows with varying sizes. Rather than using several images for different shadow styles, you can now use a few lines of CSS.

The `box-shadow` property has the following format.

```
box-shadow: horizontal-offset vertical-offset blur spread color inset;
```

The `horizontal-offset` and `vertical-offset` properties dictate the position of the shadow in pixels, `blur` sets the amount of blur in pixels, `spread` sets the shadows spread in pixels, `color` sets the shadow's color, and `inset` sets whether the shadow should be on the inside or outside of the element. The `inset` property has a value of inset or nothing.

For instance, the following CSS will produce results similar to Figure 5-15.

```
.box {
    width: 100px;
    height: 100px;
    border: 1px solid #000000;
    box-shadow: 10px 10px 20px 5px #000000;
}
```

Figure 5-15. *Box shadow*

The values for box-shadow act in the same way as text-shadow, in that if you specify negative offset values, the shadow will be rendered to the left and top of the screen.

CSS Media Queries

CSS media queries allow you to pull in CSS styles, depending on certain conditions. These conditions can include those shown in Table 5-3.

Table 5-3 *Media Query Properties*

Property	Description	Values/Options
media	The type of media for the query	screen, print, braille, embossed, handheld, projection, speech, tty, tv, and other custom options
[max-|min-]width	The width of the viewport	cm (for print), pixels, em
[max-|min-]height	The height of the viewport	cm(for print), pixels, em
[max-|min-]device-width	The width of the device's screen (equivalent to screen.width in JavaScript)	pixels

Property	Description	Values/Options
`[max-|min-]device-height`	The height of the device's screen (equivalent to `screen.height` in JavaScript)	`pixels`
`orientation`	The orientation of the device	`landscape, portrait`
`[max-|min-]aspect-ratio`	The aspect ratio of the viewport (based on height/width)	cm (for print), pixels
`[max-|min-]device-aspect-ratio`	The aspect ratio of the device's screen (based on `device-width, device-height`)	cm (for print), pixels

`[max-|min-]device-pixel-ratio`
`[max-|min-]-moz-device-pixel-ratio`
`-o-[max-|min-]device-pixel-ratio`
`-webkit-[max-|min-]device-pixel-ratio`
	The pixel ratio of the device; this can be used to pull in high-resolution images for devices with a high-pixel density; this property is also vendor specific	

The idea behind creating media queries is not necessarily to build media queries to target specific devices (e.g., not to specifically target tablets or mobile phones), but to cater for specific screen sizes and adjust the content to fit it.

By doing this, you can ensure that your CSS applies to the available space instead of the target device. We call this *responsive web design*.

Daniel Vane's web site (`http://danielvane.com/`) shows a great example of responsive web design. By providing styles for all viewport sizes, styles for displays up to 480px, and styles for displays up to 768px, the web site responds appropriately to the available space on any handset or tablet-based device, as shown in Figure 5-16 and Figure 5-17.

Figure 5-16. *Daniel Vane's responsive web site in landscape mode (tablet on left, mobile on right)*

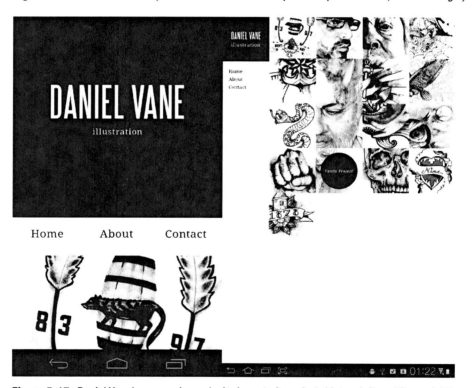

Figure 5-17. *Daniel Vane's responsive web site in portrait mode (tablet on left, mobile on right)*

Andy Clarke and Keith Clark have devised a set of media queries that you can use to target progressively larger displays. The idea behind this is to style for the smallest screen sizes with color and typography, and then progressively enhance the web site at specific screen increments until you reach screen sizes above 992px. The set of media queries also includes a media query to target displays with a high-pixel density.

```
<!-- For all browsers -->
<link rel="stylesheet" href="css/style.css">
<link rel="stylesheet" media="print" href="css/print.css">
<!-- For progressively larger displays -->
<link rel="stylesheet" media="only screen and (min-width: 480px)"
href="css/480.css">
<link rel="stylesheet" media="only screen and (min-width: 600px)"
href="css/600.css">
<link rel="stylesheet" media="only screen and (min-width: 768px)"
href="css/768.css">
<link rel="stylesheet" media="only screen and (min-width: 992px)"
href="css/992.css">
<!-- For Retina displays -->
<link rel="stylesheet" media="only screen and (-webkit-min-device-pixel-ratio:
1.5), only screen and (-o-min-device-pixel-ratio: 3/2), only screen and (min-
device-pixel-ratio: 1.5)" href="css/2x.css">
```

You should check their GitHub project for updates to this set of rules, found at https://github.com/malarkey/320andup/.

CSS Precompilers (SASS)

If you have had experience with CSS in the past, you know some of its limitations. For instance, you cannot define variables that may affect the way in which your CSS is presented or reuse elements of code. Producing and maintaining a long chain of inheritance within your CSS can also prove to be a pain as your application grows, as shown in the code below where there are several elements within an element that require similar styling.

```
/**
 * A common way to style a block in CSS
 **/

.block {
    /** style your block here **/
}

.block h1.heading {
    /** style your header here **/
}

.block ul.alternating {
    /** style your block ul here **/
}
```

```
.block ul.alternating li {
    /** style your alternating li here **/
}

.block ul.alternating li a {
    /** style your li link here **/
}

/** and the story continues **/
```

Syntactically Awesome Stylesheets (SASS) helps to get rid of this bulk with the use of nesting, variables, mixins, and selector inheritance. SASS isn't CSS, and requires a compiler to compile it into CSS.

As you can see from the preceding CSS, a lot of code is repeated. Unfortunately, there is no way to remove the bulk in a way that can be recognized by the browser, but there is a way to do this in a way that the CSS you write is easier to maintain and port. This is known as *nesting* in SASS.

In this section, you will learn how to use SASS to produce organized, reusable, and concrete CSS. You will learn how SASS can improve your development workflow and change the way you think about CSS.

You will also learn how SASS can take a lot of the repetitive work out of using similar CSS styles throughout your stylesheet and pave the way toward object-orientated CSS, a way of thinking about the relationship between CSS and HTML that treats each design element as its own independent design object.

Nesting

Nesting allows you to nest CSS styles within each other. As an example, the previous code as nested SASS code would look like the following.

```
/**
 * The SASS way to style a block in CSS
 **/

.block {
    /** style your block here **/

    h1.heading {
        /** style your header here **/
    }

    ul.alternating {
        /** style your block ul here **/
```

```scss
    li {
        /** style your alternating li here **/

        a {
           /** style your li link here **/
        }
    }
   }
}

/** and the story continues **/
```

This code is much easier to maintain. Should you change the classname for your block, it's a simple case of changing the classname once within the nested style. If you need to add more elements, you just need to add another class or element that you would like to style in the appropriate place. For instance, if you wanted to style a link within the heading, you can do the following using the preferred SCSS format.

```scss
.block {
   /** style your block here **/

   h1.heading {
      /** style your header here **/
      a {
         /** style your heading link here **/
      }
   }

   ul.alternating {
      /** style your block ul here **/

      li {
         /** style your alternating li here **/

         a {
            /** style your li link here **/
         }
      }
   }
}
```

Compiling

The preceding code will need to be compiled into CSS for it to be understandable by the web browser. You do not link SASS files directly into your HTML document; instead, you link the generated CSS file. You can compile SASS files directly from Aptana Studio using the built-in tools.

To compile a SASS file within Aptana Studio, create a new file called `mobile.scss` anywhere in your project (you can delete it after) and add the following code.

```
.test {
   background: #000000;

   .test2 {
      background: #FFFFFF;
   }
}
```

Click on Commands Sass Compile SASS. This will generate a new CSS file in the same location as the SCSS file. You will need to refresh the App Explorer to see the new file. The shortcut to Compiling SASS is cmd + shift + r (CTRL + Shift + r on Windows and Linux). Press 1 when the dialog shown in Figure 5-18 appears.

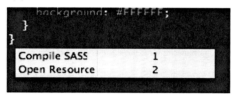

Figure 5-18. *Compiling SASS using the cmd + shift + r command*

After your new CSS file appears, open it. You should see the following code.

```
.test {
   background: #000000; }
.test .test2 {
   background: #FFFFFF; }
```

Partials

A big SASS file can become hard to maintain and very long to scroll through! In Aptana Studio, you can use code folding to show and hide SASS styles to make it easier to browse, as shown in Figure 5-10.

Figure 5-19. *Code folding in Aptana with SCSS files*

While this is convenient, SASS also supports importing partial stylesheets from external SASS files using the same @import syntax found in regular CSS. The difference between the SASS implementation and the implementation found in regular stylesheets is that SASS will pull the files in on compile time rather than loading all files in a regular CSS file one by one using HTTP requests. This provides scope for importing object- or section-specific partials at compile time. The following code shows an example.

```
/** mobile.scss **/

@import "partials/tablet";
@import "partials/phone";

/** partials/_tablet.scss **/

.test-tablet {
    background: url('../themes/mytheme/common/logo.png') no-repeat top left
#FFFFFF;
}

/** partials/_phone.scss **/
.test-phone {
    background: url('../themes/mytheme/common/logo.png') no-repeat top left
#FFFFFF;
}
```

Once compiled, the CSS will look like the following.

```
.test-tablet {
    background: url("../themes/mytheme/common/logo.png") no-repeat top left
white; }

.test-phone {
    background: url("../themes/mytheme/common/logo.png") no-repeat top left
white; }
```

As you can see from this example, the file name for each partial should be prefixed with an _ (underscore) and the reference in the import should contain the relative folder and partial name without the _ prefix or SCSS file name. You might notice that SASS also converts #FFFFF to white in the compiled CSS.

Variables and Interpolation

You are bound to eventually produce stylesheets that are color/theme based (i.e., the same stylesheet may reference the same images, but from a separate image folder, or have a different color theme).

Traditionally, you would use something like PHP, Python, or .NET to generate these stylesheets on the fly. SASS removes this need with the use of variables.

A variable in SASS acts in much the same way as in any other language. They can be of any type (string, CSS property value, integer, measurement such as pixel, em, %) and be added to the SCSS styles to make global changes to your stylesheet.

As an example, taking the code from the example in the partials section, we can modify this so that you can change the theme folder and colors from the master (mobile) stylesheet.

```
/** mobile.scss **/

$theme: "bentley";
$color: #000000;

@import "partials/tablet";
@import "partials/phone";


/** partials/_tablet.scss **/

.test-tablet {
    background: url('../themes/#{$theme}/common/logo.png') no-repeat top left
$color;
}


/** partials/_phone.scss **/

.test-phone {
    background: url('../themes/#{$theme}/common/logo.png') no-repeat top left
$color;
}
```

As you can see in `mobile.scss`, you define a theme variable with a string of "bentley". You then define a black color on the line below that. `@import` is then used to import the partials. Within each partial, you will notice that the background declaration has been modified as follows.

```
background: url('../themes/#{$theme}/common/logo.png') no-repeat top left
$color;
```

There are two ways to add variables to SASS files. To add a variable as part of a CSS string, such as a background image path, you use the following syntax.

```
#{$myvariable}
```

This is known as *interpolation*, and you can also use this to change a CSS property instead of its value. For example, `border-#{$position}-radius:` where `position` is the position defined by the variable.

The second method is simply to repeat the variable name using `$myvariable`. This is what you should use when defining a CSS property value such as a color, width, or height.

Mixins

One of the more popular features of SASS is mixins. Mixins allow you to define a piece of code in a single place and use it anywhere in your SASS stylesheet. For example, you might have a big CSS declaration for a cross browser gradient, as shown in the following code.

```
.myelement {
    background: rgb(206,220,231);
    background: -moz-linear-gradient(-45deg, rgba(206,220,231,1) 0%,
        rgba(89,106,114,1) 100%);
    background: -webkit-gradient(linear, left top, right bottom,
        color-stop(0%,rgba(206,220,231,1)),
        color-stop(100%,rgba(89,106,114,1)));
    background: -o-linear-gradient(-45deg, rgba(206,220,231,1) 0%,
        rgba(89,106,114,1) 100%);
    background: -ms-linear-gradient(-45deg, rgba(206,220,231,1) 0%,
        rgba(89,106,114,1) 100%);
    background: linear-gradient(-45deg, rgba(206,220,231,1) 0%,
        rgba(89,106,114,1) 100%);
}
```

That's a lot of code. What if you want to use it somewhere else? The most efficient way would be to simply add more classes to the definition that you want to use it with.

```
.myelement, .mysecondelement {
   background: rgb(206,220,231);
   background: -moz-linear-gradient(-45deg,
      rgba(206,220,231,1) 0%, rgba(89,106,114,1) 100%);
   background: -webkit-gradient(linear, left top, right bottom,
      color-stop(0%,rgba(206,220,231,1)),
      color-stop(100%,rgba(89,106,114,1)));
   background: -o-linear-gradient(-45deg,
      rgba(206,220,231,1) 0%,rgba(89,106,114,1) 100%);
   background: -ms-linear-gradient(-45deg,
      rgba(206,220,231,1) 0%,rgba(89,106,114,1) 100%);
   background: linear-gradient(-45deg,
      rgba(206,220,231,1) 0%,rgba(89,106,114,1) 100%);
}
```

You could use a mixin to define the gradient and include it in your styles using the following code.

```
@mixin specialgradient {
   background: rgb(206,220,231);
   background: -moz-linear-gradient(-45deg,
      rgba(206,220,231,1) 0%, rgba(89,106,114,1) 100%);
   background: -webkit-gradient(linear, left top, right bottom,
      color-stop(0%,rgba(206,220,231,1)), color-stop(100%, rgba(89,106,114,1)));
   background: -o-linear-gradient(-45deg, rgba(206,220,231,1) 0%,
      rgba(89,106,114,1) 100%);
   background: -ms-linear-gradient(-45deg, rgba(206,220,231,1) 0%,
      rgba(89,106,114,1) 100%);
   background: linear-gradient(-45deg, rgba(206,220,231,1) 0%,
      rgba(89,106,114,1) 100%);
}

#my-first-element {
   @include specialgradient;
}

#my-second-element {
   @include specialgradient;
}
```

However, that would be a bad idea, as the resulting CSS would include the gradient twice in the stylesheet, which increases bloat and isn't what we want. Selector inheritance should be the preferred option for this. Mixins come in handy when you have a chunk of CSS that will be repeated in other CSS rules, or, even better, when you have CSS that is repeated throughout your stylesheet, such as vendor-specific styles (e.g., gradients and border images) that require the same CSS to be defined several times for each browser.

To achieve this, you can pass parameters into mixins. You can now produce CSS gradients anywhere in your SASS file in a single line using the following code.

```
@mixin gradient($start, $stop, $degrees) {
    background: rgba($start, 1);
    background: -moz-linear-gradient($degrees, $start 0%, $stop 100%);
    background: -webkit-gradient(linear, left top, right bottom,
        color-stop(0%, $start), color-stop(100%, $stop));
    background: -o-linear-gradient($degrees, $start 0%,$stop 100%);
    background: -ms-linear-gradient($degrees, $start 0% $stop 100%);
    background: linear-gradient($degrees, $start 0%, $stop 100%);
}

#my-first-element {
    @include gradient(rgba(206,220,231,0.5), rgba(89,106,114,1), -45deg);
}

#my-second-element {
    @include gradient(rgba(206,220,231,1), rgba(89,106,114,1), -45deg);
}
```

As you can see, you first define a mixin called `gradient` that takes three parameters: $start, $stop, and $degrees. Within this mixin, you first define the standard background for devices that do not support gradients. You define the value of the background color using the `rgba` SASS function. In here, you explicitly set the background color to be the start color with no alpha transparency. Using the following lines, you simply pass in the start color, stop color, and degrees to the appropriate vendor gradient declarations. You can now pull the gradient with the parameters anywhere in your stylesheet using `@include gradient(start-color, finish-color, degrees);`. The resulting CSS looks like the following.

```
#my-first-element {
    background: #cedce7;
    background: -moz-linear-gradient(-45deg, rgba(206, 220, 231, 0.5) 0%, #596a72
100%);
    background: -webkit-gradient(linear, left top, right bottom,
        color-stop(0%, rgba(206, 220, 231, 0.5)), color-stop(100%, #596a72));
    background: -o-linear-gradient(-45deg, rgba(206, 220, 231, 0.5) 0%, #596a72
100%);
    background: -ms-linear-gradient(-45deg, rgba(206, 220, 231, 0.5) 0% #596a72
100%);
    background: linear-gradient(-45deg, rgba(206, 220, 231, 0.5) 0%, #596a72
100%); }

#my-second-element {
    background: #cedce7;
    background: -moz-linear-gradient(-45deg, #cedce7 0%, #596a72 100%);
```

```
background: -webkit-gradient(linear, left top, right bottom,
    color-stop(0%, #cedce7), color-stop(100%, #596a72));
background: -o-linear-gradient(-45deg, #cedce7 0%, #596a72 100%);
background: -ms-linear-gradient(-45deg, #cedce7 0% #596a72 100%);
background: linear-gradient(-45deg, #cedce7 0%, #596a72 100%); }
```

Notice how the CSS in #my-first-element has the background color in the first descriptor as a regular hex color and the rest are RGBA colors. In addition, even though the stop color was set using RGBA in the mixin call, it is also a hex color, as the opacity has been set to 1 while the start color was set to 0.5. SASS will pick the most efficient way to output your colors.

Selector Inheritance

Of course, it is tempting to use mixins throughout your SASS file, even though the CSS may well be exactly the same. Selector inheritance allows you to use the same CSS rules in a rule placed elsewhere in the SASS file. For instance, in CSS you can use the following.

```
.my-element-one, .my-element-two, .my-element-three {
    /** insert common CSS style here **/
}
```

While efficient, it can be easy to lose track of which CSS rules are associated with a group of rules. You might have to hunt around the document to find that group of rules and which elements, classes, and ids are associated with it. To add to the confusion, styles could be located in separate CSS files.

Selector inheritance helps to overcome this. Selector inheritance allows you to generate the same code as just shown, but in a much more developer-friendly way.

Using the example from the mixins section, you can define one type of gradient and use it anywhere in your SASS file on related rules without the resulting gradient being generated more than once in the CSS file.

```
.block {
    @include gradient(rgba(206,220,231,0.5), rgba(89,106,114,1), -45deg);
}
.sidebar-block {
    border-radius: 10px;
    @extend .block;
}
```

As you can see, the .sidebar-block is similar to the .block rule, aside from the rounded border. The resulting CSS looks like the following.

```
.block, .sidebar-block {
    background: #cedce7;
    background: -moz-linear-gradient(-45deg, rgba(206, 220, 231, 0.5) 0%, #596a72
100%);
    background: -webkit-gradient(linear, left top, right bottom,
        color-stop(0%, rgba(206, 220, 231, 0.5)), color-stop(100%, #596a72));
    background: -o-linear-gradient(-45deg, rgba(206, 220, 231, 0.5) 0%, #596a72
100%);
    background: -ms-linear-gradient(-45deg, rgba(206, 220, 231, 0.5) 0% #596a72
100%);
    background: linear-gradient(-45deg, rgba(206, 220, 231, 0.5) 0%, #596a72
100%); }

.sidebar-block {
    border-radius: 10px; }
```

You can see that SASS has separated the `border-radius` property and placed it within its own CSS rule for `.sidebar-block`.

You can also add chained classes to the block element and it will generate the edge cases for both the `.sidebar-block` and `.block` rules.

```
/**
 * mobile.scss
 */

.block {
    @include gradient(rgba(206,220,231,0.5), rgba(89,106,114,1), -45deg);
}

.block.wide {
    width: 100px;
}

.sidebar-block {
    border-radius: 10px;
    @extend .block;
}


/**
 * mobile.css
 */

.block, .sidebar-block {
    background: #cedce7;
    background: -moz-linear-gradient(-45deg, rgba(206, 220, 231, 0.5) 0%, #596a72
100%);
    background: -webkit-gradient(linear, left top, right bottom,
        color-stop(0%, rgba(206, 220, 231, 0.5)), color-stop(100%, #596a72));
```

```
    background: -o-linear-gradient(-45deg, rgba(206, 220, 231, 0.5) 0%, #596a72
100%);
    background: -ms-linear-gradient(-45deg, rgba(206, 220, 231, 0.5) 0% #596a72
100%);
    background: linear-gradient(-45deg, rgba(206, 220, 231, 0.5) 0%, #596a72
100%); }

.block.wide, .wide.sidebar-block {
    width: 100px; }

.sidebar-block {
    border-radius: 10px; }
```

Summary

From this chapter, you should have gained a good understanding of the new features of CSS3. You should be armed with a small toolbox from which you can expand upon, which includes how to perform basic animations, how to "tween" and create keyframes for animations, and how to apply them to elements. You should also have an understanding that some of the CSS3 features are supported by most browsers, but are still in their draft stages, which is why sometimes you need to write the same code several times.

You should also have a solid understanding of SASS, and how it can improve your productivity by drastically reducing the amount of code that you have to write.

Laying the CSS3 Foundations

In the last chapter, you focused on learning some of the new features of CSS3 and how to use SASS to make your life much easier. In this chapter you will put some of this new knowledge into practice to begin creating the visual foundations of your mobile web application. Most of the elements within the momemo application such as searching, viewing and favouriting movies are handled and generated with JavaScript, so styling those elements will be covered in Chapter 8.

Before you begin to create any application, you will usually have to go through the laborious task of bootstrapping. This entails setting everything up such as the framework of the application from which you will build upon. Although this is a very menial and boring task, it's important to get it right, as the rest of your application can really benefit from a solid foundation to work from.

In this chapter you will learn how to take advantage of partials in SASS to allow you to organize your CSS in separate files in such a way that it doesn't have an impact on load time. You will also create the basic framework of your application including creating a stylesheet to improve the quality of images on a high resolution display and creating the basic layout of your application.

You will need to download the image pack for the application and place this in your applications image (img) folder.

Getting Organized

Let's begin by creating the relevant folders within the application folder. In the CSS folder within your application folder, create two folders called mixins and partials and a new sass file in the CSS folder called mobile.scss. Your folder structure should look similar to Figure 6-1 below.

Figure 6-1. *CSS Folder Structure*

This folder structure will allow you to separate your CSS for forms, layout and typography into separate SASS files. The mobile.scss file is simply a master SASS file that will pull in all of the partials. This means that if you wanted to create a stylesheet for older mobile devices with just typography, you can create a new master SASS file and pull in just the typography SASS file and not have to duplicate any CSS.

Open the mobile.scss file and add the following SASS code:

```
@import 'mixins/animations';
@import 'mixins/gradient';
@import 'mixins/box-sizing';
@import 'partials/reset';
@import 'partials/typography';
@import 'partials/layout';
@import 'partials/forms';

@media only screen and (-webkit-min-device-pixel-ratio : 1.5),
       only screen and (min-device-pixel-ratio : 1.5) {
  @import 'partials/highres';
}
```

As shown in Chapter 5, this will import the appropriate SASS files when the SASS file is compiled.

You will also notice that there is a media query in the code above. This media query will allow you to pull in high-resolution graphics for high resoloution devices. Within the media query, you can see that rather than explicitly adding CSS, a highres partial is imported. This helps to prevent any CSS from being added to the master mobile.scss file. The mobile.scss file should simply be seen as a SASS file used to bring everything together and idealy should only contain media queries and imports.

Before compiling the mobile.scss file, you will need to create the appropriate SASS files.

  mixins/_animations.scss

  mixins/_box-sizing.scss

  mixins/_gradient.scss

  partials/_forms.scss

  partials/_highres.scss

  partials/_layout.scss

  partials/_reset.scss

  partials/_typography.scss

Go ahead and create them, remember that SASS partials require an _ (underscore) at the beginning of their file name in order for them to be recognized for importing.

You will need to create the empty files shown in Figure 6-2.

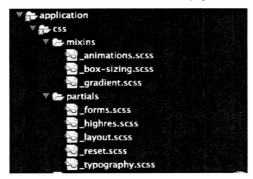

Figure 6-2. *SASS partials*

You will notice that there is a file called _reset.scss. If you're not familiar with Eric Meyer's reset css file, reset stylesheets are used to create a level playing field for CSS styling across browsers. This is because browsers can have varied default stylings for certain elements such as different margins, padding and font size. Reset stylesheets set new predictable defaults for the most used HTML elements. Be warned that some, particularly Eric Meyer's will reset fonts so that they have no stying whatsoever, this is useful, but you have to remember that for elements that have default font styling such as <pre /> will have the same typeface as the <body />.

In the mixins folder, you will see that there are several files that look like they should be CSS properties such as _animation.scss and _gradient.scss. These files are there to help remove some of the vendor specific CSS from polluting the main SASS files by using mixins to create universal versions of the properties. You can begin adding content to these files.

Open the empty _animations.scss file. This mixin will be used to create animations and apply them across all vendors. If a new vendor specific animation property is created, it can be added in one place rather than several across your SASS files. Add the following code to the opened file.

```
@mixin animation ($values) {
        animation: $values;
        -moz-animation: $values;
        -webkit-animation: $values;
}
```

As you can see, it simply acts as a proxy for the standards based, Mozilla and webkit animation properties by accepting a set of properties and then passing them to the vendor specific animation properties. Save the file and close it.

Open the empty _box-sizing.scss file. This mixin provides support for box-sizing. One of the most frustrating problems about flexible layouts in CSS is that when you set an element to be 100% wide (the width of the parent element) with padding, the browser will usually add the padding to the width of the element even when the width is specified as 100%, so the result is that your element will overstretch by the amount of padding that you add, sometimes pushing the element off screen slightly or outside of it's parent element. The box-sizing property helps to overcome this by:

  - Excluding any padding, margin or border from the width and height of the element when using the **content-box** value

  - Including any padding with the width and height of the element when using the **padding-box** value

  - Including any padding and border width with the width and height of the element when using the **border-box** value

```
@mixin box-sizing ($value) {
    -moz-box-sizing: $value;
    -webkit-box-sizing: $value;
    box-sizing: $value;
}
```

Again, this mixin simply acts as a proxy to the vendor specific properties by passing the values to the property.

Finally, open the _gradient.scss file and add the following code to it.

```
@mixin gradient($start, $stop, $degrees) {
  background: rgba($start, 1);
  background: -moz-linear-gradient($degrees,  $start 0%, $stop 100%);
  background: -webkit-gradient(linear, left top, left bottom, color-stop(0%,
$start), color-stop(100%, $stop));
  background: -o-linear-gradient($degrees,  $start 0%,$stop 100%);
  background: -ms-linear-gradient($degrees,  $start 0% $stop 100%);
  background: linear-gradient($degrees,  $start 0%, $stop 100%);
}
```

You may have seen this mixin from the previous chapter. It simply creates CSS gradients for vendor specific gradient code. It's a little bit more complex than the other mixins as each vendor at the time of writing has their own implementation for CSS gradients, which makes accepting a single value and passing it to the vendor properties impossible.

Creating the Partials

With the mixins created, it's now time to create the partials. As explained before, the partials will help to separate different parts of your CSS into different files without impacting on your end user by using the traditional @import in regular CSS files, which have a big impact on load time.

You can begin by opening the empty _reset.scss file in the partials directory. You do not have to manually type the code below into this SASS file, you can copy it from Eric Mayar's website http://meyerweb.com/eric/thoughts/2011/01/03/reset-revisited/. The code is listed below just for your reference.

```
/* http://meyerweb.com/eric/tools/css/reset/
   v2.0b1 | 201101
   NOTE: WORK IN PROGRESS
   USE WITH CAUTION AND TEST WITH ABANDON */

html, body, div, span, applet, object, iframe,
h1, h2, h3, h4, h5, h6, p, blockquote, pre,
a, abbr, acronym, address, big, cite, code,
del, dfn, em, img, ins, kbd, q, s, samp,
small, strike, strong, sub, sup, tt, var,
b, u, i, center,
dl, dt, dd, ol, ul, li,
fieldset, form, label, legend,
table, caption, tbody, tfoot, thead, tr, th, td,
article, aside, canvas, details, figcaption, figure,
footer, header, hgroup, menu, nav, section, summary,
time, mark, audio, video {
  margin: 0;
```

```
  padding: 0;
  border: 0;
  outline: 0;
  font-size: 100%;
  font: inherit;
  vertical-align: baseline;
}
/* HTML5 display-role reset for older browsers */
article, aside, details, figcaption, figure,
footer, header, hgroup, menu, nav, section {
  display: block;
}
body {
  line-height: 1;
}
ol, ul {
  list-style: none;
}
blockquote, q {
  quotes: none;
}
blockquote:before, blockquote:after,
q:before, q:after {
  content: '';
  content: none;
}

/* remember to define visible focus styles! */
:focus {
  outline: ?????;
} */

/* remember to highlight inserts somehow! */
ins {
  text-decoration: none;
}
del {
  text-decoration: line-through;
}

table {
  border-collapse: collapse;
  border-spacing: 0;
}
```

Save and close the file. The next file that you need to add code to will be the _typography.scss file. Open it in Aptana Studio. The _typography.scss file will simply style how text should be displayed within the application. As you can see from the code below, you will simply style the body and headings.

```
body {
  font-size: 0.75em;
  font-family: Arial, Helvetica, sans-serif;
}

h1, h2, h3, h4 {
  font-family: 'Arimo', sans-serif;
  font-weight: bold;
  margin-bottom: 0.5em;
  font-size: 1em;
}

h3 { font-size: 1.25em; }
h2 { font-size: 1.5em; }
h1 { font-size: 1.9em; }
```

You use em's instead of pixels for the font size. Setting the body's font-size to 0.75em is the equivelant to 12px as shown in the code snippet above where the font-size has been declared as em's for the body. 1em is equivelant to the browsers default font size, which is 16px. To work out what 10px should be in em's, you would use 10 / 16 which would equal 0.625, so 10px would be 0.625em's. em's are useful as the values are relative. For instance, if you set a div's font size to 0.75em (12px) and then set any element within that to 1em, that font size will be relative to the parent element'ss font size. So 1em in the child element becomes 0.75em from the parent element. Trying to figure out what the font sizes for EM's should be can be a nightmare, http://riddle.pl/emcalc/ has a soloution that allows you to build a DOM based tree of font sizes in pixels, the web app will convert them to em's for you and take into account what the parent elements font size is.

Save and close the _typography.scss file. Open the _layout.scss file. The _layout.scss file will control the positioning, dimensions, colour and general layout of elements within the application.

The first thing to do is to style the body, html, #shoe and .deck elements of the application. You style these at the top so that they can be overridden at a latter point in your stylesheet.

```
body, html, #shoe, .deck {
  height: 100%;
  width: 100%;
  overflow: hidden;
  margin: 0px;
}
```

As you can see, the height and width have been set to 100% so that it spans the width and height of the screen. overflow: hidden; has been added so that any content that flows outside of the elements are cut off and don't affect the layout, and for good measure, a 0px margin has been added to prevent any gaps between the elements.

The next thing to do is to style the #card-movie_search_results card. When making a search, the card should show above all elements on the page. You can do this by setting the z-index. The z-index dictates where in the stack of elements the element should exist. Setting a high number will usually place the element at the top of the stack. 50 is used in this case.

```
/**
 *  Individual Card Styles
 */
#card-movie_search_results {
  z-index: 50;
}
```

The next step is to set the deck and card styles. As you can see, SASS nesting is used here to nest the different card states within the deck. When the SASS file is rendered the appropriate CSS will be generated. You will want to set the decks position to relative. This will allow absoloutley positioned cards within the deck to be positioned relatively to the parent deck rather than the whole viewport.

```
/**
 *  Deck styles
 */
.deck {

  position: relative;

}
```

You now need to style any element with the .card class too. Each card should be the same width and height of the deck but be positioned offscreen so that the user cannot initially see it. When the .active class is added to any .card element, it should be brought back into view. This can be achieved by setting the initial left position to a negative value equivelant to the width of the card, -100% in this case. When you want the card to be brought back into view, a position of 0px has been set for the .active styling.

```
/**
 *  Deck styles
 */
.deck {

  position: relative;
```

```
.card {
  height: 100%;
  width: 100%;
  left: -100%;
  position: absolute;
}

.card.active {
  left: 0px;
}

}
```

The next things to style are the screen bars. The screenbars will sit at the top and bottom of the screen. These need to be styled in a uniform manner so that users can find them easily. As you can see below, the gradient mixin is used to create a CSS3 gradient as the background for this element.

```
/**
 *   Header taskbar styles
 */

.screenbar {
  @include gradient(#7D9DCE, #ABC1E1, 90deg);
}
```

The taskbar is quite complicated as it contains the logo of the application, the search field and a clear button. The taskbar needs to be the width of the screen and the search field needs to be flexible so that no matter the screen size, it ocupy's the majority of the space.

As you can see from the code below, you set the font colour for the taskbar to be white and the overflow has been set to hidden so that it will surround any floated elements. The taskbar also has 10px padding and a red border at the bottom.

```
header#taskbar {
  color: #FFFFFF;
  overflow: hidden;
  padding: 10px;
  border-bottom: 1px solid #BF2628;
}
```

You will now want to style the branding/logo for the app. In order to do this, you can use a header (h1) element and then use an image replacement technique to show the logo. This can be achieved by setting the width and the height of the h1 to the same width and height as the logo, setting the text-indent property to a high negative arbritary value so that the text is positioned off screen, -10000px is used in this case. Finally, the logo's background is set to the logo.

The h1 element is also floated to the left of the taskbar so that the search form can occupy the remainder of the space available.

```
header#taskbar {
  ...

  h1.branding {
    margin: 0px;
    float: left;
    width: 73px;
    height: 32px;
    text-indent: -10000px;
    overflow: hidden;
    background: url('../img/momemo.png') no-repeat top left;
  }

}
```

The next thing to do is to setup the clear-search link. You use the same image replacement technique as before to replace the text within the clear-search link. The button is floated to the right this time and hidden so that it isn't visible immadietly.

```
header#taskbar {
  ...

  h1.branding {
    ...
  }

  .clear-search {
    float: right;
    width: 35px;
    height: 35px;
    display: none;
    overflow: hidden;
    text-indent: -10000px;
    background: url('../img/clear.png') 50% 50% no-repeat;
  }

}
```

The final thing to add to the _layout.scss file is the searchactive override. When you add the css class .searchactive to the header#taskbar element, it will show the clearsearch button and provide enough space for it by adding a right margin to the add-movie form. This prevents the .searchactive buttom from dropping down onto a new line.

```scss
header#taskbar {
  ...
}

header#taskbar.searchactive {

  .clear-search {
    display: block;
  }

  form#add-movie {
    margin-right: 40px;
  }

}
```

Your final _layout.scss file should look like the code below.

```scss
header#taskbar {
  color: #FFFFFF;
  overflow: hidden;
  padding: 10px;
  border-bottom: 1px solid #BF2628;

  h1.branding {
    margin: 0px;
    float: left;
    width: 73px;
    height: 32px;
    text-indent: -10000px;
    overflow: hidden;
    background: url('../img/momemo.png') no-repeat top left;
  }

  .clear-search {
    float: right;
    width: 35px;
    height: 35px;
    display: none;
    overflow: hidden;
    text-indent: -10000px;
    background: url('../img/clear.png') 50% 50% no-repeat;
  }

}

header#taskbar.searchactive {

  .clear-search {
    display: block;
  }
```

```
form#add-movie {
  margin-right: 40px;
}
```

```
}
```

The next thing to do is to style the forms. So open the _forms.scss file. The first thing that you will want to do is set the box sizing for all of your form elements so that any padding or borders added form part of the overall width. The following line will use the box-sizing mixin to achieve this.

```
input, select, textarea, button {
  @include box-sizing(border-box);
}
```

You will then need to style the text inputs, you can do this using the new CSS3 attribute selector rather than the old way of adding CSS classes to every text input element. As you can see from the code snippet below, the text input below has a 1 pixel black border and has a 5 pixel padding whilst the submit input simply has a 10 pixel padding. There are no submit buttons used in the application so it makes no sense in styling it yet.

```
input[type="text"] {
  border: 1px solid #000000;
  padding: 5px;
}
```

At present there is only one input element that should span the full width of its parent element. You may want to add more elements like this in the future, so it's a good idea to turn this into a CSS class that can be re-used.

```
input.full-width {
  width: 100%;
}
```

By adding a left margin of 80px (greater or equal to the width of the logo) to the search form, any content within the form will appear next to the logo.

```
form#add-movie {
  margin-left: 80px;
}
```

This is a much better solution than floating the add-movie form as it will no longer be able to have the full width of it's parent task bar element without using JavaScript to calculate the size it should be.

The code below simply styles the search field. As you can see, background-size is used for the first time here. The background-size property allows you to specify how big the background should be in pixels, or as a percentage of the element the background is being added to.

```
input.search {
  padding-left: 30px;
  background: url('../img/search.png') 5px 50% no-repeat transparent;
  background-size: auto 50%;
  border: none;
  border-bottom: 1px solid #BF2628;
  color: #FFFFFF;
  font-size: 1.5em;
}
```

The background-size property accepts a width and a height, both properties can be different units. For instance, the width has been set to auto and the height has been set to 50% in this example. This allows the height to be 50% of the height of the element but the width will adjust in proportion to the height of the background image so that it doesn't appear distorted.

The following styles use vendor specific pseudo's. -webkit-input-placeholder and -moz-placeholder allow you to style the placeholder text used on input elements. For instance, the background for the search box is transparent on a blue background, so the default grey colour is barely visible. The text needs to be white, so the placeholder pseudo's allow you to customize the way the placeholder text is presented.

```
input.search::-webkit-input-placeholder, input.search::-moz-placeholder {
  color: rgba(255, 255, 255, 0.5);
}
```

Although this will not be visible immedietly on Android 4, the style below will show a loading indicator in the search box whilst movies are being searched for in the background.

```
input.search.loading {
  background-image: url('../img/loading.gif');
}
```

Your final forms SASS file should look like the code below.

```
input, select, textarea, button {
  @include box-sizing(border-box);
}

input[type="text"] {
  border: 1px solid #000000;
  padding: 5px;
}
```

```scss
input.full-width {
  width: 100%;
}

form#add-movie {
  margin-left: 80px;
}

input.search {
  padding-left: 30px;
  background: url('../img/search.png') 5px 50% no-repeat transparent;
  background-size: auto 50%;
  border: none;
  border-bottom: 1px solid #BF2628;
  color: #FFFFFF;
  font-size: 1.5em;
}

input.search::-webkit-input-placeholder, input.search::-moz-placeholder {
  color: rgba(255, 255, 255, 0.5);
}

input.search.loading {
  background-image: url('../img/loading.gif');
}
```

Save and close your file. Finally, you will need to open the _highres.scss file. This file will simply be used to replace any graphics for high resoloution displays so that they appear crisp. Add the following code to the file.

```scss
header#taskbar {

  h1.branding {
    background-image: url('../img/highres/momemo.png');
    background-size: 73px 32px;
  }

}
```

As you can see, background-size needs to be used here as CSS will still use the images full size when used as a background image despite the highres file being double the resoloution of the low resoloution image. This will ensure that the background image is scaled down to the correct pixel size. The difference between not using this and using it can be shown below in Figure 6-3.

Figure 6-3. *High-resolution images (bottom) vs low resolution (top) on a high density display*

Automatically Compiling Sass in Aptana

Until now, you haven't compiled any SASS in Aptana Studio. In the previous chapter you saw how to use SASS's built in SASS compiler command to compile SASS files. This can become labourious everytime you want to make a change to your SASS files. You can get around this by automatically compiling your SASS files using the SASS command line. In order to do this, click on your application folder in the App Explorer in Aptana Studio and click on the Commands icon, it looks like a cog and can be seen in Figure 6-4.

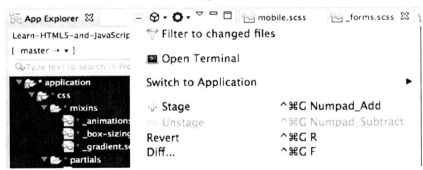

Figure 6-4. *Commands menu*

Click on the **Open Terminal** menu item. This will open a terminal view similar to Figure 6-5.

Figure 6-5. *The terminal view*

In the terminal view, enter the following command and press enter.

```
sass --watch css/*.scss
```

This will look for any changes in your SASS files and automatically generate the CSS file for you. You should see something similar to Figure 6-6.

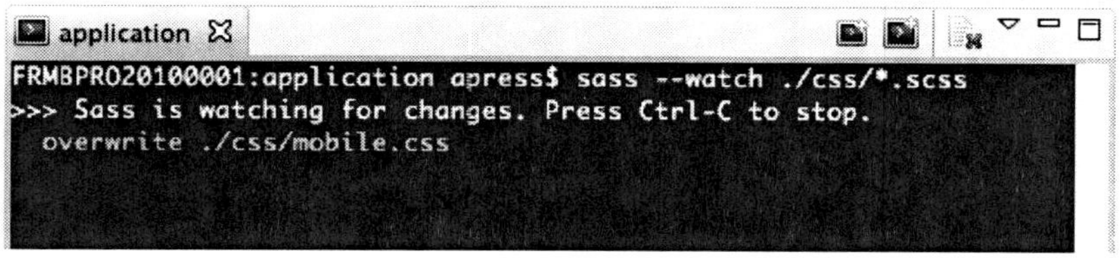

Figure 6-6. *sass --watch output*

This will also look for changes in your partial files and then automatically overwrite mobile.css with the new changes.

You will need to run this command everytime you open Aptana Studio and you should also keep this terminal view open at all times.

Now that your CSS file has succesfully been generated, run your website in Aptana Studio by right clicking on index.html going to **Run As ➤ JavaScript Web Application**. It will launch in Firefox, visit the URL displayed in the address bar on your mobile device. You should now see something similar to Figure 6-7.

Figure 6-7. *Momemo with CSS*

If you're not seeing the new styles, head back to Aptana Studio, click on the CSS folder and refresh it by pressing F5 on your keyboard. The new mobile.css file should appear. Refresh the web page on your mobile and everything should look as it should.

Summary

Although this chapter is short, you should have a greater understanding as to how to really take advantages of partilals and mixins within SASS and how to lay the foundations to start building your CSS/SASS on top of.

You should also now know how partials can be used within CSS media queries in your master SASS file (mobile.scss).

JavaScript for Mobile

JavaScript for mobile has come quite a long way since the dawn of the first consumer WAP mobile phone, the Nokia 7110, in 1999. From having absolutely no support to having full support and more in just over 10 years, JavaScript has made our mobile web experience much more interactive, interesting, and fulfilling.

The problem today is, with so much JavaScript support, how do we leverage it to our advantage, make it unobtrusive, and provide a good and smooth experience for our users?

This chapter will guide you through how to integrate JavaScript into your projects, using the different types of libraries available to make it easier for you to produce mobile web applications that should work on any platform. You will also learn about the new HTML5 JavaScript APIs (such as geolocation), storage, and how to leverage it to draw vector-based graphics for Android using the HTML5 Canvas element.

Object-Oriented JavaScript

JavaScript is a fantastic language for handling and processing user interaction in mobile web sites. In much the same way as you write JavaScript for the desktop web, you can also make use of the same design patterns and method of writing for mobile. You can write JavaScript in one of two ways. One of these methods is procedural, as shown in the following code.

```
function sayHelloWorld(foo){
    alert(foo);
}
```

The second method, which is object oriented, is shown next.

```
var World = function(){
    this.say = function say(hello){
        alert(hello);
    }
}

var myworld = new World();
myworld.say('Hello');
```

As you can see, you might need to write more code for the object-oriented approach, but there are several benefits.

- The object-oriented approach allows for expansion of your code.

- The object-oriented approach can be much more organized.

- The object-oriented approach allows for encapsulation, which means that variables or properties within your objects can be public or private.

- The object-oriented approach allows you to pass objects into other objects. This is known more commonly as *object dependencies*.

> **NOTE:** In class based languages such as Java, Objective-C and PHP a class is an object before it is instantiated by using new ClassName. An object is an instance of a class after it has been instantiated. JavaScript has basic methods for creating objects and, unfortunately, doesn't fully support encapsulation, inheritance, abstraction, and interfaces out of the box. You might need to create your own methods and practices for implementing this. JavaScript is also an object based language, so although it feels like you're creating classes, you're actually creating structures in code for your objects to take form from.

Both of the preceding code snippets have the same result; however, the object-oriented approach treats World as an object, and the function within that object, this.say, as a method that can be performed on it.

The object-oriented approach also allows you to create multiple instances of an object. For example, you can create several World instances, and by modifying the preceding code, you can begin to create instance variables that exist only within the scope of each `World object`, such as its name.

```
var World = function(_name){

    var name = _name;

    this.greet = function(guest){
        alert('Hello ' + guest + ' my name is ' + name);
    }
}

var venus = new World('Venus');
var mars = new World('Mars');

venus.greet('Antony');
venus.greet('Dan');
```

From the preceding examples, you can see that in order to create an object in JavaScript, it's as simple as creating a function. Using the function's parameters, you create what is called a *constructor*. A constructor is a method to pass parameters to the object upon instantiation. These parameters are usually used to assign variables to properties within the object itself.

A property can be declared as public or private in normal object orientation. In JavaScript there are no such declerations available for properties. So a property can either be an instance variable (private) or a public property (public). In this instance, the `name` property is an instance variable, which means that you cannot access it from outside of the object using, for example, `venus.name`. This is generally known as *encapsulation*. A property of an object is a variable that can be accessed either by using `this.propertyname` from within the object's scope, or by using `object.propertyname` from outside of the object. For example, if you attempted to access the `name` instance variable from outside of the object, you would get `undefined` as the output.

You can also create object methods, which are functions that can be accessed from within or outside of the object using `this` from within the object or the variable assigned to the instantiated object from outside. Using the previous examples, `this.greet` is a public object method and can be accessed outside of the object.

From here, you can see that objects allow for much more maintainable code. The object's properties live outside of the global namespace, so you avoid clashing variable names and other details for specific objects. You can go beyond this and create your own namespace for your application objects. This helps to avoid other JavaScript libraries from potentially overwriting them. The following example shows the most basic method for creating an application-level namespace for your objects.

```
var app = app || {};
app.world = function(_name){

    var name = _name;

    this.greet = function(guest){
        alert('Hello ' + guest + ' my name is ' + name);
    }
}
```

This allows you to create classes that belong to your application in separate files. The first line on the preceding code sample declares the variable app in the global namespace, and assigns the app global variable to it if it already exists. If it doesn't exist, it creates an empty object for you to begin populating with your objects. This can be handy if you organize your objects in such a way that they are held in separate files during development, and then merged for production. You can even go further and namespace your objects based on functionality.

These are the basics of object-oriented JavaScript, which modern mobile browsers support.

You code in this manner (instead of, for instance, creating jQuery plugins) because it separates your application code from vendor-specific code and reduces the reliance on a third-party code. You can go further than this and follow the model view controller (MVC) pattern to separate your user interaction from your domain logic (real-world objects) and the resulting view that is presented to the user.

Along with design patterns and object orientation, JavaScript is an event-driven language. This means that an event triggered in one part of your application can trigger a piece of code in a completely different part of your application at runtime.

In its simplest form, events can be triggered by user interaction. In mobile, this is commonly seen as *touch events* where a user interacts with your application through the browser using their fingers. The browser registers the event and then passes the event and its information, such as the element that the event originated from, to any subscribers in your application. For the desktop environment, these are known as *mouse events*.

Handling Touch Events

JavaScript is no slouch when it comes to handling events on the desktop, and the same can be said for mobile. Events can consist of user-level events (such as touch and drag), or device-level events (such as orientation changes or changes in the device's location). The most basic of events are user-level events. They can be tracked on any DOM element. For mobile devices, there are four main touch events:

> touchstart
>
> touchend
>
> touchmove
>
> touchcancel

The touchstart event will fire when a user touches an element on the screen. The touchend event will fire when a user lifts their finger off an element on the screen after touching it. The touchmove event will track the user's movement, and fire the event with every movement. The touchcancel event will fire when the user cancels the touch event by moving outside of the target's bounds and releasing the screen. This event seems to be unpredictable.

In order to respond to events, you must create event listeners for them using element.addEventListener(event, callbackfunction);. This method takes the event name (touchstart, touchend, etc.) and the callback function. At times, you might want to prevent the default action for the event from firing. For instance, if you add an event listener to a link, you might not want the link to open a new page when it's tapped. To do this, you must add a parameter to the callback function called e, and call e.preventDefault() at the end of the callback function. This will also prevent the element from scrolling and interfering with touchmove events, as shown in the following code snippet.

```
<div id="touch-plane" style="width: 100%; height: 100%; background: #000000;
color: #FFFFFF;"><span id="coordinates">x: 0 y: 0</span> - <span
id="touching">not touching</span></div>

<script>
   document.getElementById('touch-plane').addEventListener('touchmove',
function(e){
      document.getElementById('coordinates').innerText = 'x: ' +
e.touches[0].clientX
         + ' y: ' + e.touches[0].clientY;
      e.preventDefault();
   });
```

```
   document.getElementById('touch-plane').addEventListener('touchstart',
function(e){
      document.getElementById('touching').innerText = 'touching';
   });

   document.getElementById('touch-plane').addEventListener('touchend',
function(e){
      document.getElementById('touching').innerText = 'not touching';
   });
</script>
```

This code will fill the screen with black, with white text containing the current coordinate of the user's finger and whether the user is touching the screen or not. You can get the current coordinates by tapping into the touches list from the event passed to the touchmove event listener. You can get the first touch from the list, and use clientX and clientY to retrieve the X and Y coordinates, like so:

```
e.touches[0].clientX, e.touches[0].clientY
```

As you can see, you can prevent the document from scrolling by calling e.preventDefault().

The other two event listeners for touchstart and touch end will be called when the user touches and lifts their finger off of the screen.

Figure 7-1. *Detecting touches and movement*

Getting a User's Location

It can be handy to get a user's location when you know that they will need to enter their current location into the application. This can be useful for finding and searching for things around them such as events, places, and other people. The location API is quite simple and makes use of the mobile device's built-in GPS chip.

To get the location of the user, you can use the following code. It is asynchronous and nonblocking, so you can continue to process JavaScript events in the foreground or background while the device searches for the users location.

```
var showCurrentPosition = function(position){
    alert('Lat: ' + position.coords.longitude + ' Lon: ' +
position.coords.latitude);
}
```

This is a function that will be called after the mobile device has the position of the user. The parameter passed back to the callback function is an object that extends the Coordinates interface and has the properties shown in Table 7-1.

Table 7-1. *Coordinates Object Properties*

Property	Description
Coordinates.timestamp	The time that the position was retrieved
Coordinates.coords	A coordinates object
Coordinates.coords.accuracy	The level of accuracy of the latitude and longitude result
Coordinates.coords.altitude	If available, the altitude of the device in meters; if this cannot be determined, null is returned
Coordinates.coords.altitudeAccuracy	The accuracy of the altitude result; if this cannot be determined, null is returned
Coordinates.coords.heading	The heading of the device, or the direction of the device in degrees. If the heading cannot be determined, the value of this property is null
Coordinates.coords.latitude	The latitude of the device in decimal degrees
Coordinates.coords.longitude	The longitude of the device in decimal degrees
Coordinates.coords speed	The horizontal speed of travel in meters per second; if this cannot be determined, null is returned

To then retrieve the coordinates of the device, it is a simple case of querying the device for the user's location, like so:

```
navigator.geolocation.getCurrentPosition(showCurrentPosition);
```

If the user hasn't already authorized your application to access their location, they will first be required to approve the location request. Figure 7-2 shows what this dialog will look like.

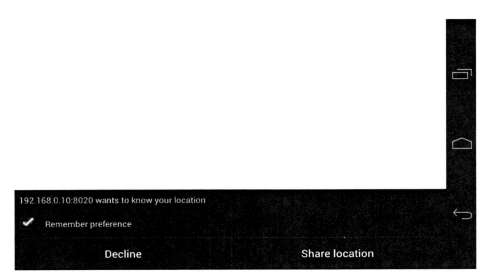

Figure 7-2. *Location request*

This presents a problem, as you should expect that some users might not wish to share their current location and might tap the decline button; or there could simply be an issue with retrieving the current location of the user. This can be handled with an error event handler, which is the second parameter of the getCurrentPosition() method. In order to handle errors in retrieving the user's current location, you must create an error handler, which will accept the error object.

```
var handleLocationError = function(error){
   alert(error.message);
}

navigator.geolocation.getCurrentPosition(showCurrentPosition,
handleLocationError);
```

The error object is part of the PositionError interface, and has the properties shown in Table 7-2.

Table 7-2. *PositionError Properties and Constants*

Property/Constant	Description
PositionError.code	The code returned by the error; use the following constants to determine the error code
PositionError.PERMISSION_DENIED	The user rejected the request to get their permission
PositionError.POSITION_UNAVAILABLE	The position could not be determined due to some other device issue
PositionError.TIMEOUT	The position could not be determined, as the request timed out
PositionError.message	The message from the error

You should use the PositionError constants PERMISSION_DENIED, POSITION_UNAVAILABLE, and TIMEOUT to handle the errors appropriately rather than relying on the error message or comparing the error code to hard-coded integers. The next code sample shows how errors should be handled using the handleLocationError function and a switch statement.

```
var handleLocationError = function(error){
    switch(error.code){
        case error.PERMISSION_DENIED:
            /**
             * Handle permission denied response here,
             * potentially display a dialog to the user
             */
            var confirmed = confirm("We really need your location!");
            if(confirmed){
                navigator.getCurrentPosition(showCurrentPosition,
handleLocationError);
            }
            break;
        case error.POSITON_UNAVAILABLE:
            /**
             * Handle position unavailable response here,
             * potentially display a dialog to the user and
             * ask them to enter their location manually
             */
            var tryagain = confirm("Sorry, something serious is wrong, would
                you like to try again?");
            if(tryagain){
```

```
            navigator.getCurrentPosition(showCurrentPosition,
handleLocationError);
        }
        break;
    case error.TIMEOUT:
        /**
         * Appologizies to the user for the delay and attempts
         * to retrieve their location again
         */
        navigator.geolocation.getCurrentPosition(showCurrentPosition,
            handleLocationError);
        break;
    }
}
```

These are very simple error handlers and they can be expanded upon to give a much better experience to users, should an error occur.

You can then pass the coordinates onto a mapping service, such as Google Maps, to show the user's current location. The following example uses the Google Maps static API to generate an image of the user's current location to be displayed on the mobile device.

```
<img src="/map.jpg" id="map" alt="Map" />
<script>
    var showCurrentPosition = function(position){
        document.getElementById('map').src =
            'http://maps.google.com/maps/api/staticmap?center=' +
            position.coords.latitude + ',' + position.coords.longitude +
            '&zoom=10&markers=' + position.coords.latitude + ',' +
            position.coords.longitude + '&size=' + window.innerWidth + 'x' +
            window.innerHeight + '&sensor=true';
    }

    var handleLocationError = function(error){
        alert(error.message);
    }

    navigator.geolocation.getCurrentPosition(showCurrentPosition,
handleLocationError);
</script>
```

The result can be seen in Figure 7-3. You can, of course, also subscribe to significant changes to the user's current position. You can do this with the navigator.geolocation.watchPosition method. This will listen for significant changes to the user's current position, and call a callback function every time the user's position changes. The watchPosition method takes the same parameters as the getCurrentPosition method.

Figure 7-3. *Showing the user's current position on Google Maps*

Drawing with Canvas

HTML5 Canvas allows you to draw vector-based shapes using JavaScript. The HTML5 Canvas element doesn't provide much inherent functionality, but it does provide a base for you to begin drawing objects upon. Think of it as a whiteboard for your device. This next exercise will take you through how to create a canvas, how to begin drawing basic shapes using JavaScript, and how to animate them.

First, create a new folder within this chapter folder called `canvas`. Create a `js` folder containing a new JavaScript file called `canvas.js` and an `index.html` file in the `canvas` folder directory root with the following contents.

```
<!DOCTYPE html>
<html lang="en">
    <head>
        <meta charset="UTF-8" />
        <meta name="viewport" content="width=device-width; initial-scale=1.0;
            maximum-scale=1.0; user-scalable=0; target-densitydpi=device-dpi;"/>
        <title>Canvas</title>
        <style type="text/css" media="screen">
            body, html {
                margin: 0;
                height: 100%;
                width: 100%;
            }
```

```
    </style>
  </head>
  <body>

    <canvas id="play" width="100" height="100"></canvas>
    <script src="js/canvas.js"></script>

  </body>
</html>
```

This will create a Canvas element with an `id` of `play` that is 100 pixels wide and 100 pixels high. You should never attempt to size a Canvas element using CSS, as it will not work as expected. This HTML will also link to the `canvas.js` file.

Open the `canvas.js` file, which will be used to control your canvas. You will use object-oriented JavaScript to create and control your play button.

In this example, you will require two objects: a `track` object (which will simulate an actual audio track) and a `playButton` object (which will control displaying track progress and playing/pausing the track). The `track` object should be responsible for the following:

Keeping track of the total length of the track

Keeping the current state of the track
(playing/paused/stopped)

Keeping the current time of the track if it is playing

Playing, pausing, and stopping the track

The `playButton` object for this example will be responsible for the following:

Drawing the play button

Showing the playback progress

Showing the track playback state

Representing the track's state by showing the play or stop
symbol

Representing the track's playback progress by moving a play
head

Inspired by the iTunes playback controls, as shown in Figure 7-4, you will create something similar.

Figure 7-4. *iTunes preview playback control*

To begin with, create the two objects in your `canvas.js` file, as shown in the following code snippet:

```
var app = app || {};

app.playButton = function(id, track){

}

app.track = function(length){

}
```

As you can see, the constructor for the `playButton` takes an `id`, which will be the ID of the Canvas element, and a `track`, which will be an instance of the `app.track` class. The `track` constructor simply takes the length of the track in seconds.

As the `track` needs to be instantiated first, you will begin by creating the code for the `track` class. To begin with, create a new property within the `track` class called `this.state`, as follows:

```
app.track = function(length){
    this.state = {
        STOPPED: 0,
        PLAYING: 1,
        PAUSED: 2
    };
}
```

The `state` property contains variables that can be used to determine the current state of the application. The alternative to doing this is to store the current state as a string (i.e., playing, paused, or stopped). This can be problematic as you add more states or change the state names in your application. By doing this, to change the application's state it's as simple as using `state = this.state.STOPPED`. This helps, too, because as you type `this.state.` the code completion will appear to show you the possible states, which is better and more efficient than having to dig through your code to find out what the available states are.

Next, you define a few variables within the scope of the `track` class, as shown in the following code snippet:

```
app.track = function(length){

   ...

   var length = (length * 1000),
      currentTime = 0,
      interval,
      _self = this,
      state = this.state.STOPPED,
      updateInterval = 1000 / 30;
}
```

In JavaScript, you can declare variables in a single line, by separating them with commas. This also works on mobile.

Your first variable, `length`, will convert the track length passed to the class from seconds to milliseconds by multiplying it by 1000. You also set the `currentTime` to 0, and declare a variable called `interval`. The `interval` variable is responsible for holding a reference to the interval declared to repeatedly adjust the timing of the track.

It seems strange, but you also declare a variable called `_self` and assign `this` to it. This creates a global variable so that any callback events that are called out of the scope of the object by event listeners will still be able to access the parent class, as `this` will be in the scope of the callback event or target and not the parent class (which, in this case, is `track`).

You then declare the current state of the application and set its default state to `this.state.STOPPED`.

Finally, you create a new variable called `updateInterval`, which will be used to set the number of times per second the time will be updated. For instance, if you wanted to update the interval 500 times per second, you would set the `updateInterval` as `updateInterval = 1000 / 500`. Increasing this time will have an impact on performance, as this affects the frame rate of the Canvas animation.

You will need to update the `currentTime`. `setCurrentTime` is a private method that will allow you to set the current time for the playback head. It will also make a callback to any function or method that has assigned itself as the callback to that method using `_self.callbacks.didUpdateTime.call(_self, currentTime);`. `call` is a method that allows you to invoke a function within the scope of another object. This will allow the callback function to use `this` within its code, and `this` will be a reference back to the object that made the callback, rather than the callback function's parent object. The first parameter for `call` is the object that you would like to pass scope from. The parameters after that are the parameters that the callback method will accept.

Next, you must create the private method called `updateTime`. This will update the current playback time for the track. This method also checks to see whether the total track length has been reached by the `currentTime`. If it has, then it will stop the track.

```
app.track = function(length){

   ...

      var setCurrentTime = function(time){
         currentTime = time;
         _self.callbacks.didUpdateTime.call(_self, currentTime);
      };

      var updateTime = function(){

         if(currentTime < length){
            setCurrentTime(currentTime + updateInterval);
         } else {
            _self.stop();
         }

      };
}
```

You will notice that `_self` is being used here. This is not a global JavaScript variable but the `_self` variable that you declared earlier. `updateTime` is called out of the scope of the track class/object, so `_self` maintains a reference back to it. This is better known as a *closure*.

Next, you will declare several getter and setters. You create this so that you can access the private variables outside of the scope of the object. This is handy when you do not want objects to change properties of another object. For instance, the `currentTime` should never be manipulated outside of the object, but outside objects should be able to find out the current playback time of the track. Using a getter without a setter prevents outside objects from changing this value.

```
app.track = function(length){

   ...

   this.getCurrentTime = function(){
      return currentTime;
   };

   this.getLength = function(){
      return length;
   };
```

```
    this.getState = function(){
        return state;
    };
}
```

The getters in this example will simply return the private variable; however, you may define a getter, such as getCurrentTimeInSeconds, that will modify the return value so that the function returns the playback time in seconds. For example:

```
this.getCurrentTimeInSeconds = function(){
    return (currentTime / 1000);
}
```

Next, you must define the controls for the track, such as play, pause, and stop.

```
app.track = function(length){

    ...

    this.stop = function(){
        window.clearInterval(interval);
        state = _self.state.STOPPED;
        setCurrentTime(0);
        _self.callbacks.didStop.call(_self);
    };

    this.play = function(){
        if(state != _self.state.PLAYING){
            interval = window.setInterval(updateTime, updateInterval);
            state = _self.state.PLAYING;
            _self.callbacks.didStartPlaying.call(_self);
        }
    };

    this.pause = function(){
        window.clearInterval(interval);
        state = _self.state.PAUSED;
        _self.callbacks.didPause.call(_self);
    };
}
```

this.stop will stop the track and clear the interval timer using window.clearInterval(interval). The stop method will also set the current state of the track to 0 or STOPPED using state = _self.state.STOPPED. This method will also reset the current time and make a call to the didStop callback method.

`this.play` will check to see whether the track is playing by checking the current state. If the track is not playing, then it will create a new interval timer. `window.setInterval` takes two parameters: the callback method and the interval time in milliseconds. If you wish to assign a callback that takes a parameter from the function that set the initial interval, you could use the following:

```
var globalParam = 'foo';
window.setInterval(function(){
    callbackFunction.call(this, globalParam);
}, intervaltime);
```

Remember that `globalParam` must be declared with `var` in order for it to exist within the closure.

Finally, you define the default callback functions.

```
app.track = function(length){
    ...
    this.callbacks = {
        didUpdateTime: function(time){},
        didStartPlaying: function(){},
        didPause: function(){},
        didStop: function(){}
    };
};
```

As you can see, these are empty functions. This allows you to call the callback functions even if they haven't been assigned. There are four callback functions: `this.callbacks.didUpdateTime`, `this.callbacks.didStartPlaying`, `this.callbacks.didPause`, and `this.callbacks.didStop`.

Now it's time to start creating the play button and digging into Canvas! Before you begin, it's important to understand how Canvas really works. In order to draw on the canvas, you need to get its *context*. If you are not familiar with what a context is, it is like a hidden space where you can draw. The context will be presented to the user after you have finished drawing onto it. There is currently only one context in the Canvas API, and all shapes are drawn onto it. In an ideal world, you would have several contexts, draw individual components onto them, and merge each context onto one single context. For now, this is not possible, and will be explained further into this chapter.

The Canvas context works on a coordinate-based system with 0,0 starting at the top left, as shown in Figure 7-5.

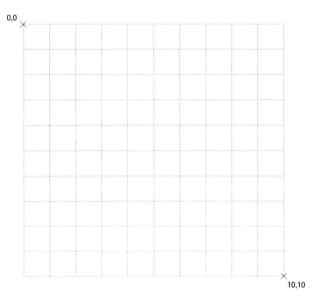

Figure 7-5. *Canvas grid*

To begin, you will need to define a few global variables.

```
app.playButton = function(id, track){
    var canvas = document.getElementById(id),
    context = canvas.getContext('2d'),
    track = track,
    _self = this;
}
```

As you can see, you get the Canvas element by using `getElementById`. You then get the Canvas context by using `canvas.getContext('2d')`, which will return a 2d Canvas context for you to draw on. You then explicitly declare the track variable and again define `_self` as `this` for any callback methods.

You can make it easier to calculate certain aspects of the canvas by creating new properties for the Canvas element. This is done using the following code:

```
app.playButton = function(id, track){

    ...

    canvas.center = {
        x: (canvas.offsetHeight / 2),
        y: (canvas.offsetHeight / 2)
    };
```

```
    canvas.dimensions = {
        width: (canvas.offsetWidth),
        height: (canvas.offsetHeight)
    };
}
```

This will now allow you to quickly retrieve the center coordinates and the width and height of the canvas without storing them in global variables. You simple use `canvas.center.x`, for example, to get the center x coordinate for the canvas.

Next you will need to assign callbacks for when the track updates its timer and for when the track is paused.

```
app.playButton = function(id, track){

    ...

    track.callbacks.didUpdateTime = function(time){
        _self.draw();
    };

    track.callbacks.didPause = function(){
        _self.draw();
    }

}
```

As you can see, both callbacks simply call the `draw` method within the `playButton` class.

Next, you will need to create the playback control methods. This will be used to play and stop the track via the play button. This also allows other objects or function to start or stop the track through the play button.

```
app.playButton = function(id, track){

    ...

    this.togglePlay = function(){

        switch(track.getState()){
            case track.state.STOPPED:
            case track.state.PAUSED:
                _self.play();
                break;
            case track.state.PLAYING:
                _self.stop();
                break;
        }

    };
```

```
this.play = function(){
   track.play();
};

this.stop = function(){
   track.pause();
};
}
```

As you can see, there is a method called `this.togglePlay`. The toggle play method will check the track's state. If it is stopped or paused, it will trigger the play method; if it is playing, it will trigger the `stop` method. These conditions are wrapped within a `switch` statement. The `switch` statement is a good alternative to using `if` statements to reduce clutter. The statement is formed of the following:

```
switch(value){
   case condition:
      /** condition code **/
      break;
   case condition:
      /** condition code **/
      break;
   default:
      /** default code **/
      break;
}
```

As you can see, it takes a `value`. Each `case` represents a `condition` to compare the value to. If the `condition` matches, it executes the code within the `case` and then breaks out of the `switch`. If none of the `conditions` match, you can specify a default action to take using `default:`. It's best practice to only compare integer values in a `switch` statement.

With the `togglePlay` method complete, the `this.play` and `this.stop` methods both act as wrappers to pause or play the track.

The full code for the track is as follows:

```
app.track = function(length){

   this.state = {
      STOPPED: 0,
      PLAYING: 1,
      PAUSED: 2
   };
```

```javascript
var length = (length * 1000),
    currentTime = 0,
    interval,
    _self = this,
    state = this.state.STOPPED,
    updateInterval = 1000 / 30;

var setCurrentTime = function(time){
    currentTime = time;
    _self.callbacks.didUpdateTime.call(_self, currentTime);
};

var updateTime = function(){

    if(currentTime < length){
        setCurrentTime(currentTime + updateInterval);
    } else {
        _self.stop();
    }

};

this.getCurrentTime = function(){
    return currentTime;
};


this.getLength = function(){
    return length;
};

this.getState = function(){
    return state;
};

this.stop = function(){
    window.clearInterval(interval);
    state = _self.state.STOPPED;
    _self.setCurrentTime(0);
    _self.callbacks.didStop.call(_self);
};

this.play = function(){
    if(state != _self.state.PLAYING){
        interval = window.setInterval(updateTime, updateInterval);
        state = _self.state.PLAYING;
        _self.callbacks.didStartPlaying.call(_self);
    }
};
```

```
    this.pause = function(){
        window.clearInterval(interval);
        state = _self.state.PAUSED;
        _self.callbacks.didPause.call(_self);
    };

    this.callbacks = {
        didUpdateTime: function(time){},
        didStartPlaying: function(){},
        didPause: function(){},
        didStop: function(){}
    };

};
```

Now it's time to draw the stop button. The draw methods are called in the `this.draw` method and the context is taken from the private variable within the class.

Drawing the Stop Icon

The stop button is 20px × 20px and should be a filled rectangle. To draw a rectangle of any proportion, you can use the `context.fillRect()` method. The `fillRect` method takes the four parameters shown in Table 7-3.

Table 7-3. *fillRect Method Parameters*

Parameter	Description
x	Where to place the upper-left x coordinate of the rectangle in relation to the canvas
y	Where to place the upper-left y coordinate of the rectangle in relation to the canvas
width	The width of the rectangle
height	The height of the rectangle

To draw a simple rectangle, 20px × 20px, you would use the following code:

```
context.fillStyle = '#000000';
context.fillRect(0, 0, 20, 20);
```

This would produce a rectangle similar to that shown in Figure 7-6.

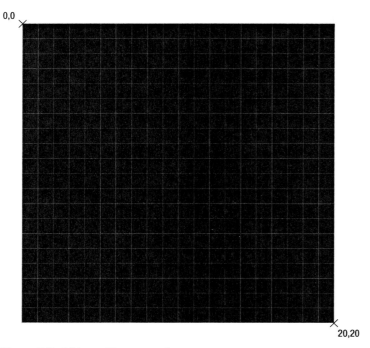

Figure 7-6. *A 20px × 20px rectangle*

`context.fillStyle` will set the fill for any new closed shape, such as a rectangle or a circle, to black or #000000.

In the code to draw the rectangle on the play button for the stop symbol, you need to take into consideration the position of the stop symbol in relation to the canvas. You will want to place the stop symbol directly in the center of the canvas. To center the stop symbol, you will need to calculate the x and y offsets for the top-left corner of the stop symbol. To calculate this, you need to divide the canvas width and height in half to give you the offsets. You can then subtract the canvas centers from the center of the shape to give you the x and y coordinates. This method simply aligns the center of the shape to be drawn with the center of the canvas.

The following code will center the stop icon on the canvas in relation to the size of the canvas itself.

```
app.playButton = function(id, track){

    ...
```

```
this.drawStop = function(){
   var width = 20,
      height = 20,
      x = canvas.center.x - (width / 2),
      y = canvas.center.y - (height / 2);

   context.beginPath();
   context.fillStyle = '#A0A0A0';
   context.fillRect(x, y, width, height);

};
}
```

As you can see, you declare the width and height of the stop icon as 20, so that they can be referenced later. You also calculate the x coordinate by getting the canvas's center x coordinate minus half of the width of the rectangle. This will center the stop icon horizontally.

Next, the y coordinate is set in much the same way, by halving the height of the canvas (its center) and subtracting half of the stop icon's height. This then places the stop icon in the center of the canvas vertically, as shown in Figure 7-7. Combining these two calculations will completely center the stop icon within the canvas.

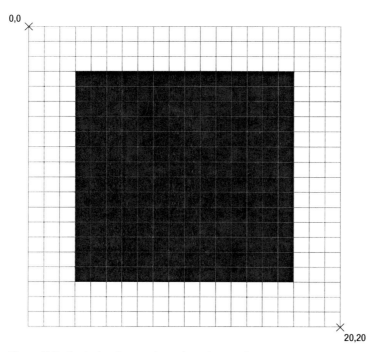

Figure 7-7. *Centering the stop icon along the x and y axes*

Before you begin to draw new shapes in Canvas, it's a good idea to call `context.beginPath()`. This will create a new path within the context for you to start drawing. It's the equivalent of lifting your pen off of the page before you draw a new shape on a piece of paper.

Next, you will need to set the `fillStyle` of the shape you are about to draw. The 2D context API has several methods for drawing. The API's most basic methods and properties are shown in Tables 7-4 and 7-5.

Table 7-4. *Basic 2D Context API Properties*

Property	Description
context.fillStyle	Sets the fill color of the shape to be drawn. This can be a solid color using either a hex color (#000000), an RGB color (rgb(0,0,0)), or an alpha color (rgba(0,0,0,0.5)).
context.lineWidth	This will set the width of any lines drawn after this is set. Values are doubles, such as 1.5.
context.lineCap	This will set the cap style of any line. Valid values are butt, round, and square.
context.strokeStyle	This is the stroke style for the context. It sets the color of any line drawn after setting this. This can be a solid color using either a hex color (#000000), an RGB color (rgb(0,0,0)), or an alpha color (rgba(0,0,0,0.5)).

Table 7-5. *Basic 2D Context API Methods*

Method	Description
context.fillRect(x, y, width, height)	This will create a rectangle with the properties specified.
context.strokeRect(x, y, width, height)	This will create a rectangle with no fill, but a stroke with the properties specified.
context.clearRect(x, y, width, height)	This will draw a "white" rectangle with the properties specified.
context.arc(x, y, center, start angle, end angle, anticlockwise)	This will draw an arc using the properties specified. The start and end angles are defined as radians. anticlockwise is a Boolean value and is used to specify in which way to draw the arc.

With the style properties set, you can now draw the stop icon using context.fillRect().

The method defined will draw a rectangle within the current context. Next, you will need to create a method to draw the play button.

Drawing the Play Icon

The play button is slightly more complex. To draw the play button you will need to drop down to drawing paths on the context.

In order to draw paths, you use the `moveTo` and `lineTo` methods. These methods allow you to move to a certain point without drawing a line, and draw a line between two points.

```
app.playButton = function(id, track){

    ...

    this.drawPlay = function(){
        var width = 20,
            height = 20,
            x = canvas.center.x - (width / 2),
            y = canvas.center.y - (height / 2);

        context.beginPath();
        context.moveTo(x, y);
        context.lineTo(x + width, y + (height / 2));
        context.lineTo(x, (y + height))
        context.fillStyle = '#A0A0A0';
        context.fill();
    };
}
```

To begin with, you set the `width` and the `height` of the play icon to `20` (i.e., 20px × 20px). You then set the center point to be half of the width of the canvas, minus half of the width of the play button. You also do the same for the y axis, just as you did for the stop icon.

In order to draw the play button, you will essentially premap three points on the canvas to draw lines from and to. Figure 7-8 shows the approximate coordinates for this on a 20px × 20px drawing context.

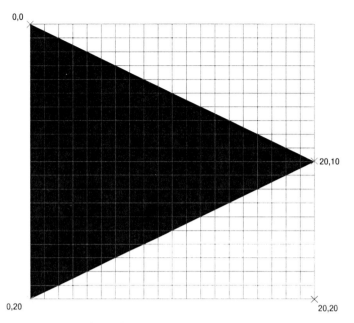

Figure 7-8. *Drawing a triangle*

As you can see, there are three points to the triangle: (0,0), (20,10), and (0,20). In much the same way as you did on the square, you must calculate where the points on the triangle should be, based on its width and height. You know that the first point should begin at 0,0. The second point should be positioned where x = shape width and y = shape height / 2. With this in mind, the third and final point should be positioned where x = origin x and y = shape height. This will create an equilateral triangle. The following code will create this:

```
var width = 20, height = 20, startx = 0, starty = 0;
context.beginPath();
context.fillStyle = '#A0A0A0';

context.moveTo(startx, starty);
context.lineTo((startx + width), (starty + (height / 2)));
context.lineTo(startx, (starty + height));
context.fill();
```

As you can see, you draw two lines to form the equilateral triangle. You do not have to draw another line to connect the final position to the original position. By calling context.fill(), you will automatically close the gap between the original and final point and fill the rectangle with the context.fillStyle color. The preceding method also takes into consideration the starting point to draw the shape. You can change the `startx` or `starty` values and it will always draw an equilateral triangle at that position.

With the icons created, it's now time to set up the playback head. The playback head is simply a circle that gradually opens. Below the semicircle is another circle with a contrasting color to help distinguish the progress of the audio playback, as shown in Figure 7-9.

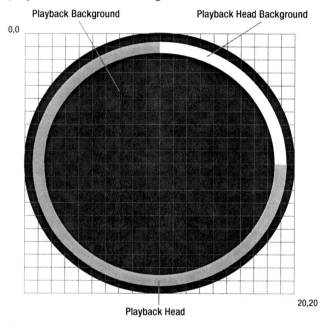

Figure 7-9. *The playback head*

Drawing the Playback Head

The problem with Canvas is that you cannot animate each shape on its own. Moving or animating Canvas elements requires a complete redraw of the canvas. Animating in Canvas requires keeping track of each object's state in JavaScript and then rendering it with each call to `draw`. It's a long and laborious process, but with the correct implementation, it can be less time consuming..

To track the progress of the track, you first need to work out its current progress as a percentage.

```
app.playButton = function(id, track){
   ...
   this.draw = function(){
      var percentage = 100 - ((track.getCurrentTime() / track.getLength())
* 100);

   };
}
```

This is simply calculated as (current time / length) * 100. This will give you a predictable number between 1 and 100. You will need to return a percentage, where 100% is when the track is at the beginning, and 0% is when the track is at the end. To do this, you simply subtract the percent played from 100 to give you the percent of the track that is remaining.

The next step is to calculate the angle of the playback head based on the percentage of track remaining. You know that the result of $2 * \pi$ (PI) will equal the angle of a full circle in radians. $0 * \pi$ (PI) will result in 0, which will result in an empty circle.

```
app.playButton = function(id, track){
   ...
   this.draw = function(){
      var percentage = 100 - ((track.getCurrentTime() / track.getLength()) *
100);
      var endradians = (percentage * (2 / 100)) * Math.PI;

   };
}
```

Figure 7-10 shows the significant positions of the PI calculations.

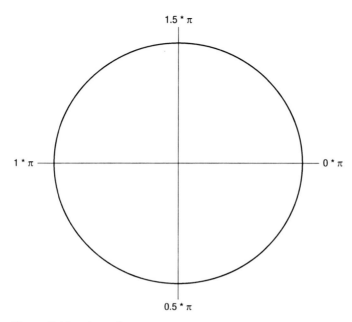

Figure 7-10. *n * π radians*

As you can see, 0 starts at the immediate right of the circle, and 2 will also result in the same position. If you set the start position of the arc to 0 and the end position as 2 * PI, the result will be nothing, as the circle will have no circumference due to the 0˚ angle.

You will be redrawing the canvas at regular intervals, so you will need to clear the canvas with every redraw to prevent displaying the previous context shapes below the new ones. This can be achieved by calling `context.clearRect(0, 0, canvas width, canvas height);`. This will essentially draw a clear rectangle over the whole canvas. You don't have to worry about memory or shapes existing after the rectangle is drawn, as only the current context is held within memory.

```
app.playButton = function(id, track){
   ...
   this.draw = function(){
      var percentage = 100 - ((track.getCurrentTime() / track.getLength()) *
100);
      var endradians = (percentage * (2 / 100)) * Math.PI;

      context.clearRect(0, 0, canvas.dimensions.width,
canvas.dimensions.height);
   };
}
```

The next step is to draw the circle that will provide the background of the play
button. Drawing a full circle and filling it with the color black achieve this.

```
app.playButton = function(id, track){
    ...
    this.draw = function(){
        var percentage = 100 - ((track.getCurrentTime() / track.getLength()) *
100);
        var endradians = (percentage * (2 / 100)) * Math.PI;

        context.clearRect(0, 0, canvas.dimensions.width,
canvas.dimensions.height);

        /**
         * Draw the play button backdrop
         */
        context.beginPath();
        context.fillStyle = '#000000';
        context.arc(canvas.center.x, canvas.center.y,
            canvas.center.x - 10, 0, 2 * Math.PI, false);
        context.fill();

    };
}
```

The next step is to draw the circle with no fill and apply a stroke to it to provide
the background that will be revealed as the play head moves.

```
app.playButton = function(id, track){
    ...
    this.draw = function(){
        var percentage = 100 - ((track.getCurrentTime() / track.getLength()) *
100);
        var endradians = (percentage * (2 / 100)) * Math.PI;

        context.clearRect(0, 0, canvas.dimensions.width,
canvas.dimensions.height);

        /**
         * Draw the play button backdrop
         */
        context.beginPath();
        context.fillStyle = '#000000';
        context.arc(canvas.center.x, canvas.center.y,
            canvas.center.x - 10, 0, 2 * Math.PI);
        context.fill();

        /**
         * Draw the background for the play head
         */
        context.beginPath();
```

```
        context.arc(canvas.center.x, canvas.center.y,
            canvas.center.x - 20, 0, 2 * Math.PI);
        context.lineWidth = 5;
        context.strokeStyle = "#FFFFFF";
        context.stroke();

    };
}
```

Finally, it's a case of drawing the play head based on the track's current playback position. The code is the same as that of drawing the background for the play head, except the end angle is set to the endradians previously declared in the code to represent the progress of the track.

```
app.playButton = function(id, track){
    ...
    this.draw = function(){
        var percentage = 100 - ((track.getCurrentTime() / track.getLength()) *
100);
        var endradians = (percentage * (2 / 100)) * Math.PI;

        context.clearRect(0, 0, canvas.dimensions.width,
canvas.dimensions.height);

        /**
         * Draw the play button backdrop
         */
        context.beginPath();
        context.fillStyle = '#000000';
        context.arc(canvas.center.x, canvas.center.y,
            canvas.center.x - 10, 0, 2 * Math.PI);
        context.fill();

        /**
         * Draw the background for the play head
         */
        context.beginPath();
        context.lineWidth = 5;
        context.strokeStyle = "#FFFFFF";

        context.arc(canvas.center.x, canvas.center.y,
            canvas.center.x - 20, 0, 2 * Math.PI);

        context.stroke();

        /**
         * Draw the progress head
         */
        context.beginPath();
        context.lineWidth = 5;
```

```
        context.strokeStyle = "#A8A8A8";
        context.arc(canvas.center.x, canvas.center.y,
            canvas.center.x - 20, 0, endradians);
        context.stroke();

    };
}
```

The final step in this method is to decide whether to draw the stop or the play icons on the button with every canvas redraw. This is achieved with a `switch` statement.

```
app.playButton = function(id, track){
    ...
    this.draw = function(){
        var percentage = 100 - ((track.getCurrentTime() / track.getLength()) *
100);
        var endradians = (percentage * (2 / 100)) * Math.PI;

        context.clearRect(0, 0, canvas.dimensions.width,
canvas.dimensions.height);

        /**
         * Draw the play button backdrop
         */
        context.beginPath();
        context.fillStyle = '#000000';
        context.arc(canvas.center.x, canvas.center.y,
            canvas.center.x - 10, 0, 2 * Math.PI);
        context.fill();

        /**
         * Draw the background for the play head
         */
        context.beginPath();
        context.lineWidth = 5;
        context.strokeStyle = "#FFFFFF";

        context.arc(canvas.center.x, canvas.center.y,
            canvas.center.x - 20, 0, 2 * Math.PI);

        context.stroke();

        /**
         * Draw the progress head
         */
        context.beginPath();
        context.lineWidth = 5;
        context.strokeStyle = "#A8A8A8";
        context.arc(canvas.center.x, canvas.center.y,
```

```
        canvas.center.x - 20, 0, endradians);
    context.stroke();

    /**
     * Decide whether to draw the play or the stop button
     */
    switch(track.getState()){
      case track.state.PAUSED:
      case track.state.STOPPED:
        this.drawPlay();
        break;
      case track.state.PLAYING:
        this.drawStop();
        break;
    }

  };
}
```

As you can see, if the track state is paused or stopped, the play icon is drawn; if the track is playing, the stop icon is drawn.

The full code for the `playButton` follows. You will notice that at the bottom of the code sample, there is an event listener to bind the touch event for the canvas. This will trigger the `togglePlay()` method.

```
app.playButton = function(id, track){

    var canvas = document.getElementById(id),
        context = canvas.getContext('2d'),
        track = track,
        _self = this;

    canvas.center = {
      x: (canvas.offsetHeight / 2),
      y: (canvas.offsetHeight / 2)
    };

    canvas.dimensions = {
      width: (canvas.offsetWidth),
      height: (canvas.offsetHeight)
    };

    /**
     * Track callback methods
     */
    track.callbacks.didUpdateTime = function(time){
      _self.draw();
    };
```

```javascript
track.callbacks.didPause = function(){
   _self.draw();
}

/**
 * Track controls
 */

this.togglePlay = function(){

   switch(track.getState()){
      case track.state.STOPPED:
      case track.state.PAUSED:
         _self.play();
         break;
      case track.state.PLAYING:
         _self.stop();
         break;
   }

}

this.play = function(){
   track.play();
};

this.stop = function(){
   track.pause();
};

this.drawStop = function(){
   var width = 20,
      height = 20,
      x = canvas.center.x - (width / 2),
      y = canvas.center.y - (height / 2);

   context.beginPath();
   context.fillStyle = '#A0A0A0';
   context.fillRect(x, y, width, height);

};

this.drawPlay = function(){
   var width = 20,
      height = 20,
      x = canvas.center.x - (width / 2),
      y = canvas.center.y - (height / 2);

   context.beginPath();
   context.moveTo(x, y);
```

```
        context.lineTo(x + width, y + (height / 2));
        context.lineTo(x, (y + height))
        context.fillStyle = '#A0A0A0';

        context.fill();

    };

    this.draw = function(){
        // Draw the progress bar based on the
        // current time and total time of the track
        var percentage = 100 - ((track.getCurrentTime() / track.getLength()) *
100);
        var endradians = (percentage * (2 / 100)) * Math.PI;

        context.clearRect(0, 0, canvas.dimensions.width,
canvas.dimensions.height);

        context.beginPath();
        context.fillStyle = '#000000';
        context.arc(canvas.center.x, canvas.center.y,
           canvas.center.x - 10, 0, 2 * Math.PI);
        context.fill();

        context.beginPath();
        context.arc(canvas.center.x, canvas.center.y,
           canvas.center.x - 20, 0, 2 * Math.PI);
        context.lineWidth = 5;
        context.strokeStyle = "#FFFFFF";
        context.stroke();

        context.beginPath();
        context.arc(canvas.center.x, canvas.center.y,
           canvas.center.x - 20, 0, endradians);
        context.lineWidth = 5;
        context.strokeStyle = "#A8A8A8";
        context.stroke();

        switch(track.getState()){
            case track.state.PAUSED:
            case track.state.STOPPED:
               this.drawPlay();
               break;
            case track.state.PLAYING:
               this.drawStop();
               break;
        }

    };
```

```
canvas.addEventListener('touchend', function(e){
    _self.togglePlay();
    e.preventDefault();
});

    this.draw();
};
```

Figure 7-11. *Final play button*

Storing Data

Traditionally, to persist data (such as a user's name) within a mobile web application, you would store this information within a cookie. The problem with cookies is that while they are prefect for storing small amounts of data, they quickly become hard to manage for large amounts of data, such as a JavaScript object. This can be perfect for when you wish to store the current state of the application so that when the users come back it it, they can pick up from where they left off, much like a native application.

Unfortunately, local storage does not support storing objects, only string values. But you can convert objects into strings using JSON.stringify and convert them back into objects using JSON.parse.

To store data using local storage, simply use the `localStorage` APIs. These consist of the properties and methods shown in Table 7-6.

Table 7-6. *Local Storage Methods and Properties*

API Method	Description
`localStorage.clear()`	Clears all data in the local storage
`localStorage.setItem(key, value)`	Sets a key value pair in local storage
`localStorage.getItem(key)`	Gets an item from local storage based on its key
`localStorage.key(0)`	Gets an item from local storage based on its index value; you can get the last item in local storage by calling `localStorage.key(localStorage.length)`
`localStorage.removeItem(key)`	Removes an item from local storage based on its key
`localStorage.length`	Returns the number of items in local storage

For example, if you wanted to store an object with a user's name, e-mail address, and contact phone number, you would create something like this:

```
var user = {name: "John Seagate", email: "john.seagate@hello.com",
contactNumber: "012345678910"}
localStorage.setItem('user', JSON.stringify(user));
```

To retrieve the item, you would use the following code:

```
var user = JSON.parse(localStorage.getItem('user'));
```

JavaScript Libraries for Mobile

JavaScript libraries can help with some of the heavy lifting of any type of front-end development. They can help with providing a consistent API for anything from DOM manipulation to all the way through to the kitchen sink. There are three libraries that will be used as examples in this chapter.

- XUI
- jQuery Mobile
- Sencha Touch

Figure 7-12. *jQuery Mobile (left), and Sencha Touch (right)*

XUI is targeted specifically for mobile and provides a jQuery-like syntax with lightweight DOM manipulation, simple API abstraction for making and processing Ajax requests, and performs basic JavaScript-based animation. It has a plugin architecture much like jQuery, so you can extend XUI to suit your needs and create additional plugins for your project.

jQuery Mobile and Sencha Touch are both heavyweights, in the sense that they can provide not just an abstraction from what you might call "vanilla JavaScript," but also a framework from which you can easily build mobile web applications.

jQuery mobile can help you to rapidly prototype projects and then skin them further on down the line. Its UI relies on Plain Old Simple HTML (POSH). The POSH is then enhanced with CSS and JavaScript. jQuery works on both phone- and tablet-based devices through the use of CSS media queries to alter layout.

Sencha Touch offers a much more complex and fully featured development methodology. You do not write cards or pages in HTML. Instead, you configure each page and provide content through JavaScript. Sencha Touch offers lots of UI enhancements and widgets including the ability to store data offline and online out of the box through the use of proxies. This allows you to store and retrieve data through a common interface and specify the type of store you use in the configuration.

jQuery and Sencha Touch are great; however, what you end up creating is an application built in the jQuery mobile or the Sencha way of thinking. There is nothing wrong with using a mobile library to complete a mobile-based project, but you should be aware of the things you should look for when picking a framework or library.

File Size

It is important to ensure that any library has a small footprint. Some mobile operators, unfortunately, do not offer unlimited data plans, so it's important to make sure that accessing your mobile web site doesn't have a large impact on your user's pockets. It's also important to remember that although 3G and LTE offer relatively high data speeds, not all users will have access to 3G or LTE all of the time. This has an impact on load time, as a 500kB library along with your entire application's image and CSS assets could take several seconds to download through 3G/LTE; it could take much longer on EDGE. So, cater for the lowest common denominator, which would be EDGE in this case.

Number of Files

At the time of writing, the number of requests that a mobile browser can make is quite restricted. This means that if you have many assets to download to the browser, this can affect loading time. You can overcome this by ensuring that the JavaScript library you are using offers the following:

- A minified and concatenated version of the source
- A sprite sheet for things such as icons and buttons
- A content delivery network (CDN) hosted version of the library

Activity

You should check to see when the most recent update was for the library and how often new versions are released (the release cycle). This has an effect on your development, and if you're one for keeping up to date with bug fixes and major releases, you might find yourself constantly updating your code with the latest release; or even worse, if the library is abandoned and no longer maintained, it means that you will have to learn a new library or maintain the one that has just been abandoned.

CSS3 Support

Many libraries are now updating their code to take advantage of the enhancement in GPU support for CSS3 animations and transitions. You should check your library to ensure that it supports or has a roadmap for CSS3 transitions and animations over JavaScript animations and transitions. This will provide performance enhancements for your application.

Summary

From this chapter, you should have a much greater understanding of JavaScript in general and the new capabilities that mobile brings you.

You should be able to distinguish the difference between procedural JavaScript and object-oriented JavaScript, and that passing objects into each other is a much better concept and principle than calling functions in the global namespace.

You should also have a brief understanding of scope within JavaScript and how to maintain it between objects through closures and the use of _self = this.

You should also have a brief understanding of how to handle touch events in JavaScript and that by tapping into this, you can produce much richer applications.

This chapter has touched on Canvas in great detail. You should have an understanding of how HTML5 Canvas works and the idea behind context and the drawing APIs, such as arc, fillRect, and the style APIs, such as lineStyle and fillStyle.

JavaScript: Models, Views, and Controllers

There are many development design patterns. One that has really stood out and can be applied across almost all programming languages is MVC (Model View Controller). MVC breaks down how an application should be structured into various layers of responsibility.

It's all too common that we, as developers, jump in and begin working on a project with no real understanding of how that project will eventually evolve or grow. For example, we pull in data from external resources using Ajax and then simply render that data in HTML in the same code block. What happens when you then want to use that same HTML in another part of your application, but for a different purpose, using a different data source? The quickest thing to do is to copy and paste that code and alter the variables.

As you begin to bolt more features onto your application in this manner, it might begin to look more like you've built your application out of jelly and chocolate rather than code and logic. As tasty as that sounds, the point is that if you build your application from the beginning in such a way that it can easily be built upon later, it will cost less time and money to add more features in the future.

Part of making this happen is to standardize or create rules for certain aspects of your application. This can make the code longer to write, but easier to work with by developers other than yourself. By adopting MVC, you adopt a method of working that's easy to understand. Your skill level shouldn't dictate whether you should learn about design patterns. You may implement MVC any way that you like; however, this chapter will show you only one way of working with MVC in JavaScript.

Through this chapter, you will learn how to create and implement your own MVC framework. You will learn what models are and how they act as the lifeblood of your application. You will learn how a controller can help to bind and manage events in your application and how view can be built to be reused.

> **NOTE:** Before you begin, you will need a Rotten Tomatoes developer account. To create one, head over to `http://developer.rottentomatoes.com` and follow the steps to create a developer account and get an API key.

Cleaning Up Your Code

Before you begin to write any code for this chapter, you will need to clean up `index.html` in the root directory of your application that you made for Chapter 4. Most of the HTML, such as the favorites list and the movie preview list, will now be generated using JavaScript. We'll be covering quite a bit in this chapter; in order to focus on all these issues in detail, looking for cinemas and playing back audio tracks will be removed from the final feature list.

Open `index.html` and ensure your HTML looks like the following code.

```
<!DOCTYPE html>
<html lang="en-GB" dir="ltr">

    <head>

        <meta charset="UTF-8" />
        <meta name="viewport" content="width=device-width; initial-scale=1.0;
            maximum-scale=1.0; user-scalable=0; target-densitydpi=device-dpi;"/>
        <title>Mo Memo</title>
        <link rel="stylesheet" type="text/css" href="css/mobile.css" />
        <link rel="apple-touch-icon-precomposed" href="img/home-screen-icon.png">
    </head>

    <body>

        <div id="shoe">

            <!-- Begin Taskbar -->

            <header id="taskbar" class="screenbar">
                <h1 class="branding">Mo Memo</h1>
                <!-- Taskbar Search form -->
                <form method="post" id="add-movie" class="horizontal">
                    <input type="text" class="full-width search" name="query"
                        placeholder="enter your movie name&hellip;" />
```

```
            </form>

        </header>

        <!-- End Taskbar -->

        <!-- Begin Movie List Deck -->

        <div class="deck">

            <div class="card active" id="card-favorite_list">

            </div>

            <div class="card" id="card-movie_search_results">

            </div>

            <div class="card" id="card-movie_info">

            </div>

        </div>

        <!-- End Movie List Deck -->

    </div>
  </body>

</html>
```

As you can see from the preceding code, there are several changes to `<div />`
IDs and classes. The content from the individual cards has also been removed.
This is because, in this chapter, you will learn about how to create reusable
HTML snippets, called *views*, in JavaScript. This will allow you to keep your
HTML and view logic outside of the application's main code and in its own
maintainable file.

MVC and a JavaScript Primer

JavaScript is based on the ECMAScript standard. We were blessed by
JavaScript's popularity toward the end of the twentieth century, when the web
site dynamicdrive.com helped to bring JavaScript to the forefront of the Web.
Then, just as Web 2.0 was the buzzword for the collection of popular web
technologies (such as Ajax, JavaScript, CSS, and HTML) and concepts
(including APIs, RSS, social media, and mass content production and
consumption) several years ago, DHTML became the buzzword for making use

of JavaScript, DOM manipulation, and CSS (e.g., making web pages with snowflakes that float on top of them).

Soon, JavaScript became much more popular and, in the hands of serious developers with experience in enterprise software development in languages such as Java and C/C++, JavaScript matured. However, browsers were inconsistent in implementation; JavaScript developers often coded in hatred, knowing that other browsers' implementation of Ajax/XMLHttpRequest was completely different to the then-popular Internet Explorer (the opposite of what we see today). Even simple tasks such as binding events or selecting elements could be a pain, as you had to do them twice—once for Internet Explorer and once for everybody else.

We later got libraries such as MooTools, DoJo, JQuery, and YUI to take a lot of the heavy lifting away from us. These did away with many of the browser inconsistencies by providing one method for us to use to perform simple tasks (such as DOM selection and manipulation), which worked across all browsers. For example, rather than writing several lines of code to create an Ajax request that was compatible with both Internet Explorer and Firefox, you could cover both at once with jQuery, as follows.

```
$.ajax('/my/data/provider.json');
```

What this unfortunately left us with was a group of new developers who had every right to believe that jQuery, DoJo, MooTools, or YUI was true JavaScript—because that's the way they were taught or self-taught.

Procedural JavaScript mixed with library code became the norm, and cramming `$(document).ready(function(){});` with spaghetti code would eventually become hard to maintain for growing web applications.

These tools are amazing and powerful, but it's easy to become reliant on them and not understand how they really work and why you should or shouldn't use one or the other for mobile. If you primarily work with jQuery, then that's great. I have been working with jQuery as a developer since 2007/version 1.1, and script.aculo.us (although I hate to admit it) since 2005. However, I learned JavaScript first, and I looked through jQuery and script.aculo.us's code before I even began to use it.

This is even more important in mobile, as the majority of the code found in the libraries will be barely used by your mobile web application. At a minimum, you might potentially use DOM selectors, traversal, event binding, and Ajax, which accounts for a small percentage of the libraries code. That said, it doesn't make sense to pull the whole thing down a network that's already struggling with supply and demand.

Instead, sometimes it's actually much more beneficial to roll your own mini JavaScript library or framework. You're never too much of a novice to learn how to do this; in fact, it's actually better to get set in your ways now.

A framework is simply a method, standard, or practice for working with your code. You create a framework to also separate the vital parts of your application so they're easier to manage as your application grows. The framework also manages how data flows through your application. You will mainly see JavaScript objects passed from one method to another for presentation. These objects will usually represent some form of entity, and are known as *models*. The models will usually be passed to a method or a function that will then display that to the user. In MVC, the method that handles and manipulates the model for presentation is called the *controller*, and the code that generates the HTML incorporating the model is called the *view*. Figure 8-1 shows how the MVC framework is structured.

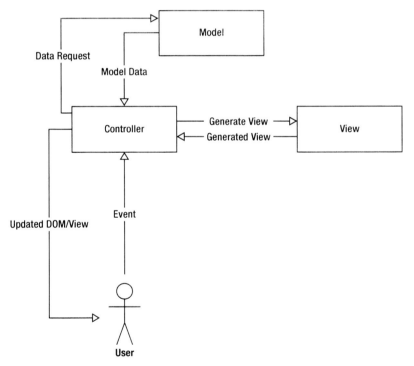

Figure 8-1. *MVC diagram for JavaScript*

The Model

The M in MVC stands for Model. A model is the part of the application that dictates how different types of data are handled. A model is simply a JavaScript object that can represent an entity of some kind. For instance, you might create a model for a user within your application, like so:

```
var user = function user(){}
```

> **TIP:** You will notice that I have named the function, as well as assigned it to a variable. This essentially creates a named function instead of an anonymous one. This is useful in many instances, such as debugging, as you can see the method name in a stack trace.

A user will typically have attributes, such as name, password, and pet. It's best to create these attributes by using instance variables (variables that are only accessible from within the object/model) and then creating privileged getters and setters to modify or retrieve those values. This allows you to then create rules around those attributes. For instance, you can have a setter for the password that accepts a plain text password and then encrypts its value within the object. By omitting a getter, you can also prevent the user's password from being retrieved from the user object by another piece of code. The next code example shows the evolution of the user model.

```
var user = function user(name, password, pet){

    var _name = null,
    _password = null,
    _pet = null,
    _self = this;

    this.setName(name);
    this.setPassword(password);
    this.setPet(pet);

    name = null;
    password = null;
    pet = null;

    /**
     * Returns the user's name
     */
    this.getName = function(){
        return _name;
    }
```

```
/**
 * Sets the user's name
 */
this.setName = function(name){
    _name = name;
}

/**
 * Sets the user's password and encrypts it before assignment
 */
this.setPassword = function(password){
    _password = password.encrypt(); // .encrypt() doesn't really exist!
}
    /**
 * Returns the user's favorite pet
 */
this.getPet = function(){
    return _pet;
}

/**
 * Sets the user's favorite pet
 */
this.setPet = function(pet){
    _pet = pet;
}

}
```

As you can see, there's a significant amount of code here to achieve what feels like very little. However, the idea is that you can use this new user model anywhere in your application, and no matter what data you provide to it, it will act in a predictable manner throughout your application.

The beauty of using models is that you can create relationships between them. For instance, using the previous example, every user has a pet, but wouldn't it be nice to find a way to describe that pet? To do this, you can create a pet model.

You could just as easily add pet attributes to the user model, but if you need to describe the pet in more detail in the future, you end up with a cluttered user model. Having a separate model allows you to create new pet attributes in the future, without damaging the integrity of your application. The pet model is as follows .

```
var pet = function pet(name, type){
    var _name = null,
        _type = null;
```

```
        this.setName(name);
        this.setType(type);

        /**
         * Gets the pet's name
         */
        this.getName = function(){
            return _name;
        }

        /**
         * Sets the pet's name
         */
        this.setName = function(name){
            _name = name;
        }

        /**
         * Gets the pet's type
         */
        this.getType = function(){
            return type;
        }

        /**
         * Sets the pet's type
         */
        this.setType = function(type){
            _type = type;
        }
}
```

As you can see, the pet model follows the exact same structure as the user model. To use these together, you can do the following.

```
var sue = new user('Suzanne', 'password', null); // First create a new user with
no pet
var jack = new pet('Jack', 'dog'); // Create a new pet
sue.setPet(jack); // Assign the new pet to the user

/**
 * By calling getPet, you now have access to all of the pet's methods and
 * attributes from the user
 */

alert(sue.getName() + 'has a favorite ' + sue.getPet().getType() + ' called ' +
sue.getPet().getName());
```

You might want to go further and allow a user to have many pets. You can do this by creating an array of pets within the user model. You will have to create several new methods to manage the pets array from outside of the user object.

addPet will add a single pet to the pet array.

getPet gets a single pet at a specific index from the pet array.

removePet removes a single pet using an index value.

setPets sets the pet array using an array of pets, overwriting the existing pet array.

getPets retrieves all of the pets assigned to a user object.

The new changes to the user object are as follows.

```
/**
 * Now that you can have multiple pets, it doesn't make sense to add it to
 * the constructor
 */
var user = function user(name, password){

    var _name = null,
        _password = null,
        _pets = [], // The default value is now an array instead of null
        _self = this;

    this.setName(name);
    this.setPassword(password);
    // favoritePet is not part of the constructor anymore, so it doesn't need to
be set

    name = null;
    password = null;

    ...

    /**
     * Adds a pet to the pet array
     */
    this.addPet = function(pet){
        // You can add object validation here before adding to the pet array
        _pets.push(pet);
    }

    /**
     * Gets a pet from the array at a specific index
     */
    this.getPet = function(index){
        return _pets[index];
```

```
    }

    /**
     * Removes a pet from the array
     */
    this.removePet = function(index){
        /**
         * Splice can remove items from an array. It accepts a start index
         * and number of items
         */
        _pets.splice(index, 1);
    }

    /**
     * Sets the pet array
     */
    this.setPets = function(pets){
        /**
         * Clear the pets array, using Array.length = 0 will remove
         * every element in the array as apposed to creating a new array
         * using _pets = [];
         */
        _pets.length = 0;

        /**
         * Instead of completely replacing the pets array with the new array,
         * each pet should go through the same validation in the addPet method.
         * Instead of duplicating any validation code, it makes sense to just
         * call the addPet method for every pet using a for loop.
         */
        for(var i = 0; i < pets.length; i++){
            _self.addPet(pets[i]);
        }
    }

    /**
     * Gets the pet array
     */
    this.getPets = function(){
        return _pets;
    }

}
```

As you can see from the preceding code, most of the methods are fairly self-explanatory, except for the setPets method. From the setPets code, you can see that you have to first clear the pets array using _pets.length = 0. This is slower than assigning a new empty array to the _pets variable using _pets = []; however, it will simply remove all of the array elements rather than create a new empty array. Rather than assigning the pets array passed to the method to the _pets array in the pets object, you iterate through every pet in the new array and call the addPet method. The reason for this is to ensure that any new pets still pass through the same code used to add a pet to the user object, which may contain validation or modify each pet object. To make use of the new code, you can do something similar to the following JavaScript code.

```
var user = new user('Suzanne', 'password');
var pet1 = new pet('Jack', 'dog');
var pet2 = new pet('Snoop', 'dog');
user.appPet(pet1);
user.addPet(pet2);

var message = user.name + ' has ' + user.getPets().length + ' pets. ' +
user.name + ' has';
for(var i = 0; i < user.getPets().length; i++){
   message += ' a ' user.getPet(i).getType() + ' called ' +
user.getPet(i).getName();
}

alert(message);
```

This should output something similar to "Suzanne has 2 pets. She has a dog called Jack a dog called Snoop".

It's important to remember that your models are simply JavaScript objects, so you can add any methods to manipulate the variables within them or output things in a certain way.

There aren't that many models within MoMemo. The best way to explain how the models work with each other is through a class diagram.

Although JavaScript is a classless language, you can still use the class analogy to describe how an object is formed through creating a constructor, methods, and instance variables within that object.

A class diagram shows what methods and properties a class will have, and how they interact with other classes.

> **NOTE:** To keep things as simple as possible in this book, I will only cover how to read basic UML class diagrams including properties, methods, and common associations. If you'd like to learn more about UML and the different diagrams available, feel free to check out www.agilemodeling.com/essays/umlDiagrams.htm.

A basic class diagram for MoMemo is shown in Figure 8-2.

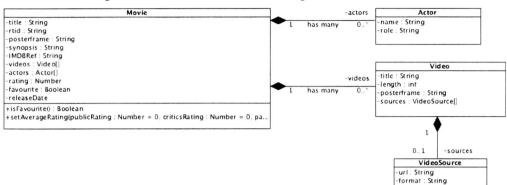

Figure 8-2. *Classes in a class diagram*

As you can see from Figure 8-2, each box shows a name at the top (e.g., Movie, Actor, etc.), which represents the name of each class. Just below the box name are several lines prefixed with a - symbol. These are attributes of the class. The symbol before the name of the attribute dictates whether the attribute should be public (+) or private (-). You can specify types as well as other properties for attributes in UML class diagrams.

Just below the attributes, there is a line followed by a method name. In the example in Figure 8-2, you can see that the only method for Movie is isFavorite, which returns a Boolean and determines whether the movie is a favorite.

The black diamonds next to the class indicate that there is an association between the Movie class and the Actor and Video classes. The black diamond tells you that the association is a composite, meaning that the Movie class owns an Actor and Video, and that the Actor and/or Video cannot exist without the Movie within the context of this application. The composite association also says that if the parent (Movie, in this case) dies, then child (Actor/Video) will cease to exist. It's always important to remember that, when creating associations between classes, they are made within the context of the application. There are other types of associations, which are listed in Table 8-1.

Table 8-1. *The Different UML Association Types*

Symbol	Name	Description
◆—	Composite	This is when a parent owns the child, and the child cannot exist without the parent. If the parent is destroyed, the child is destroyed too. This is known as a "contains a" relationship.
◇—	Aggregate	This is when the parent does not own the child, but the child can exist without the parent. If the parent is destroyed, the child will still exist. For instance, an Actor can exist without a Movie. This is known as a "has a" relationship. A child in an aggregate association can only belong to a single parent entity (i.e., an Actor cannot belong to more than one Movie).
——	Association	This is a loose association, meaning that there is no ownership between entities and that they can exist without each other. Each entity can be associated with many other entities.

Next to the association line you will see either a 1 or 0..*. This is called *multiplicity*. It indicates what the type of association is between each class. A 1 indicates that there is only one associated object, 0..* indicates that there are zero or more associated objects.

In the example in Figure 8-2, an Actor only has one Movie, but a Movie has zero or more Actors. A Movie has zero or more Videos, but a Video can only have a single Movie.

In general, a UML diagram will also never show getters and setters for attributes. Using the previous model, you can begin to create your models for MoMemo.

Let's start with the smallest and most insignificant model, VideoSource.

The Video Source Model

The video source model is the simplest of all of the models used within the MoMemo application. The video source model is used to store the different video formats for a video. Rather than adding webm, mp4, and ogv attributes to the Video model, it makes sense to associate the video with video sources for flexibility.

Imagine a new mobile web browser has just been released with support for several new formats. If you wanted to support those formats, you would need to modify the `Video` model, which could have an adverse effect on your application. By creating an association with a video source, you don't need to worry about modifying your code if new formats appear, as you can simply create new instances for the new video formats, and then add them to the association with the `Video` model. To make life even easier, you can create a loop in your view (which will be discussed further into this chapter) so that you don't have to modify the application to support the new video formats.

To begin, create a new JavaScript file, called `videosource.js`, for the video source model within the `js/app/model/` folder. You can now begin to define your model's structure using the following code.

```
var app = app || {};

app.model = app.model || {};

/**
 * A video source used within a video
 * You must add this object to a video once instantiated
 * @param {String} url
 * @param {app.type.format} format
 */
app.model.videosource = function appModelVideoSource(url, format){
    // Your implementation goes here
}
```

As you can see, the model is declared in much the same way as the pets model, except you use the `app.model` namespace for all of your models.

The constructor accepts a URL for the video, and a format that could be webm, ogv, mp4, and so forth.

The next thing to do will be to declare the instance variables. Just to recap, an instance variable is a variable that exists only within the scope of the object instance. The instance variables aren't accessible or modifiable outside of the instance, unless a getter or setter is created for the instance variable.

```
...
app.model.videosource = function appModelVideoSource(url, format){

    /**
     * The video source's instance variables
     */
    var _url,
        _format,
        _self = this;

}
```

As you can see, there are only two instance variables that corrospond to the constructor parameters. The instance variables are prefixed with underscores (_) so that they don't clash with variables passed through the constructor. You also declare a reference to the instance using _self = this, as the this keyword references the privileged method and not the object.

The next thing to do is to create an instantiation method, which gets called toward the end of the model. The code is as follows.

```
...
app.model.videosource = function appModelVideoSource(url, format){
...

   /**
    * Set the instance variables using the constructor's arguments
    */
   this.init = function(){
      this.setUrl(url);
      this.setFormat(format);
   }

   // Insert getters and setters

   this.init();

}
```

As you can see, the init method simply calls the setters for the attributes passed through the constructor.

> **NOTE:** Variables passed through a constructor are within the scope of the constructor and privileged methods that are contained within the constructor. This means that constructor parameters can be used and modified within privileged methods. When you create new variables within privileged methods, it's important to declare them using var to prevent the privileged method from modifying the constructor parameter.

This prevents code repetition, as you might perform other operations when modifying instance variables from outside of the object, such as error checking or changing the value based on a condition.

You might be thinking, why not simply call the setters without wrapping them with the init method at the top of the JavaScript object as shown in the previous code sample. The simple answer is that the setters haven't been declared yet, so calling the methods will create a JavaScript error.

When you declare a normal named function in JavaScript, the interpreter will look for the function when it's called, regardless of its placement in the script. However, when you assign a function to a variable, you have to wait until that assignment happens before calling the function.

To get around this, you must either put all of your initialization code at the end of the object, or wrap it in a method at the top and call it from the bottom. I have opted for the later, as getters and setters tend to create a lot of white noise, and scrolling through lots of what feels like pointless code to get to your main code is a bit irritating. You can see that the `init` method is called toward the end of the object in the previous example.

The next thing to do is to create the getters and setters. This is a really simple task. Just to recap, the getters return an instance variable, and the setters assign values to instance variables as anything outside the object can't modify the instance variables from outside of the object.

The getters and setters are fairly self explanitory, you can see in the following code.

```
...
app.model.videosource = function appModelVideoSource(url, format){
...
  /**
   * Getters and setters
   */

  /**
   * Gets the url of the video source
   * @return {String}
   */
  this.getUrl = function(){
    return _url;
  }

  /**
   * Sets the url of the video source
   * @param {String} url
   */
  this.setUrl = function(url){
    _url = url;
  }

  /**
   * Gets the mimetype of the video source
   * @return {app.type.format}
```

```
    */
  this.getFormat = function(){
     return _format;
  }

  /**
   * Sets the mimetype of the video source
   * @param {app.type.format} format
   */
  this.setFormat = function(format){
     _format = format;
  }
  ...
}
```

That concludes the VideoSource model. As you can see, it's very simple. Next, you'll create the Video model, which is also relatively simple.

The Video Model

The Video model is also relatively simple, except that it has a composite association with the VideoSource model in which it can be composed of many video sources.

Create a new empty file called video.js within js/app/model. This will contain the new video model.

The constructor accepts a title, length in milliseconds, and a URL to a posterframe or preview frame, which will be an image.

```
var app = app || {};

app.model = app.model || {};

/**
 * A video associated with a movie
 * You must add video sources in order for videos to play
 * @param {String} title
 * @param {Integer} length
 * @param {String} posterframe
 */
app.model.video = function appModelVideo(title, length, posterframe){
  // Code implementation goes here
}
```

The instance variables for this object are title, length, posterframe, and an array of sources. As you can see from the following code snippet, the sources variable isn't part of the constructor's parameters.

```
app.model.video = function appModelVideo(title, length, posterframe){
   /**
    * The video's instance variables
    */
   var _title,
      _length,
      _posterframe,
      _sources = [],
      self = this;
}
```

You can create accessors for the _sources instance variable. As it isn't imperative toward the function of the object's immediate instance, it doesn't need to be in the constructor.

The accessors for the _sources instance variable consists of a method to add single source instances, remove and get instances from the array based on an index, retrieve the full array, or overwrite the array with a new array. The accessors can be seen in the following code snippet.

```
app.model.video = function appModelVideo(title, length, posterframe){
   ...

   /**
    * Gets all of the video sources used for embedding video
    * in POSH
    * @return {Array}
    */
   this.getSources = function(){
      return _sources;
   }

   /**
    * Sets all video sources using an array
    * @param {Array} sources
    */
   this.setSources = function(sources){

      /**
       * Clears the sources array
       */
      __sources.length = 0;

      /**
       * Rather than setting the sources all in one go,
       * you use the addSource method, which can handle
       * any validation for each source before it's
       * added to the object
```

```
      */
    for(var i = 0; i < sources.length; i++){
      _self.addSource(sources[i]);
    }
  }

  /**
   * Adds a source to the sources array
   * @param {app.model.videosource} source
   */
  this.addSource = function(source){
    _sources.push(source);
  }

  ...
}
```

As you can see, the accessors follow the same implementation from the pet example shown earlier in this chapter.

You might also want to add some type of filtering on the _length setter so that any value is parsed as an integer to prevent any issues within the model. You can use the parseInt method in the setter's implementation. This will ensure that any value passed to the model will be an integer or zero. The setter can be seen in the following code snippet.

```
app.model.video = function appModelVideo(title, length, posterframe){
  ...
  /**
   * Sets the length of the video in milliseconds
   * @param {Integer} length
   */
  this.setLength = function(length){
    /**
     * Use parseInt here just to ensure the length
     * is an integer. If it's not, then it will
     * return NaN. The isNaN method will check to
     * see whether the value is not a number.
     */
    _length = parseInt(length);

    if(isNaN(_length)){
      _length = 0;
    }
  }
  ...
}
```

You can now complete the Video model, which should look like the following.

```javascript
var app = app || {};

app.model = app.model || {};

/**
 * A video associated with a movie
 * You must add video sources in order for videos to play
 * @param {String} title
 * @param {Integer} length
 * @param {String} posterframe
 */

app.model.video = function appModelVideo(title, length, posterframe){

   /**
    * The video's instance variables
    */
   var _title,
       _length,
       _posterframe,
       _sources = [],
       _self = this;

   /**
    * Set the instance variables using the constructor's arguments
    */

   this.init = function(){
      this.setTitle(title);
      this.setLength(length);
      this.setPosterframe(posterframe);
   }

   /**
    * The getters and setters
    */

   /**
    * Gets the title of the video
    * @return {String}
    */
   this.getTitle = function(){
      return _title;
   }

   /**
    * Sets the title of the video
    * @param {String} title
    */
   this.setTitle = function(title){
```

```
        _title = title;
    }

    /**
     * Gets the length of the video in milliseconds
     * @return {Integer}
     */
    this.getLength = function(){
        return _length;
    }

    /**
     * Sets the length of the video in milliseconds
     * @param {Integer} length
     */
    this.setLength = function(length){
        /**
         * Use parseInt here just to ensure the length
         * is an integer. If it's not, then it will
         * return NaN. The isNaN method will check to
         * see whether the value is not a number.
         */
        _length = parseInt(length);

        if(isNaN(_length)){
            _length = 0;
        }
    }

    /**
     * Gets all of the video sources used for embedding video
     * in POSH
     * @return {Array}
     */
    this.getSources = function(){
        return _sources;
    }

    /**
     * Sets all video sources using an array
     * @param {Array} sources
     */
    this.setSources = function(sources){

        _sources.length = 0;

        /**
         * Rather than setting the sources all in one go,
         * you use the addSource method, which can handle
         * any validation for each source before it's
```

```
     * added to the object
     */
    for(var i = 0; i < sources.length; i++){
        _self.addSource(sources[i]);
    }
}

/**
 * Gets the source at a specific index
 * @param {Integer} index
 * @return {app.model.videosource} source
 */
this.getSource = function(index){
    return _sources[index];
}

/**
 * Removes a source at a specific index
 * @param {Integer} index
 */
this.removeSource = function(index){
    _sources.splice(index, 1);
}

/**
 * Adds a source to the sources array
 * @param {app.model.videosource} source
 */
this.addSource = function(source){
    _sources.push(source);
}

this.init();

}
```

With the Video model complete, you can move onto the last small model, the Actor model.

The Actor Model

The Actor model is another simple object, which contains only the actor's name and role within the Movie. Create a new file within js/app/models/ called actor.js. There's not much to explain here, so go ahead and create the model. It should have two instance variables called _name and _role that are set through the constructor. Your complete code will look like the following.

```javascript
var app = app || {};

app.model = app.model || {};

/**
 * The actor object handles the actors for a movie
 * Actors should only be included in a full movie listing
 * @param {String} name
 * @param {String} role
 */
app.model.actor = function appModelActor(name, role){

  /**
   * The actor's instance variables
   */
  var _name,
     _role,
     _self = this;

  /**
   * Set the instance variables using the constructor's arguments
   */
  this.init = function(){
     this.setName(name);
     this.setRole(role);
  }

  /**
   * Getters and setters
   */

  /**
   * Returns the full name of the actor
   * @return {String}
   */
  this.getName = function(){
     return _name;
  }

  /**
   * Sets the actor's full name
   * @param {String} name
   */
  this.setName = function(name){
     _name = name;
  }

  /**
   * Gets the role of the actor in
   * relation to the associated film
```

```
 * @return {String}
 */
this.getRole = function(){
   return _role;
}

/**
 * Sets the actor's role in relation
 * to the associated film
 * @param {String} role
 */
this.setRole = function(role){
   _role = role;
}

this.init();

}
```

The Movie Model

The Movie model is one of the biggest models within the MoMemo application. It has composite associations with the Actor and Video models, so if the movie is destroyed, the associated object instances will also be destroyed. The attributes for the associations are also arrays, so you will need to create add and remove methods for the arrays objects, which aren't outlined in the UML class diagram.

To begin with, create the movie.js model file within js/app/model/. The Movie model will mimic some of the properties available from the Rotten Tomatoes API.

> **NOTE:** Only some of the Rotten Tomatoes APIs will be covered in this book. You can find out more about what the APIs are capable of at http://developer.rottentomatoes.com/.

The following code snippet shows the instance variables that you will need to create accessors for.

```
var app = app || {};

app.model = app.model || {};

/**
 * A movie model used for all movies within the application
 *
```

```
 * @alias app.model.movie
 * @constructor
 * @param {String} title
 * @param {String} rtid
 * @param {String} posterframe
 * @param {String} synopsis
 */
app.model.movie = function appModelMovie(title, rtid, posterframe, synopsis) {

    /**
     * The video's instance variables
     */
    var _title,
        _rtid,
        _posterframe,
        _synopsis,
        _releaseDate,
        _videos = [],
        _actors = [],
        _rating,
        _favorite = false,
        _self = this;

}
```

Your complete Movie model should look like the code snippet in Listing A-1 in the appendix.

The code for this model is very simplistic. For something that's quite crucial to the application, it makes sense to validate values passed to accessors to prevent the application from falling over when the wrong type is passed to a model.

Validation

JavaScript, unfortunately, doesn't support what is known as *type hinting*. Type hinting is the process of specifying what type of parameter a method can accept. Type hinting in other languages will allow you to specify that a parameter for a method should be a certain type in the method declaration. For instance, in PHP, you can specify that a parameter should be an array or object type as shown in the following code snippet.

```
function doSomething(MyObject $object, array $myarray){
    /** some implementation **/
}
```

This eases the need to perform vast amounts of validation to check to see whether an object passed to a method is of a certain type, as upon execution, if it isn't, the method will automatically throw an exception or error.

To get around this, you need to validate parameters passed to your accessors. The most common type of validation will be to validate against type. You can check to see whether a value is an object, array, number, or string.

You will want to use some of these validators more than once, so it's worth creating an object to store all of the validation methods. To do this, create a new JavaScript file called `validator.js` within the `js/app/utility` folder (if the folder doesn't exist, create it).

You will create a constructorless object. This will allow you to use the object's methods without having to instantiate it. Use the following code snippet to start creating your validation object.

```
var app = app || {};

app.utility = app.utility || {};

/**
 * Validator object has static methods
 * to check to easily validate values
 */

app.utility.validator = {}
```

With the validator utility in place, we can begin to create the validation methods.

isEmpty

The first easy validation method will be to check to see whether a value is empty. Create a new method within the validator called `isEmpty`, as shown in the following code example.

```
...
app.utility.validator = {

   /**
    * Checks to see whether a value is empty or not
    * Returns true if it is, or false if it isn't
    * @param {String|Object} value
    * @return {Bool}
    */
   isEmpty: function(value){
      return false;
   }
```

```
}
```

As you can see, the isEmpty method accepts a single parameter, which is the value to be validated. By default, it will return false unless the rest of the implementation returns true.

Use the following validation code to complete the validator.

```
...
app.utility.validator = {

   /**
    * Checks to see whether a value is empty or not
    * Returns true if it is, or false if it isn't
    * @param {String|Object} value
    * @return {Bool}
    */
   isEmpty: function(value){
      if(value == '' || value == null || value === false){
         return true;
      }
      return false;
   }

}
```

From the preceding implementation, you can see that the conditional statement returns true if the value is an empty string, null, or false.

> **NOTE:** As you can see, I have used === to compare the value with false. A == comparison loosely compares values. For example, 0 == false will return true. 0 is not necessarily an empty value, so using 0 === false will return false, as 0 and false are two completely different types.

isTypeOf

The next validator will check to see whether a value is a type of object. This is a relatively simple method. It uses instanceof to see whether an object is an instance of another object. The method accepts a value and a type. However, the type must not be a string but the original object, as shown in the following code snippet.

```
...
app.utility.validator = {
   ...
   /**
    * Checks to see whether a value is a type of object
    * Returns true if it is, or false if it isn't
    * @param {Object} value
    * @param {Object} type
    * @return {Bool}
    */
   isTypeOf: function(value, type){

      if(value instanceof type){
         return true;
      }

      return false;
   }
}
```

This is great, but what happens when you want to check primitive types like
Booleans, strings, and numbers? Creating a new method just to check those
would be confusing and slightly annoying. To get around this, you can use the
typeof operator. This will check the type of a variable. As strings, numbers, and
Booleans are primitive types, you can check for these by allowing the type
parameter to accept a string. To do this, simply add the following code.

```
...
app.utility.validator = {
   ...
   /**
    * Checks to see whether a value is a type of object
    * Returns true if it is, or false if it isn't
    * @param {Object} value
    * @param {Object} type
    * @return {Bool}
    */
   isTypeOf: function(value, type){

      // First check to see if the type is a string
      if(typeof type == "string"){
         // If it is, we're probably checking against a primative type
         if(typeof value == type){
            return true;
         }
      } else {
         // We're dealing with an object comparison
         if(value instanceof type){
            return true;
         }
```

```
    }
        return false;
    }
}
```

As you can see from the preceding code, the main changes are that the isTypeOf method checks to see whether the type parameter is a string type or not. If it's a string, the assumption is that you want to check for a primitive type; otherwise, you're going to check for an object type. If the primitive type is the same as the type you require, it will return true.

This is by no means a bulletproof solution. There are libraries available that can do even better type checking. The idea is that as you begin to require more validation techniques, you can add to the validation object as and when you need to. If a validation method that you create doesn't quite match up to a specific edge case, you can adjust to compensate. With these in place, we can now enforce type in the models' accessor methods based on the UML class diagrams.

Applying Validation to Models

When you apply validation to models, you have one of two choices: either you fail silently if the validation fails, or you throw an exception and allow the caller to handle it. I prefer the later. Nothing is more frustrating than when something seriously bad happens in your application and you have no idea about it and, thus, can't react to it in your code.

Throwing and Handling Exceptions

Exceptions should be known as critical errors that can be thrown by user code. You shouldn't throw an exception in every bit of code that you write, as you have to wrap that code from the caller in try/catch blocks in the code calling it. An uncaught thrown exception will appear in the console of the browser. Throwing an exception is fairly simple. It consists of the throw operator along with either a string, Boolean, integer, or (believe it or not) an object.

```
// Throwing a string
if(true !== false){
    throw "True definitely isn't equal to false"
}

// Throwing an object
if(true !== false){
    throw {
        message: "True definitely isn't equal to false",
```

```
        type: "pointless_exception",
        code: 1000
    }
}
```

If you want to see what type of exception has been thrown, it's usually better to throw an object. As you can see from the preceding code, you can put pretty much anything in there, including a code, type, and a message. If you were to throw a primitive type exception (string, Boolean, integer), nobody other than you will probably be able to figure out what the exception was, what it meant, and most importantly, how to handle it. By using an object, you have the ability to check against a code or type, rather than trying to compare a complex string.

The next step is to catch the exception after it's been thrown. This is a simple task. To test this out, you can wrap your conditional statement in a function and call it from the try/catch block, just to show you how it would work in a real-world situation.

```
function doSomething(){
if(true !== false){
    throw {
        message: "True definitely isn't equal to false",
        type: "pointless_exception",
        code: 1000
    }
}
}

try {
    doSomething();
} catch (e){
    alert(e.message);
}
```

If you try out this code, you'll find that the exception is thrown, and e.message will retrieve the message for you and alert it.

It's important to understand that exceptions should be used only when there is no other way to handle the error in your block of code.

The next section will take you through hardening the models so that the setters will throw exceptions if the wrong type of value is passed to them. The getters have been omitted to make it easier to read.

Strengthening the Models

The new validation rules (shown in bold in the following code) simply check the type. If the value is not of a certain type, it will throw a validation exception and break out of the method. This prevents the instance variable from being set by the invalid value.

Also, for convenience, the `app.utility.validator` object has been assigned to the validator variable. This makes it a little bit easier to access validation methods, rather than having to constantly type out the extremely long namespace. Because it's an instance variable, it's also accessible to privileged methods.

```javascript
app.model.videosource = function appModelVideoSource(url, format){

/**
 * The video source's instance variables
 */
var _url,
    _format,
    _self = this,
    validator = app.utility.validator;

...
    /**
     * Sets the url of the video source
     * @param {String} url
     */
    this.setUrl = function(url){

        // Check to see whether the value is a primitive string type
        if(!validator.isTypeOf(url, "string")){
            throw {
                message: "The url property in the videosource model requires a
'string' type",
                type: "validation_exception"
            }
            return;
        }

        _url = url;
    }

    ...
    /**
     * Sets the mimetype of the video source
     * @param {app.type.format} format
     */
    this.setFormat = function(format){

        // Check to see whether the value is an app.type.format
        if(!validator.isTypeOf(format, app.type.format)){
            throw {
```

```
        message: "The format property in the videosource model requires
a 'app.type.format' type",
            type: "validation_exception"
        }
        return;
    }

    _format = format;
}

this.init();

}
```

Based on this example, you should now be able to add validation to your setters based on the code comments from this book. Feel free to add them for each model.

Creating New Types

The types currently available in JavaScript are great. However, sometimes you might find yourself in a situation where you would like to pass a structured object to a model that might not necessarily be a model itself. These are usually known as *types*, and have the same structure throughout your application. For instance, you might want to create a new location type to store location information and retrieve it in a predictable way.

From the models comments, you would have seen that there are two custom types in the application: format and releaseDate. format simply allows you to store a video format so that it's easy to get the mime type, file format (such as mp4, webm, etc.), and the name of the format for reference. The releaseDate type simply stores a film's cinema release date and DVD release date.

To create the new types, simply create two new files within the js/app/type directory called format.js and releaseDate.js. (If the directory doesn't exist, you should create it.)

In the format.js file, add the following code.

```
var app = app || {};

app.type = app.type || {};

/**
 * The media type, can be used to
 * define mime types of objects
 * @param {String} name
```

```javascript
 * @param {String} format
 * @param {String} mime
 */

app.type.format = function(name, format, mime){

   /**
    * The media's instance variables
    */
   var _name,
      _format,
      _mime,
      _self = this;

   /**
    * Set the instance variables using the constructor's arguments
    */
   this.setName(name);
   this.setFormat(format);
   this.setMime(mime);

   /**
    * Getters and setters
    */

   /**
    * Gets the name of the media type
    * @return {String}
    */
   this.getName = function(){
      return _name;
   }

   /**
    * Sets the name of the media type
    * @param {String} name
    */
   this.setName = function(name){
      _name = name;
   }

   /**
    * Gets the format of the media (e.g., webm, ogv)
    * @return {String}
    */
   this.getFormat = function(){
   return _format;
   }

   /**
```

```
 * Sets the format of the media
 * @param {String} format
 */
this.setFormat = function(format){
    _format = format;
}

/**
 * Gets the mime type of the media
 * @return {String}
 */
this.getMime = function(){
    return _mime;
}

/**
 * Sets the mime type of the media
 * @param {String} mime
 */
this.setMime = function(mime){
    _mime = mime;
}

}
```

As you can see, there are just three instance variables called mime, format, and name. With accessors, that's all that is required to create a new type. You can create the release type in just the same way, by adding the following code to releaseDate.js.

```
var app = app || {};

app.type = app.type || {};

/**
 * The movie release date
 * The constructor takes the cinema release date and dvd release date
 * @param {Date} cinema
 * @param {Date} dvd
 */
app.type.releaseDate = function(cinema, dvd){

    /**
     * The release date instance variables
     */
    var _dvd,
        _cinema;

    /**
     * Sets the instance variables using setters
```

```
 */
this.setDvd(_dvd);
this.setCinema(_cinema);

/**
 * Gets the DVD release date
 */
this.getDvd = function(){
    return _dvd;
}

/**
 * Sets the DVD release date
 */
this.setDvd = function(dvd){
    _dvd = dvd;
}

/**
 * Gets the cinema release date
 */
this.getCinema = function(){
    return _cinema;
}

/**
 * Sets the cinema release date
 */
this.setCinema = function(cinema){
    _cinema = cinema;
}

}
```

Again, the model works in just the same manner as the `format` type.

Application Utilities

As you have seen from the validator utility, a utility allows you to place code that may not necessarily belong to a controller, model, view, or type in its own object. A utility object will usually perform some kind of repetitive action. In this application, there are three other utilities, in addition to the validator utility. These are:

- `deck.js`—This utility is used to manage the cards within a deck. It allows you to show and hide cards.

> `layout.js`—This utility allows you to refresh the layout when the orientation of the device changes. Some elements require a dynamic width and height, which this utility facilitates.

> `jsonp.js`—This utility allows you to make cross-site requests for web services that support the JSONP (JavaScript Object Notation with Padding) format.

Managing the Deck

The deck manager is a simple object used to show and hide cards. This utility was created to avoid having to repetitively type out class names in the application's main code. The reason for this is because a class name might change and it would mean having to update that class name throughout the application and retest all of the code. The other reason for doing this is that you might want to change the way in which cards are shown or hidden. For example, you might use CSS3 animations to flip cards, fade them out, and so forth.

Create a new file within `js/app/utility` called `deck.js` that contains the following code.

```javascript
var app = app || {};

app.utility = app.utility || {};

app.utility.deck = (function(){

    // Keep all of the cards in a local scope
    var _cards = document.getElementsByClassName('card');

    // Return an object with methods
    return {
        // Shows a card by adding the active class
        showCard: function(id){
            document.getElementById(id).classList.add('active');
        },
        // Hides a card by removing the active class
        hideCard: function(id){
            document.getElementById(id).classList.remove('active');
        },
        /*
         * Hides all cards by iterating through the card list
         * and removing the active classname
         */
        hideAllCards: function(){
            for(var i = 0; i < _cards.length; i++){
```

```
            _cards[i].classList.remove('active');
        }
    }
}
})();
```

This object simply exposes methods that allow you to add or remove the active class name from an element with a specific ID. There is also a method to facilitate hiding all cards within the deck. The `_cards` instance variable holds a list of all cards within the deck.

As you can see, rather than creating an anonymous function, the function itself is wrapped in parentheses, and the function itself returns an object with methods. This is known as the *revealing module pattern*. It differs from the normal way of creating objects in JavaScript by creating a function and using `this.methodName` to create methods. The code within the function is automatically executed when the script loads, and returns an object.

```
var myObject = (function(){
    return {
        sayHi: function(){
            alert('Hi!');
        }
    }
})();
```

This means that you don't have to create a new object using the new operator. You can simply call the object by using its assigned variable (myObject, in this case), as the constructor has already executed. You can then access the "public" methods in much the same way as any object.

```
myObject.sayHi();
```

The downside to this method is that there is no obvious way to create a new object and assign it to a new variable.

Sending Cross-Site Requests

There might be times when you need to pull in data from external web services other than your own. To do this, you would normally use Ajax. If the other server supports Cross-Origin Resource Sharing (CORS), you will be able to make remote Ajax requests. Unfortunately, not all web services support this.

To get around this issue, some web services support JSONP. JSONP allows you to send a callback parameter to a web service. Normally, you'll receive a JSON object as part of a JSON request much like the following.

```
{
    " name": " Dave",
    "occupation": " General Manager"
}
```

With JSONP, this data become inaccessible, due to the method used to create the request.

With an Ajax request, you send the request and create a callback method as an event listener. With JSONP, you actually embed the request as a `<script />` in the web page. As part of the script source, you will append a callback method. The resulting HTML looks like the following code snippet.

```
<script src="http://myservice.com/staff/101/?callback=showProfile"
async="async"></script>
```

This will load the script, the web service will wrap the result in the method, and the response will look like the following.

```
showProfile({
    "name": "Dave",
    "occupation": " General Manager"
});
```

The `showProfile` function will then be executed with the data as its parameter.

Creating a JSONP request can be a laborious task, and one which `jsonp.js` can handle for you.

Begin by creating a new JavaScript file called `jsonp.js` within `js/app/utility/`. Add the following code.

```
var app = app || {};

app.utility = app.utility || {};

app.utility.jsonp = function(url, callbackmethod){

    /**
     * Create a new _src variable to append the callback param to the url
     */
    var _src = url + '&callback=' + callbackmethod;

    /**
     * Create the script element
     */
    var _script = document.createElement('script');

    /**
     * Set the source of the script element to be the same as the one specified
above
```

```
  */
  _script.src = _src;

  /**
   * To prevent the script from blocking other requests, load it
   * asynchronously where possible
   */
  _script.async = "async";

  /**
   * Once the script has loaded, the function will execute and the
   * script tag can be removed from the head of the document
   */
  _script.onload = _script.onreadystatechange = function(load){
      var script = document.head.removeChild(load.target);
      script = null;
  }

  /**
   * This privileged method will send the request by appending the script to
the
   * DOM
   */
  this.send = function(){
      document.head.appendChild(_script);
  }
}
```

The utility itself isn't very complicated. It simply creates a script element and embeds it into the document. After the script has finished loading, the onload event listener will automatically remove it from the DOM.

To make a request, it's as simple as calling.

```
var request = new app.utility.jsonp("http://myservice.com/staff/101/",
"showProfile");
request.send();
```

The problem with JSONP is that unlike Ajax, you can't cancel a request. So if you are sending requests frequently for an autocomplete field, you may find that several requests are sent, but they do not come back in the order that you expect. How to handle this will be covered in the Movies Controller further into this chapter.

Controlling the Layout and Handling Resizes

Sometimes, you might find a circumstance where using CSS alone can't produce the layout that you want. For instance, you might have three elements on a page that have unpredictable heights. Using JavaScript to handle this should really be seen as a last resort, as there may be a delay between when your page loads and when the layout utility adjusts the dimensions of the elements.

The code for this utility looks slightly different than the other objects. It uses a self-executing function so that as soon as the script finishes loading, it automatically executes. Create a new file within js/app/utility/ called layout.js that contains the following code.

```javascript
var app = app || {};

app.utility = app.utility || {};

app.utility.layout = (function(){

    /**
     * This method will adjust the height of all decks
     * so that there is space at the top for the taskbar,
     * which has an unpredictable height
     */
    var fixdeckheight = function(){

        /**
         * First loop through each deck
         */
        [].forEach.call(document.getElementsByClassName('deck'), function(el){
            /**
             * And set the height of the deck by subtracting the height of
             * the taskbar from the height of the document body
             */
            el.style.height = (document.body.offsetHeight -
                document.getElementById('taskbar').offsetHeight) + 'px';
        });

    };

    /**
     * Create a timeout variable, as it may take a while
     * for the new sizes to update in some browsers
     */
    var timeout;
```

```
/**
 * Add an event listener to the window so that when
 * it's resized, it will clear the timeout
 */
window.addEventListener('resize', function(){
    // Clear the timeout just in case it's set, to prevents multiple calls
    clearTimeout(timeout);
    /*
     * Set the timeout to 100ms and execute fixdeckheight at the end of
     * the timeout
     */
    timeout = setTimeout(function(){ fixdeckheight(); }, 100);
});

// Call fixdeckheight for the first time
fixdeckheight();
```

```
})();
```

As you can see from the code comments, the self-executing function contains a method called fixdeckheight. This simply sets the height of the deck to be the size of the viewport, taking into account the size of the taskbar. The event listener will listen for the resize event to fire and call the fixdeckheight function. A timer is used, as the viewport size isn't immediately available when the resize event is fired.

The View

When I first encountered views in MVC for JavaScript, I assumed that the view was simply a piece of HTML defined on an HTML web page, just like MVC in PHP. My ideas on views have since evolved. The best explanation that I can give for a view in JavaScript MVC is that it is a piece of HTML that will be reused within your application.

The view may contain some kind of logic, but not much. The idea behind a view is that no piece of HTML is ever visible in a model or controller. With this in mind, the view is usually a piece of HTML, encapsulated in a JavaScript object, with logic to modify it before it's rendered. The controller will create a new view object and pass appropriate variables to the constructor. An example of a view object is as follows.

```
var view = function(name){

    /**
     * Create a root element. This allows you to add to it using innerHTML
     * so that you don't need to manually create new DOM elements for large
     * chunks of HTML.
```

```
    */
    var _rootElement = document.createElement('div');

    /**
     * You can use innerHTML here to add content to the root element. As you can
see,
     * rather than concatenating a very long string, an array is used. This is
     * cleaner and easier to read than a long string. .join('') is used to merge
the
     * array into a string with no spaces.
     */
    _rootElement.innerHTML = [
      '<p>Hello, my name is ', name, '</p>'
    ].join('');

    this.render = function(){
      return _rootElement;
    }
}
```

As you can see, the constructor accepts a parameter called name. You can have any number of parameters you like, which can then be used in the view itself.

The second line creates a new element and assigns it to the _rootElement instance variable. This is useful, as a DOM parser won't be needed to traverse the DOM for any new elements added to the root element.

The third line of code sets the innerHTML of the root element using an array. This is preferable to using a long string, as it's far easier to read and maintain. join('') is used to merge the array into a string so that innerHTML can accept it.

The only privileged method within the view is this.render, which simply returns the _rootElement. You can add methods later to manipulate the view after it has been instantiated. To retrieve the complete view, you can run the render method on the object from your controller, which will return a DOM object.

It's important to remember that views do not have to be full cards to be used within a deck; they can also be partial views that are used within other views. For instance, in MoMemo, there are two types of movie lists: favorite movies and movie search results.

The presentation of the list itself might differ, but because the individual movie rows are the same, it doesn't make sense to duplicate the HTML for each movie list item. This is where using a view within a view comes in handy. Our controller doesn't need to know how each type of list is rendered; the view is responsible for that.

We can take the HTML used in the original HTML file to create the views for us. There are three views in the MoMemo application: `movielistitem`, `movielist`, and `movie`. We'll discuss these next.

The Movie List Item View

The movie list item view is quite simple. Rather than having to create the same movie list item for various movie lists in the future, the movie list item view can be used in different movie lists to avoid having to rewrite the POSH for every view.

Create a new file within `js/app/view` called `movielistitem.js`. (If the folder doesn't exist, then create it.)

Add the following code to the file.

```
var app = app || {};
app.view = app.view || {};

/**
 * Creates a new view for a movie list item
 * @param {app.model.movie} movie
 */
app.view.movielistitem = function(movie){

    var _movie = movie,
        _rootElement = document.createElement('li');
        _rootElement.innerHTML = [
            '<a data-controller="movies" data-action="find"
                data-params="{&quot;id&quot;: &quot;', movie.getRtid() ,'&quot;}"
                class="more" href="movie/view/", movie.getRtid() ,'">',
                '<div class="preview-image">',
                    '<img src="', movie.getPosterframe(), '" alt="',
movie.getTitle(), '" height="82" />',
                '</div>',
                '<h2>', movie.getTitle(), '</h2>',
                '<p>', movie.getSynopsis(), '</p>',
            '</a>'
        ].join('');

    this.render = function(){
        return _rootElement;
    }
}
```

As you can see, it follows the same standard structure as a regular view. The root element is a list item (`li`), and the view accepts a movie model. Within the array for the POSH, you can see that array value separators (commas) are used to separate the movie accessors from the POSH itself. This is much easier to read and maintain than using concatenated strings. Within the link for the movie, you can see that various data attributes have been created.

```
<a data-controller="movies" data-action="find"
    data-params="{&quot;id&quot;: &quot;', movie.getRtid() ,'&quot;}"
    class="more" href="movie/view/", movie.getRtid() ,'">
```

The `params` will be used for the event delegate for the application to trigger controller events/actions and pass parameters to them.

The rest of the code is quite simple and creates a list item to hold the movie's title, synopsis, and preview image/posterframe.

The Movie List View

The movie list view is simply an unordered list used to hold the various movies. In this application, the movie list view is used once for the favorites list and once for the search results list. Again, this outlines the benefit of using views. If you didn't create this view, you would have to create and maintain the same POSH in two places within your application.

Create a new file within the `js/app/view/` folder called `movielist.js` and add the following code.

```
var app = app || {};

app.view = app.view || {};

/**
 * Creates a new view based on the search results
 * @param {Array} results
 */
app.view.movielist = function(results){

    var _results = results,
        _rootElement;

    // Create the root UL element
    _rootElement = document.createElement('ul');
    _rootElement.classList.add('list');
    _rootElement.classList.add('movie-list');

    for(var i = 0; i < results.length; i++){
        var itemView = new app.view.movielistitem(results[i]);
        _rootElement.appendChild(itemView.render());
    }
```

```
   this.render = function(){
      return _rootElement;
   }

}
```

As you can see, the view constructor accepts an array of results. No error checking is done within this view to verify each model within the array, but you can use the validator utility to enforce this. From the code, you can see that the root element is an unordered list.

```
_rootElement = document.createElement('ul');
_rootElement.classList.add('list');
_rootElement.classList.add('movie-list');
```

From here, several classes are added for styling later.

You then loop through each model within the array and create a new movielistitem object with the model. It's then simple to append the movielistitem by calling the appendChild method and rendering the list item.

```
for(var i = 0; i < results.length; i++){
   var itemView = new app.view.movielistitem(results[i]);
   _rootElement.appendChild(itemView.render());
}
```

The result is an unordered list filled with a list of movies.

The Movie View

The movie view simply holds the full view for the movie when a user taps on a movie item from their favorites or a search. It's slightly more complicated than the other views, as it side scrolls so that a user can get more information about a movie. This works especially well when you want to add new content blocks for a model. There is a limit, however, as adding too many blocks and side scrolling forever can be a pain for the user.

As it's quite a large view, we'll go through it line by line.

First, create the standard view object layout in js/app/view/movie.js with the following code.

```
var app = app || {};
app.view = app.view || {};

/**
 * Creates a new view for a movie list item
 * @param {app.model.movie} movie
 */
```

```
app.view.movie = function(movie){

    var _rootElement = document.createElement('div');
    _rootElement.innerHTML = [].join('');

    this.render = function(){
        return _rootElement;
    }

}
```

As you can see, the root element is a `div`. The first section that should be created is the header for the movie view. This contains the posterframe, the movie title, a button to add/remove the movie from your favorites, and the movie release date.

```
...
app.view.movie = function(movie){

    ...
    _rootElement.innerHTML = [
        '<header class="movie-header">',
        '<img src="', movie.getPosterframe() ,'" alt="', movie.getTitle() , '"
            class="poster" width="100%" />',
        '<hgroup class="movie-title">',
        '<a href="#" class="btn-favorite add" data-controller="favorites"
            data-action="add" data-params=\'{"id": "', movie.getRtid() ,'",
"title": "',
            escape(movie.getTitle()) ,'", "synopsis": "',
escape(movie.getSynopsis()) ,
            '", "posterframe": "', movie.getPosterframe() ,'"}\'>favorite</a>',
        '<h2>', movie.getTitle(),'</h2>',
        '<p class="movie-release-date">Cinematic Release - ',
            movie.getReleaseDate().getCinema().getDate(), '/',
            movie.getReleaseDate().getCinema().getMonth() + 1 , '/',
            movie.getReleaseDate().getCinema().getFullYear() ,'</p>',
        '</hgroup>',
        '</header>',
    ].join('');
    ...
}
```

As you can see, the movie header `<header />` contains the posterframe, which spans the width of the header. It also contains the movie information such as the title and release date. The `Date` object returns a month number starting from zero, so you will need to increase its value by one to get the correct month number.

```
movie.getReleaseDate().getCinema().getMonth() + 1 , '/',
```

The next thing to create will be the movie content blocks. These blocks contain the movie information, such as the synopsis, cast, and videos.

```
...
app.view.movie = function(movie){

   ...
   _rootElement.innerHTML = [
   ...
   '<div class="movie-content">',
      '<div class="block-container span-three">',
         '<section class="block" id="block-synopsis">',
            '<div class="content">',
               '<p>', movie.getSynopsis() ,'</p>',
            '</div>',
         '</section>',

         '<section class="block" id="block-cast">',
            '<div class="content">',
               '<h3>Cast List</h3>',
               '<ul class="list"></ul>',
            '</div>',
         '</section>',

         '<section class="block" id="block-video">',
            '<div class="content">',
               '<h3>Video Clips</h3>',
               '<ul class="list grid"></ul>',
            '</div>',
         '</section>',
      '</div>',
   '</div>',
   ].join('');
   ...
}
```

The POSH is quite simple for this section; it simply outputs the synopsis of the movie. The cast list and video clips remain empty, as these will be populated a bit later.

Finally, you will need to create a footer navigation button to return to the favorites screen.

```
...
app.view.movie = function(movie){

   ...
   _rootElement.innerHTML = [
   ...
   '<footer class="footer screenbar">',
```

```
     '<a class="back" href="/" data-controller="favorites" data-
action="list">my favorites</a>',
  '</footer>'
  ].join('');
  ...
}
```

The next lines of code will check to see whether a movie is in the user's favorites. If it is, it will change the state, data attributes, and text within the favorite button.

```
...
app.view.movie = function(movie){

  ...
  // Check to see whether the movie is in the user's favorites
  if(movie.isFavorite()){
    var _favoriteButton = _rootElement.querySelector('a.btn-favorite');
    _favoriteButton.setAttribute('data-action', 'remove');
    _favoriteButton.classList.remove('add');
    _favoriteButton.classList.add('remove');
    _favoriteButton.textContent = 'un-favorite';
  }
  ...
}
```

Last but not least, you will need to loop through all of the actors that are in the movie and append them to the cast list.

```
...
app.view.movie = function(movie){

  ...
  for(var i = 0; i < movie.getActors().length; i++){
    var actor = movie.getActor(i);
    var element = document.createElement('li');
    element.innerHTML = [
      '<p>', actor.getName(), '<br />',
      '<em>', actor.getRole(), '</em></p>'
    ].join('');
    _rootElement.querySelector('#block-cast ul.list').appendChild(element);
  }
  ...
}
```

The Bootstrap and Controller

Unlike other MVC frameworks, the controller doesn't necessarily have to be assigned to a route or URI/URL in JavaScript. In this book, controllers can be assigned to events too. A controller manages the flow of data through your application, passes that information on to the view, and then is responsible for rendering that back to the user using DOM manipulation. The controller is also responsible for handling user events. In my previous attempts at creating an MVC framework for JavaScript, events were handled outside of the controller, which became cluttered. Common events (such as binding to links to trigger controller actions) should be handled in one place; however, other unique events (such as form events) should be bound by the controller itself. There are other more efficient ways of doing this, but for the purpose of the application being developed for this book, it makes sense to do it this way. Other alternatives include using a library called Sammy.js, which can be used to create restful URLs based on hashbangs (e.g., index.html#/mypage). Sammy can pick up these URLs and then execute JavaScript based on routing rules. If you would like to find out more about Sammy.js, head over to http://sammyjs.org.

The construction of a controller is quite simple; it's simply an object with privileged methods that act as event actions. A controller can be related to a specific entity in your application. In MoMemo, there is a single controller to manage movies and a controller to manage your favorites.

The Bootstrap

The bootstrap is a big object, as it handles delegating link events to various parts of the application. It's responsible for initializing all of the controllers, and becomes the one place to go to access controllers from the rest of the application.

Begin by creating a new file within js/ called bootstrap.js with the following code.

```
var app = app || {};

app.bootstrap = (function(){

})();
```

Begin by declaring an instance variable called _controller.

```
var app = app || {};
```

```
app.bootstrap = (function(){

  /**
   * Create the controller object
   * You explicitly declare the movies and favorites
   * controllers
   */
  var _controller = {
    movies: null,
    favorites: null
  }

})();
```

This will hold the controller objects. It's a good idea to explicitly create this so that you know which controllers should exist within your application.

The next step is to create a click event listener for the whole document. This will pick up any taps and check to whether the element tapped is a link with a request to trigger an action within a controller.

```
var app = app || {};

app.bootstrap = (function(){
  ...
  /**
   * Add a click event listener over the entire document
   * It will delegate clicks for controllers to the
   * controller and action
   */
  document.addEventListener("click", function(event){
  });

})();
```

When you tap an item on the screen, the event listener won't necessarily return the link that you tapped on; it will more than likely return an element within the link itself. As you will want to grab data from the link itself, you will need to traverse up the DOM tree to either grab the link and set it as the target or set the target as null if the user didn't tap on a link.

To do this, you will need to create a while loop. This will assign the target to the current target's parent and gradually loop up the DOM tree. If the target is a link, contains the data-controller attribute, and has a data-action attribute, then it will break out of the while loop and continue with the execution. If the DOM element is the HTML element (at the top of the DOM tree) it will break out of the while loop and assign the target to a null value as the link hasn't been found.

```
var app = app || {};
```

```
app.bootstrap = (function(){
   ...
   /**
    * Add a click event listener over the entire document
    * It will delegate clicks for controllers to the
    * controller and action
    */
   document.addEventListener("click", function(event){
      var target = event.target;

      /**
       * Crawl up the DOM tree from the target element until
       * the link surrounding the target element is found
       */

      while(target.nodeName !== "A" && target.getAttribute('data-controller')
         == null && target.getAttribute('data-action') == null){
         // We've reached the body element break!
         if(target.parentNode.nodeName == 'HTML'){
            target = null;
            break;
         }

      // Assign the target.paretNode to the target variable
      target = target.parentNode;
      }

   });
})();
```

If you have a target, you now need to call the controller's action and pass the parameters (if there are any) to it.

```
var app = app || {};

app.bootstrap = (function(){
   ...
   /**
    * If there's a target, then process the link action
    */
   if(target){

      /**
       * You have the target link, so it makes sense to prevent the
       * link from following through now.
       * This will allow any JavaScript to fail silently!
       */

      event.preventDefault();
   }
```

```
...
})();
```

The first thing to do is to prevent the event from being handled by the browser. This will prevent the browser from attempting to load a dead link. You will then need to get the controller, action, and params data attributes from the element.

```
var app = app || {};

app.bootstrap = (function(){
    ...
    /**
     * If there's a target, then process the link action
     */
    if(target){
    ...

        // Get the controller, action, and params from the element
        var controller = target.getAttribute('data-controller'),
            action = target.getAttribute('data-action'),
            params = target.getAttribute('data-params');

    }
    ...

})();
```

You will then need to verify that the controller and action exists. Check to see whether the controller exists in the _controller instance variable, and that the action exists within the controller, as shown in the following conditional statement.

```
var app = app || {};

app.bootstrap = (function(){
    ...
    /**
     * If there's a target, then process the link action
     */
    if(target){
        ...
        /*
         * Check to see whether the controller exists in
         * the bootstrap and the action is available
         */

        if(typeof _controller[controller] === 'undefined'
           || typeof _controller[controller][action] === 'undefined'){
```

```
            // If they don't exist, throw an exception
            throw "Action " + action + " for controller " + controller + " doesn't
appear to exist";
            return;
        }
    }
    ...

})();
```

You can access properties within an object much like an array. Except rather than passing an index, you can pass a string or a variable. For example:

```
_controller["movie"]["show"]
```

is the same as calling

```
_controller.movie.show
```

except you can now use variables to make the call within the brackets in the first example.

The parameters passed to the controller's action will need to be converted from a string to a JSON object. You can do this with the JSON.parse() method, as shown in the following code.

```
var app = app || {};

app.bootstrap = (function(){
    ...
    /**
     * If there's a target, then process the link action
     */
    if(target){
        ...
        // Check to see whether the params exist
        if(params){
            try {
            // If they do, then parse them as JSON
            params = JSON.parse(params);
            } catch (e) {

                /*
                 * If there's a parsing exception, set the
                 * params to be null
                 */
                params = null;
                    return;
            }
```

```
        }
    }
    ...

})();
```

JSON.parse will throw an exception if the JSON validation fails. You will need to catch this and set the params to null.

The final thing to do is to execute the controller action.

```
app.bootstrap = (function(){
    ...
    /**
     * If there's a target, then process the link action
     */
    if(target){
        ...
        /**
         * Execute the controller within the context of the target.
         * This will allow you to access the original element from
         * the controller action. Also pass the parameters from the
         * data-params attribute.
         */
        _controller[controller][action].call(target, params);

    }
    ...

})();
```

Because the application uses localStorage to store movie favorites, you will need to initialize the local storage variables.

```
app.bootstrap = (function(){
    ...
    /**
     * Set up the local storage by checking to see whether
     * the favorites item exists
     */
    if(!localStorage.getItem('favorites')){
        // if it doesn't, create an empty array and assign it to the storage
        var favorites = [];
        localStorage.favorites = JSON.stringify(favorites);
    }

})();
```

As mentioned before, you will need to create methods to access the controllers and initialize them.

The getController method accepts a string parameter representing the name of the controller with its namespace. It will split the string into parts using the dot character (fullstop) and then loop through the separate namespaces, gradually building it up into an object.

```
app.bootstrap = (function(){
   ...
   return {
   /**
    * Create an accessor for the controller,
    * which accepts a string representation of the
    * controller's namespace
    */
   getController: function(name){

      /**
       * Split the string into an array using the .
       * character to separate the string
       */
      var parts = name.split('.');

      /**
       * Initially set the returned controller to null
       */
      var returnController = null;

      /**
       * If the number of parts is greater than 0
       */
      if(parts.length > 0){
         /**
          * Set the return controller to the parent object
          */
         returnController = _controller;
         /**
          * Loop through each part, gradually assigning the
          * action to the return controller
          */
         for(var i = 0; i < parts.length; i++){
            returnController = returnController[parts[i]];
         }
      }

      /**
       * Return the controller
       */
      return returnController;
   },

   /**
```

```
    * Initializes all of the controllers. You might not want to do this
    * automatically, so you can use the initScripts method to execute it.
    */
  initScripts: function(){
    _controller.movies = new app.controller.movies();
    _controller.favorites = new app.controller.favorites();
    _controller.favorites.list();
    }
  }
})();
```

The init method will simply initialize all of the controllers and load the first
controller.

For your convenience, the full bootstrap is shown next.

```
var app = app || {};

app.bootstrap = (function(){

  /**
   * Create the controller object
   * You explicitly declare the movies and favorites
   * controllers
   */
  var _controller = {
    movies: null,
    favorites: null
  }

  /**
   * Add a click event listener over the entire document
   * It will delegate clicks for controllers to the
   * controller and action
   */
  document.addEventListener("click", function(event){

    var target = event.target;

    /**
     * Crawl up the DOM tree from the target element until
     * the link surrounding the target element is found
     */
    while(target.nodeName !== "A" && target.getAttribute('data-controller')
      == null && target.getAttribute('data-action') == null){

      // We've reached the body element break!
      if(target.parentNode.nodeName == 'HTML'){
        target = null;
        break;
      }
```

```
      // Assign the target.paretNode to the target variable
      target = target.parentNode;
   }

   /**
    * If there's a target, then process the link action
    */
   if(target){

      /**
       * You have the target link, so it makes sense to prevent the link from
following through now.
       * This will allow any JavaScript to fail silently!
       */
      event.preventDefault();

      // Get the controller, action, and params from the element
      var controller = target.getAttribute('data-controller'),
         action = target.getAttribute('data-action'),
         params = target.getAttribute('data-params');

      // Check to see whether the controller exists in the bootstrap and the
action is available
      if(typeof _controller[controller] === 'undefined'
         || typeof _controller[controller][action] === 'undefined'){
         // If they don't exist, throw an exception
         throw "Action " + action + " for controller " + controller + "
doesn't appear to exist";
         return;
      }

      // Check to see whether the params exist
      if(params){
         try {
            // If they do, then parse them as JSON
            params = JSON.parse(params);
         } catch (e) {
            // If there's a parsing exception, set the params to be null
            params = null;
            return;
         }

      /**
       * Execute the controller within the context of the target.
       * This will allow you to access the original element from
       * the controller action. Also pass the parameters from the
       * data-params attribute.
       */
      _controller[controller][action].call(target, params);
```

```
      }

});

/**
 * Set up the local storage by checking to see whether
 * the favorites item exists
 */
if(!localStorage.getItem('favorites')){
    // if it doesn't, create an empty array and assign it to the storage
    var favorites = [];
    localStorage.favorites = JSON.stringify(favorites);
}

return {
    /**
     * Create an accessor for the controller,
     * which accepts a string representation of the
     * controller's namespace
     */
    getController: function(name){

        /**
         * Split the string into an array using the .
         * character to separate the string
         */
        var parts = name.split('.');

        /**
         * Initially set the returned controller to null
         */
        var returnController = null;

        /**
         * If the number of parts is greater than 0
         */
        if(parts.length > 0){
            /**
             * Set the return controller to the parent object
             */
            returnController = _controller;
            /**
             * Loop through each part, gradually assigning the action to the
             * return controller
             */
            for(var i = 0; i < parts.length; i++){
                returnController = returnController[parts[i]];
            }
        }
```

```
    /**
     * Return the controller
     */
    return returnController;
},

    /**
     * Initializes all of the controllers. You might not want to do this
     * automatically, so you can use the initScripts method to execute it.
     */
    initScripts: function(){
      _controller.movies = new app.controller.movies();
      _controller.favorites = new app.controller.favorites();
      _controller.favorites.list();
    }
  }
})();
```

The Movies Controller

The movies controller is quite complex, as it handles searching for movies through the Rotten Tomatoes API, and providing a list of results as the user types through JSONP.

First, start by creating a new controller within js/app/controller called movies.js with the following code.

```
var app = app || {};

app.controller = app.controller || {};

app.controller.movies = function(){

this.init = function(){}

this.init();

}
```

All controllers contain an init method that is executed at the end of the object.

You will want to declare a few instance variables.

    _searchfield—contains the DOM element for the search field

    _searchform—contains the DOM element for the search form

_searchresultcard—contains the DOM element for the search results card

_searchTimeout—contains the search timeout timer

_viewScrolls—contains the iScroll objects for the views

_searchScroll—contains the iScroll object for the search results

Declare these instance variables using the following code.

```
var app = app || {};

app.controller = app.controller || {};

app.controller.movies = function(){

var _self = this,
    _searchfield = document.querySelector('#add-movie input[name="query"]'),
    _searchform = document.getElementById('add-movie'),
    _searchresultscard = document.getElementById('card-movie_search_results'),
    _searchTimeout,
    _viewScrolls = [],
    _searchScroll = null;

this.init = function(){}

this.init();

}
```

Binding the Search Form

The first method you will create will bind the event listeners to the search form.

```
var app = app || {};

app.controller = app.controller || {};

app.controller.movies = function(){

   ...
   /**
    * Binds the search form
    */
   this.bindSearchForm = function(){

   }
   ...
```

```
}
```

When a user focuses on the search field, if there is a search query in
the text box, you will want to show the current results to the user using
the deck utility.

```javascript
var app = app || {};

app.controller = app.controller || {};

app.controller.movies = function(){

    ...
    /**
    * Binds the search form
    */
    this.bindSearchForm = function(){
        /**
         * Here you add an event listener to the search filed using
         * the focus event listener. If there's a value, then show the
         * results.
         */
        _searchfield.addEventListener('focus', function(){
            if(this.value.length > 0){
                app.utility.deck.showCard('card-movie_search_results');
            }
        });

    }
    ...
}
```

The next event that you will need to bind is the submission of the form.
This is to prevent a user from accidentally pressing the go button on
the Android keyboard and submitting the form through the browser.
Instead, a search will be performed and the application will no longer
wait for the input timeout.

```javascript
var app = app || {};

app.controller = app.controller || {};

app.controller.movies = function(){

    ...
    /**
     * Add an event listener to the submission of the form.
     * This will prevent the form from being submitted
     * and sent to another page. Instead, we capture the
     * event and trigger the search action.
```

```
        */
    _searchform.addEventListener('submit', function(e){

        e.preventDefault();

        // Clear the _searchTimeout timeout
        clearTimeout(_searchTimeout);

        var value = _searchfield.value;

        if(value.length > 0){
            _self.search(value);
        }

    });

    ...
}
```

Finally, you will need to bind an event to the actual input field. This will take the value from the field, clear the searchtimeout (if it is set), check to see whether the length of the string for the value is greater than zero, and then set a timeout to perform a search.

```
var app = app || {};

app.controller = app.controller || {};

app.controller.movies = function(){

    ...
    _searchfield.addEventListener('input', function(){

        /**
         * This is the value of the input field
         */
        var value = this.value;

        /**
         * This will clear the search timeout
         */
        clearTimeout(_searchTimeout);

        /**
         * You don't want to run search straight after every
         * key press. This will set a timeout of 1 second
         * (1000 ms) before the search function is called.
         */
```

```
        if(value.length > 0){
            document.getElementById('taskbar').classList.add('searchactive');
        } else {
            document.getElementById('taskbar').classList.remove('searchactive');
        }

        _searchTimeout = setTimeout(function(){
            _self.search(value);
        }, 1000);
    });
    ...
}
```

The reason for setting a timeout on the input is so that a request isn't sent as soon as a user types a letter. As you can't cancel a JSONP request and the request may come back in a random order, it's best to avoid a situation where lots of requests are made at any one time by setting a one-second timer.

The full code for the bind method can be seen next.

```
/**
 * Binds the search form
 */
this.bindSearchForm = function(){

    /**
     * Here you add an event listener to the search filed using
     * the focus event listener. If there's a value, then show the
     * results.
     */
    _searchfield.addEventListener('focus', function(){
        if(this.value.length > 0){
            app.utility.deck.showCard('card-movie_search_results');
        }
    });

    /**
     * Add an event listener to the submission of the form.
     * This will prevent the form from being submitted
     * and sent to another page. Instead, we capture the
     * event and trigger the search action.
     */
    _searchform.addEventListener('submit', function(e){

        e.preventDefault();

        clearTimeout(_searchTimeout);

        var value = _searchfield.value;
```

```
            if(value.length > 0){
                _self.search(value);
            }

        });

        _searchfield.addEventListener('input', function(){

            /**
             * This is the value of the input field
             */
            var value = this.value;

            /**
             * This will clear the search timeout
             */
            clearTimeout(_searchTimeout);

            /**
             * You don't want to run search straight after every key press.
             * This will set a timeout of 1 second (1000 ms) before the
             * search function is called.
             */

            if(value.length > 0){
                document.getElementById('taskbar').classList.add('searchactive');
            } else {
                document.getElementById('taskbar').classList.remove('searchactive');
            }

            _searchTimeout = setTimeout(function(){
                _self.search(value);
            }, 1000);
        });

    }
```

Performing a Search

The search action will be used to perform a JSONP request to Rotten Tomatoes, based on a search value.

```
var app = app || {};

app.controller = app.controller || {};

app.controller.movies = function(){
```

```
...
this.search = function(query){
    // Check to see whether the query length is longer than 0 characters
    if(query.length > 0){

        /*
         * Encode the query so that it can be passed
         * through the URL
         */
        query = encodeURIComponent(query);

        /**
         * Create a new JSONP request
         */
        var jsonp = new app.utility.jsonp(
            'http://api.rottentomatoes.com/api/public/v1.0/movies.json?apikey=
            YOURAPIKEY&q=' + query, 'app.bootstrap.getController(
            "movies").showSearchResults');

        /**
         * Send the request
         */
        jsonp.send();

        /**
         * Add the loading class to the search field
         */
        _searchfield.classList.add('loading');
    }

}
...
}
```

You will need to replace YOURAPIKEY in the JSONP request URI with your API key for Rotten Tomatoes. As you can see, you use the bootstrap to get the movies controller and execute the showSearchResults after the results have loaded.

Showing the Results

The showSearchResults action/event accepts a Rotten Tomatoes result set.

> **NOTE:** If you would like to see all of the values in the Rotten Tomatoes API result set, check out the API documentation at `http://developer.rottentomatoes.com/docs/read/json/v10/Movies_S earch`.

Next, it will loop through the results and create movie models to be used within the application, based on the data. It will then create the view for the results, and then replace the contents of the search results `div` with the results HTML.

```javascript
var app = app || {};

app.controller = app.controller || {};

app.controller.movies = function(){

    ...
    /**
     * Shows the search results in the search results card
     */
    this.showSearchResults = function(rtresults){

        /**
         * This is the Rotten Tomatoes API data.
         * The following code will process the data
         * returned and convert it to models
         * that the application will understand.
         * You could wrap these API calls into
         * a separate library, but for now having
         * them in the controller will suffice.
         */

        // First, create an empty array to hold the results
        var results = [];

        // Next, loop through the results from Rotten Tomatoes
        for(var i = 0; i < rtresults.movies.length; i++){
            var rtmovie = rtresults.movies[i];
            // For every result you create a new movie object
            var title = rtmovie.title || '', rtid = rtmovie.id, posterframe =
                rtmovie.posters.original || '', synopsis = rtmovie.synopsis || '';
            results.push(new app.model.movie(title, rtid, posterframe, synopsis));
        }

        // Create the view using the data
        var view = new app.view.movielist(results);
```

```
    // Set the contents of the search results div
    _searchresultscard.innerHTML = '';
    _searchresultscard.appendChild(view.render());
    // Controlling page needs to be handled by it's own utility or class
    _searchresultscard.classList.add('active');
    _searchfield.classList.remove('loading');
    results = null;

    // Check to see whether the search scroll is null
    if(_searchScroll !== null){
        // If it isn't, destroy it
        _searchScroll.destroy();
        _searchScroll = null;
    }

    // Initialize the search scroll for the results card
    _searchScroll = new iScroll(_searchresultscard);

    }
    ...
}
```

As you can see, a JavaScript library called iScroll handles the scrolling functionality. Android browsers below Honeycomb do not support overflow, hidden in CSS, so iScroll is used to facilitate this. You will need to download the latest version of iScroll and place it in the `js/lib/cubiq` folder (create the directory, if it doesn't already exist). Name the file `iscroll.js`.

Viewing a Movie

In order to view a movie, you will need to make a request for the movie info from Rotten Tomatoes and then process the results with an event handler within the controller. Add the following code to the controller.

```
var app = app || {};

app.controller = app.controller || {};

app.controller.movies = function(){

    ...

    this.find = function(data){

        // Check to see whether the ID exists in the action params/data
        if(typeof data.id === 'undefined'){
            throw "No ID supplied to find action in view controller";
                return;
```

```
        }

        // Create a new JSONP request
        var jsonp = new app.utility.jsonp(
            'http://api.rottentomatoes.com/api/public/v1.0/movies/' +
            data.id + '.json?apikey=YOURAPIKEY,
'app.bootstrap.getController("movies").view');

        // Send the request
        jsonp.send();
    }


    this.view = function(rtresult){

        // Check to see whether an object has been returned
        if(!app.utility.validator.isTypeOf(reresult, 'object')){
            // If it's not an object, don't show the movie
                return;
        }

        // Create a new movie object
        var movie = new app.model.movie(rtresult.title,
            rtresult.id, rtresult.posters.original, rtresult.synopsis),
        // Get the movie info card
        viewcard = document.getElementById('card-movie_info');

        /**
         * Set the DVD and cinema release dates
         */

        var releaseDate = new app.type.releaseDate(
            new Date(rtresult.release_dates.theater),
            new Date(rtresult.release_dates.dvd));
        movie.setReleaseDate(releaseDate);

        /**
         * Set the movie's rating
         */
        movie.setRating(rtresult.mpaa_rating);

        /**
         * Check to see whether the movie is in the user's favorites
         * by looping over the favorites localStorage object
         */
        var _favorites = JSON.parse(localStorage.favorites);

        for(var i = 0; i < _favorites.length; i++){
            if(_favorites[i].id == movie.getRtid()){
                /**
```

```
             * If a match is found, set the
             * favorite flag to true
             */
            movie.setFavorite(true);
        }
    }

    /**
     * Add actors to the movie
     */
    for(var i = 0; i < rtresult.abridged_cast.length; i++){
        var cast = rtresult.abridged_cast[i],
            character = (typeof cast.characters === 'undefined') ? '' :
cast.characters[0];
        var actor = new app.model.actor(cast.name, character);
        movie.addActor(actor);
    }

    // Create the movie view
    var view = new app.view.movie(movie);
    viewcard.innerHTML = view.render().innerHTML;

    // Intialize iScroll
    _viewScrolls.push(new iScroll(viewcard.querySelector('.movie-content'),
        {vScroll: false, vScrollbar: false}));

    [].forEach.call(viewcard.getElementsByClassName('block'), function(el){

        _viewScrolls.push(new iScroll(el, {hScroll: false, hScrollbar:
false}));

    });

    /**
     * Add an event listener to the window. If it resizes,
     * reset the iScroll so that it adjusts to the new size.
     */

    window.addEventListener('resize', function(){
        setTimeout(function(){

            _searchScroll.refresh();

            for(var i = 0; i < _scrolls.length; i++){
                _viewScrolls[i].refresh();
            }

        }, 100);
    });
```

```
    /**
     * Hide all of the cards
     */
    app.utility.deck.hideAllCards();

    /**
     * Show the movie info card
     */
    app.utility.deck.showCard('card-movie_info');

  }

  ...
}
```

Finally, you will need to add the `this.bindSearchForm();` call to the `init` method.

```
var app = app || {};

app.controller = app.controller || {};

app.controller.movies = function(){

   ...

   this.init = function(){
      this.bindSearchForm();
   }

   ...

   this.init();

}
```

The Favorites Controller

The favorites controller is much simpler than the movies controller. It will simply handle listing the user's favorites, adding and removing items from the user's favorites in `localStorage`.

Begin by creating a new file within `js/app/controller` called `favorite.js` with the following code.

```
var app = app || {};

app.controller = app.controller || {};
```

```
app.controller.favorites = function(){

    var _listScroll = null;
    this.init = function(){}

    this.init();

}
```

The `_listScroll` instance variable will hold the iScroll object for the favorites scrolling.

Listing Favorites

The first action/event that you will need to create is the `list` action. This will list all of the favorites for the user.

Begin by creating a new action within the favorites controller called `list`.

```
var app = app || {};

app.controller = app.controller || {};

app.controller.favorites = function(){

    ...
    this.list = function(){

    }
    ...

}
```

The next thing that you will need to do is to grab the favorites from `localStorage`. As you saw in the bootstrap file, you created an empty favorites `localStorage` property with an empty array. This will allow you to get the application's favorites without having to check whether the property exists, and then create it throughout your code. It might be a good idea to create a `localStorage` utility to store your data; this won't be covered in this book, as you'll only be storing and retrieving `localStorage` properties in three places in the application.

```
var app = app || {};

app.controller = app.controller || {};

app.controller.favorites = function(){
```

```
...
this.list = function(){
   // Get the favorites from local storage
   var _favorites = JSON.parse(localStorage.favorites),
   // Create an empty movies variable
   _movies = [],
   // Get the favoritesList card from the DOM
   _favoriteslist = document.getElementById('card-favorite_list');
}
...

}
```

You can see from the code, that you also created an empty movies array. This will be used to hold all of the movie models created from the user's favorites further into the code. You'll also get the favorite card list DOM element.

The next thing to do is to loop through each of the favorites retrieved from `localStorage`. The for loop might look a little strange, as you are subtracting a value of one from the iterator each time the for loop is run. This essentially reverses the array, so that the last/most recent element is looped over first.

```
var app = app || {};

app.controller = app.controller || {};

app.controller.favorites = function(){

   ...
   this.list = function(){
      ...
      /**
       * Loop through each of the favorites backward
       * to ensure that the most recent favorite
       * is displayed at the top of the list
       */

      for(var i = _favorites.length; i > 0; i--){
         var _favorite = _favorites[i - 1];

         // Push the movie model to the movies array

         _movies.push(new app.model.movie(unescape(_favorite.title),
            _favorite.id, _favorite.posterframe, unescape(_favorite.synopsis)))
      }
      ...
   }
   ...

}
```

As you can see from the code, the unescape method is used to escape the characters used for each of the favorites properties. This is because the add method escapes each property value so that the object can be stored in local storage.

The next step is to create a movies view from the array of movies.

```
var app = app || {};

app.controller = app.controller || {};

app.controller.favorites = function(){

    ...
    this.list = function(){
        ...
        /**
         * Create a new movielist view with the _movies model
         */
        var view = new app.view.movielist(_movies);

        // Set the contents of the search results div
        _favoriteslist.innerHTML = '';

        // Append the view to the favorites list
        _favoriteslist.appendChild(view.render());
        ...
    }
    ...

}
```

Finally, you will need to create a new iScroll object for the view and show it. This will allow users on devices older than Honeycomb to be able to scroll for long lists.

```
var app = app || {};

app.controller = app.controller || {};

app.controller.favorites = function(){

    ...
    this.list = function(){
        ...

        // Destroy the listScroll if it exists
        if(_listScroll !== null){
            _listScroll.destroy();
            _listScroll = null;
```

```
            }

            // Create a new one
            _listScroll = new iScroll(_favoriteslist);

            // Hide all of the cards
            app.utility.deck.hideAllCards();
            // Show only the favorites card
            app.utility.deck.showCard('card-favorite_list');

            ...
        }
        ...

}
```

Your final list method should look like the following code.

```
var app = app || {};

app.controller = app.controller || {};

app.controller.favorites = function(){

    ...
    this.list = function(){

        // Get the favorites from local storage
        var _favorites = JSON.parse(localStorage.favorites),
        // Create an empty movies variable
        _movies = [],
        // Get the favoritesList card from the DOM
        _favoriteslist = document.getElementById('card-favorite_list');

        /**
         * Loop through each of the favorites backward
         * to ensure that the most recent favorite
         * is displayed at the top of the list
         */

        for(var i = _favorites.length; i > 0; i--){
            var _favorite = _favorites[i - 1];

        // Push the movie model to the movies array

        _movies.push(new app.model.movie(unescape(_favorite.title),
            _favorite.id, _favorite.posterframe, unescape(_favorite.synopsis)))
        }

        /**
         * Create a new movielist view with the _movies model
```

```
    */
    var view = new app.view.movielist(_movies);

    // Set the contents of the search results div
    _favoriteslist.innerHTML = '';
    // Append the view to the favorites list
    _favoriteslist.appendChild(view.render());

    // Destroy the listScroll if it exists
    if(_listScroll !== null){
        _listScroll.destroy();
        _listScroll = null;
    }

    // Create a new one
    _listScroll = new iScroll(_favoriteslist);

    // Hide all of the cards
    app.utility.deck.hideAllCards();
    // Show only the favorites card
    app.utility.deck.showCard('card-favorite_list');

    }
    ...

}
```

Adding Favorites

With the movie list complete, you will now need an action to add favorites to the list. This is a really simple action, as it will loop through the user's favorites from localStorage to check whether it exists. If it doesn't, it will then proceed to add the movie to the user's favorites and change the state of the button that called it, so that the user can remove the movie from his favorites without having to refresh the page.

```
var app = app || {};

app.controller = app.controller || {};

app.controller.favorites = function(){
    ...
    this.add = function(data){

        // Get the movie data
        var _movie = data;
        // Load the favorites from localStorage
        var _favorites = JSON.parse(localStorage.favorites);
```

```
/**
 * Check to see whether the movie
 * is already in the user's favorites
 */
for(var i = 0; i < _favorites.length; i++){
  if(_favorites[i].id == _movie.id){
    return;
  }
}

/**
 * Change the button's attributes
 */
if(this.nodeName == 'A'){
  this.setAttribute('data-action', 'remove');
  this.classList.remove('add');
  this.classList.add('remove');
  this.textContent = 'un-favorite';
}

// Push the movie to the favorites array
_favorites.push(_movie);

// Save it back to localStorage
localStorage.favorites = JSON.stringify(_favorites);

  }
  ...
}
```

Removing Favorites

Now that adding is in place, you will need to write the action to remove items from the user's favorites. This is quite a simple process and the method looks similar to that of the add action. The difference is that when you loop to check whether a favorite already exists, if the favorite exists in the array, you will remove it. The code can be seen here.

```
var app = app || {};

app.controller = app.controller || {};

app.controller.favorites = function(){
  ...
  this.remove = function(data){
    // Get the ID of the favorite to remove
    var _id = data.id;
```

```
      // Get the user's favorites from localStorage
      var _favorites = JSON.parse(localStorage.favorites);

      // Loop through the favorites
      for(var i = 0; i < _favorites.length; i++){
         // If there's a match
         if(_favorites[i].id == _id){
            // Remove the item from the favorites using splice
            _favorites.splice(i, 1);
         }
      }

      // Save the changed favorites object back to localStorage
      localStorage.favorites = JSON.stringify(_favorites);

      /**
       * Change the add/remove favorites button
       * so that it will either add/remote the item
       * from the favorites
       */
      if(this.nodeName == 'A'){
         this.setAttribute('data-action', 'add');
         this.classList.remove('remove');
         this.classList.add('add');
         this.textContent = 'favorite';
      }

   }
   ...
}
```

Styling the Content

Even with all the hard work you've put into the JavaScript framework, MoMemo looks pretty ugly. In Chapter 6, we touched upon using SASS to create a basic framework to work from. We're now going to put that into practice to style the various elements of the application a bit further.

We'll start by styling the movie list, as it's the first thing that a user will interact with.

Styling the Movie List

The movie list will be used in two places within the MoMemo application. One of these places will be in the search results, and the second will be in the favorites list on the main screen. As there are two lists, you might want to style these differently. We can break out common styles for a list, such as each list item's size and its common child elements' positions in a "global" list class, which can be overridden using specificity.

First, create the global style for lists.

```
.list {

    margin: 0;
    padding: 0;

    li {

        padding: 10px;
        overflow: hidden;
        height: 82px;
        display: block;
        border-bottom: 1px solid #CCCCCC;
        background: #FFFFFF;

        .preview-image {
            float: left;
            width: 60px;
            height: 82px;
            text-align: center;
            margin-right: 10px;
        }

    }

}
```

The .list style will provide a framework for all lists to be styled upon. This is a good way to design your web applications if you know that a particular design component may be used multiple times, but not necessarily look the same. You could create just a movie-list style and then override it using specificity, but there could be certain CSS styles that you don't want in your new style, which will mean extra code to reset them. Add the SASS style in the previous code snippet just below the deck style in the css/partials/_layout.scss SASS file.

Recompile the SASS file and reload the web app in your mobile browser and search for a movie. The results should look like Figure 8-3.

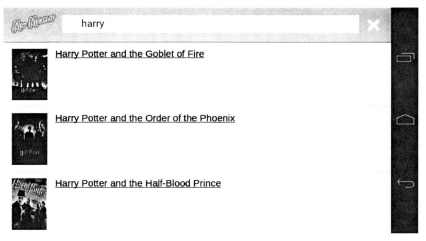

Figure 8-3. *Vanilla search results*

The next thing to do is to style the movie list so that it looks a bit better. In the view for the movie list, you can see that there are multiple classes assigned to it, as follows.

```
_rootElement.classList.add('list');
_rootElement.classList.add('movie-list');
```

These provide essential hooks that the CSS styles can latch onto. The following SASS/CSS style will style the additional content within each list item, such as cutting off the synopsis so that it doesn't flow beyond the size of the list item's height.

```
.movie-list {

  li {

    background: #A5CCEB;
    border-bottom-colour: #FFFFFF;

    .more {

      display: block;
      height: 100%;
      overflow: hidden;
      text-decoration: none;

      h2 {
        margin: 0 0 10px;
        color: #BF2628;
      }
```

```
        p {
            margin: 0;
            color: #000000;
        }

    }

}

li:nth-child(odd) {
    background: #97B2D9;
}

}
```

Add the preceding code to your SASS file just underneath the .list style. If you place it before the .list style, the styles that you intended to overwrite will be overridden by the styles placed below the .movie-list style, which in this case is .list. As you can see, there's a li:nth-child(odd) style, which will style every odd list item. This will style the background color of every odd list item differently to help the user distinguish the different items in the list and make it easier for them to target where to tap.

Your final movie-list and list SASS should look like the following code.

```
/**
 *   Standard list
 */

.list {

    margin: 0;
    padding: 0;

    li {

        padding: 10px;
        overflow: hidden;
        height: 82px;
        display: block;
        border-bottom: 1px solid #CCCCCC;

        .preview-image {
            float: left;
            width: 60px;
            height: 82px;
            text-align: center;
            margin-right: 10px;
        }
```

```
    }

}

/**
 *   Movie list
 */

.movie-list {

   li {

       background: #A5CCEB;
       border-bottom-color: #FFFFFF;

       .more {

          display: block;
          height: 100%;
          overflow: hidden;
          text-decoration: none;

          h2 {
             margin: 0 0 10px;
             color: #BF2628;
          }

          p {
             margin: 0;
             color: #000000;
          }

       }

   }

   li:nth-child(odd) {
       background: #97B2D9;
   }

}
```

With this in place, reload your mobile browser and perform another search. The results view will look like Figure 8-4. You can now move on to style the movie view.

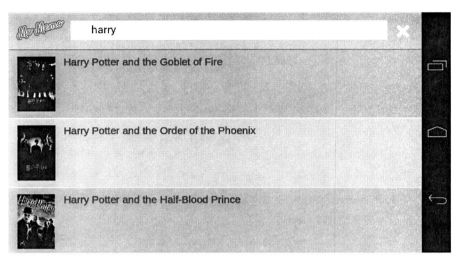

Figure 8-4. *Final search results view*

Styling the Movie View

The movie view is slightly different than the movie list view as it's slightly more complex. The idea is that you can side-scroll through content using iScroll. When the content is too long for the size of the viewport, the user can then scroll down.

In order for the user to understand that there is more content, the width of each content block has to be smaller than the size of the screen, so the next content element peaks out a bit from the left- or right-hand side.

We'll also make the poster image animate within the header using CSS. This will make the view a bit more interesting.

Let's begin by styling the header. Declare a new style just under the `movie-list` style, as shown in the following code.

```
.movie-header {

    position: relative;
    overflow: hidden;
    height: 20%;

}
```

This code will position the movie header relative to its parent element and any absolutely positioned element within it will be contained within the `.movie-`

header. The height is set to 20%, which will ensure that it will appear just as big on a tablet device as it would on a mobile device. The overflow has been set to hidden to prevent the poster from being visible outside of the element, as it's quite big.

Within the movie style, we can begin to style the poster. Create a new style within the .movie-header style, as shown in the following code.

```
.movie-header {
   ...
   .poster {
      position: absolute;
      top: 0%;
      @include animation(posteranimation 10s ease 0 infinite alternate);
   }

}
```

This will place the poster image at the top of the element. You can see that there's an animation attached to it. We'll get to that in a bit. Now, it's time to style the movie title element. Add the following code within the .movie-header style.

```
.movie-header {
   ...
   .movie-title {
      position: absolute;
      bottom: 0px;
      background: rgba(255, 255, 255, 0.75);
      padding: 5px;
      bottom: 0;
      left: 0;
      width: 100%;
      @include box-sizing(border-box);
   }

}
```

This will position the movie title at the bottom of the movie header. It will take up 100% of the width of the header, and has a slightly transparent white background color so that the text can be seen even on dark poster images. You can see that we're also using the box-sizing trick to ensure the padding doesn't affect the specified width of the element.

Within the .movie-title, you will also need to style the the favorite button. This can be done using the code highlighted next.

```
.movie-header {
   ...
   .movie-title {
```

```
    ...
    .btn-favorite {
        float: right;
        padding: 10px;
        color: #FFFFFF;
        background: #7D9DCE;
        font-weight: bold;
        border-radius: 5px;
        text-decoration: none;
        border: 1px solid #A5CCEB;
    }
  }

}
```

This will create a blue button, floated to the right of the movie title. You will also want to alter the release date a bit, so that it stands out from the title of the movie. You can see the additions next.

```
.movie-header {
  ...
  .movie-title {
    ...
    .movie-release-date {
        text-transform: uppercase;
        font-weight: bold;
    }
  }

}
```

Your full movie header style should look like the following code.

```
.movie-header {

  position: relative;
  overflow: hidden;
  height: 20%;

  .poster {
    position: absolute;
    top: 0%;
    @include animation(posteranimation 10s ease 0 infinite alternate);
  }

  .movie-title {
    position: absolute;
    bottom: 0px;
    background: rgba(255, 255, 255, 0.75);
    padding: 5px;
    bottom: 0;
```

```
      left: 0;
      width: 100%;
      @include box-sizing(border-box);

      .btn-favorite {
          float: right;
          padding: 10px;
          color: #FFFFFF;
          background: #7D9DCE;
          font-weight: bold;
          border-radius: 5px;
          text-decoration: none;
          border: 1px solid #A5CCEB;
      }

      .movie-release-date {
          text-transform: uppercase;
          font-weight: bold;
      }
   }

}
```

Refresh your mobile browser and take a look by searching for a movie and taping on it. It should now look like Figure 8-5.

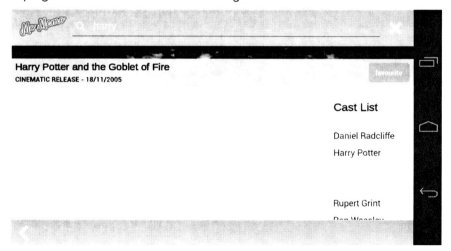

Figure 8-5. *Movie header*

The next task is to style the actual content for the movie itself. Because the blocks are relatively the same, there's not a lot of code required to achieve this.

Let's start by styling the `.movie-content` element.

```
.movie-content {
   height: 80%;
   width: 100%;
   padding-bottom: 40px;
   @include box-sizing(border-box);
}
```

There's nothing special to see here. We're just setting the `height` to be 80% of the screen height to accommodate for the movie header's 20 percent height.

There's also a `padding-bottom` of 40px that allows the movie footer to sit at the bottom and have no content appear behind it.

The block container, which holds all of the block elements, needs to be the width of the screen × the number of elements – the difference between the width of each block element. This is really easy to do in SASS, as you can create a variable to hold the width of each block element and then create an equation to set the width of the container element, as follows.

```
$blockWidth: 33%;
$blocks: 3;
...
.block-container {
   width: (100% * $blocks) - (100% - 33%);
...
```

We can now style the block and its content. This parts really simple and the only complex thing is to ensure that the width of the block is set based on the variable set previously. Add the following code to the `movie-content` style.

```
.movie-content {
   ...
   .block-container {

      $blockWidth: 33%;
      $blocks: 3;

      width: (100% * $blocks) - (100% - 33%);
      height: 100%;

      .block {
         width: 33%;
         float: left;
         height: 100%;

         font-size: 1.3em;
         line-height: 2em;
```

```scss
    .content {
        @include box-sizing(border-box);
    }

    h3 {
        padding: 10px 10px 0 10px;
    }

    .content {
        padding: 10px;
    }

        }

    }
}
```

Refresh your browser, and your web application should now look like Figure 8-6.

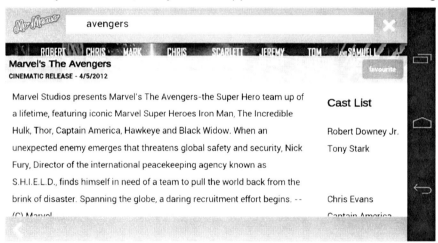

Figure 8-6. *Movie block styling*

You'll need to create the keyframes for the header animation. All this does is move the poster image up and down repeatedly. We use percentages so that, depending on the screen size, the image will move in proportion to it. Add the following code to your SASS file.

```scss
@keyframes posteranimation {
    0% { top: 0%; }
    100% { top: -80%; }
}
```

```
@-moz-keyframes posteranimation {
    0% { top: 0%; }
    100% { top: -80%; }
}

@-webkit-keyframes posteranimation {
    0% { top: 0%; }
    100% { top: -80%; }
}
```

Last but not least, we need to style the movie footer, which is a really simple style. It will position the footer at the bottom of the view. The footer can also contain a back button which needs to be styled with an image. Place the code from Listing A-2, found in the appendix, at the end of the SASS file.

Your final movie view should look like Figure 8-7.

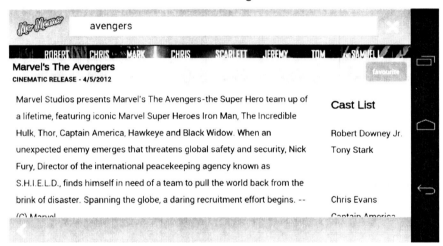

Figure 8-7. *Final movie info page*

Putting It All Together

With all of your JavaScript and SASS files in place, it's now time to update your HTML to make use of all of the new code.

This is a really simple process. Open the index.html file and add the following code to the bottom, just before the closing body tag.

```
...
    <!-- Load all of the JavaScript dependencies -->
```

```
    <!-- Load any lib files -->
    <script src="js/lib/eligrey/classlist.js"></script>
    <script src="js/lib/cubiq/iscroll.js"></script>

    <!-- Load the utility files -->
    <script src="js/app/utility/validator.js"></script>
    <script src="js/app/utility/layout.js"></script>
    <script src="js/app/utility/deck.js"></script>
    <script src="js/app/utility/jsonp.js"></script>

    <!-- Load the custom types -->
    <script src="js/app/type/format.js"></script>
    <script src="js/app/type/releaseDate.js"></script>

    <!-- Load the models -->
    <script src="js/app/model/actor.js"></script>
    <script src="js/app/model/movie.js"></script>
    <script src="js/app/model/video.js"></script>
    <script src="js/app/model/videosource.js"></script>

    <!-- Load the views -->
    <script src="js/app/view/movie.js"></script>
    <script src="js/app/view/movielistitem.js"></script>
    <script src="js/app/view/movielist.js"></script>

    <!-- Load the controllers -->
    <script src="js/app/controller/movies.js"></script>
    <script src="js/app/controller/favorites.js"></script>

    <!-- Bootstrap the application -->
    <script src="js/app/bootstrap.js"></script>
    <script>
      app.bootstrap.initScripts();
    </script>
  </body>
</html>
```

You will also need to load a new font from Google's font directory. This is a simple enough task. In the <head /> tag, add the following code, just after the mobile.css link declaration.

```
<!DOCTYPE html>
<html lang="en-GB" dir="ltr">
  <head>

    <meta charset="UTF-8" />
    <meta name="viewport" content="width=device-width; initial-scale=1.0;
      maximum-scale=1.0; user-scalable=0; target-densitydpi=device-dpi;"/>
    <title>Mo Memo</title>
    <link rel="stylesheet" type="text/css" href="css/mobile.css?v=22" />
```

```
    <link href='http://fonts.googleapis.com/css?family=Arimo' rel='stylesheet'
        type='text/css'>
    <link rel="apple-touch-icon-precomposed" href="img/home-screen-icon.png">
</head>
...
```

Reload your mobile web browser, and everything should be working as expected.

Concatenating, Minifying, and Caching

Although having several JavaScript files can be useful for development and debugging purposes, it's not a good idea to send each and every JavaScript file to the user while in production, as it could create a loading bottleneck in the application. To get around this and to achieve the best performance, it's a good idea to concatenate all of the JavaScript files into a single JS file, much like we have done with the CSS files using SASS.

To improve performance, you can also minify the JavaScript and CSS files. This is the process of removing as much unused data (such as spaces and carriage returns) as possible to create a much more compact file.

To further improve performance, you will need to update the cache's manifest file. This will allow your application to store JavaScript and images on the user's mobile device, reducing the need to constantly fetch them from the server every time the page is loaded. This also allows the user to use parts of the web application while there is no connection to the network or your server.

Concatenating

Concatenating JavaScript can be done in several ways. The most popular is to use server-side script to automatically combine all of the files and cache the final result on the server. The least popular is to manually combine all of the files by copying them all into a single JavaScript file. This section will cover manually concatenating the application's JavaScript files.

Create a new file within the js directory called app.dev.js. Begin by copying and pasting the code from the application's JavaScript file into app.dev.js in the following order, and where the JavaScript file at the top of the list appears at the top of the file.

- js/lib/eligrey/classlist.js
- js/lib/cubiq/iscroll.js

```
js/app/utility/validator.js
js/app/utility/layout.js
js/app/utility/deck.js
js/app/utility/jsonp.js
js/app/type/format.js
js/app/type/releaseDate.js
js/app/model/actor.js
js/app/model/movie.js
js/app/model/video.js
js/app/model/videosource.js
js/app/view/movie.js
js/app/view/movielistitem.js
js/app/view/movielist.js
js/app/controller/movies.js
js/app/controller/favorites.js
js/app/bootstrap.js
```

Save the file and remove the current list of JavaScript files from the bottom of `index.html`.

The following code snippet shows how this should now look.

```
...
    <!-- Load the applications JavaScript -->
    <script src="js/app.dev.js"></script>
    <script>
        app.bootstrap.initScripts();
    </script>
  </body>
</html>
```

If you refresh your mobile browser, everything should be working correctly.

Minifying

Minifying/minification is the process of removing as much white space and comments as possible from your code. It sounds silly, but that extra data can account for a large part of your JavaScript's file size.

Have a look at the size of your app.dev.js file by right-clicking on it in Aptana and selecting Properties. It should weigh in at around 54,000 bytes, which is about 53KB. You can further reduce the size of the file for production by running it through a minification script.

Just like concatenation, you can also minify your JavaScript automatically at server-side or using YUI compressor. For the example in this book, you will use the online JavaScript compression tool found at http://jscompress.com.

Create a new file within js/ called app.min.js. This will contain your production-ready minified code. Copy the code from app.dev.js and paste it into the text box called "Javascript Code Input" at http://jscompress.com. Then press the "Compress Javascript" button.

Copy the compressed output and paste it into app.min.js. Save the file, and then right-click on it in the app explorer and select Properties. You should see a big reduction in the file size, from about 54,000 bytes down to about 24,318 bytes. That's a file size reduction of about a half.

You can also compress your CSS files using SASS by taking advantage of the -- style compress option. To do this, open up the terminal from the application folder and enter the following command.

```
sass ./css/*.scss ./css/mobile.min.css --style compress
```

This will output a minified version of the CSS file to the CSS directory. To use it, change the href of the CSS stylesheet in the head of index.html from mobile.css to mobile.min.css. Your new head should now look like the following code.

```
<head>
    <meta charset="UTF-8" />
    <meta name="viewport" content="width=device-width; initial-scale=1.0;
        maximum-scale=1.0; user-scalable=0; target-densitydpi=device-dpi;"/>
    <title>Mo Memo</title>
    <link rel="stylesheet" type="text/css" href="css/mobile.min.css" />
    <link href='http://fonts.googleapis.com/css?family=Arimo' rel='stylesheet'
type='text/css'>
    <link rel="apple-touch-icon-precomposed" href="img/home-screen-icon.png">
</head>
```

Caching

All of the file-saving techniques work perfectly for reducing the amount of bandwidth that your application takes up per page load. Now, wouldn't it be perfect if the user only ever had to make a request for assets that changed only once in a blue moon? You can do this with the cache manifest.

We briefly touched upon this in Chapter 4. Caching can be useful, but can also be a pain when you need to clear it. Fortunately, application caching has a JavaScript API that allows you to dynamically clear it.

Not only can you cache files from your web application, but you can also cache files that you pull in from external web sites, such as the user's favorite movie images. Be warned, however, as your application's cache may be limited to a certain size on some devices.

Open the momemo.cache file that you created in Chapter 4. We know that the application files (such as the images, JavaScript files, and CSS) will need to be cached, so update the momemo.cache so that the following files are cached.

```
index.html

css/mobile.min.css

js/app.min.css

img/
```

Your manifest file should now look like the following code.

```
CACHE MANIFEST

# We'll make these files cachable
CACHE:
index.html
css/mobile.min.css
js/app.min.js
img/highres/momemo.png
img/lowres/momemo.png
img/back.png
img/clear.png
img/loading.gif
img/search.png
```

You can see that every file that needs to be cached has been explicitly specified. Unfortunately, you can't use wildcards, as the browser cache will cache all of the files in the manifest file before the page is loaded. It doesn't know which files exist on your server, so using a wildcard (*) won't have any effect.

We're caching the minified CSS and JS files, instead of the JavaScript and CSS files that haven't been minified. This will prevent frustration when you need to change files for development, so that you don't have to manually change the manifest file to bring in the changed files.

With the cache manifest, you can also specify which files require a network connection. We definitely want the Rotten Tomatoes API to have the latest data.

To do this, you have to place the URL or location of the files under the NETWORK definition in the manifest file. Your new cache file should look like the following.

```
CACHE MANIFEST

# We'll make these files available offline
CACHE:
index.html
css/mobile.min.css
js/app.min.js
img/highres/momemo.png
img/lowres/momemo.png
img/back.png
img/clear.png
img/loading.gif
img/search.png

# These files require a network connection
NETWORK:
http://api.rottentomatoes.com/
```

If you cache a file, you must remember that it has to exist on the server; otherwise, the application cache won't cache any of your files.

To reload the cache, simply change/amend the cache file.

Debugging with Chrome for Android

If you have experience creating web sites, you know how frustrating it used to be debugging anything in IE6. There was no JavaScript console, DOM inspector, profiler, and so forth. Up until now, it's been the same for mobile, as there has been no native way to easily run and debug a mobile web application. Finally, Chrome for Android has introduced a smart and clever way to debug your mobile web applications, just like your desktop web applications.

With Chrome for Android, you can initiate a remote debugging session from the console, and use the web inspector on your computer to interact with the web page on your android device. Unfortunately, this works only for Android 4+ (Ice Cream Sandwich), as Chrome supports only this version of Android.

To do this, head over to the Play Store on your device, and download the free Google Chrome browser. Remember, you'll only find the app if you're on Android 4+.

You'll need to enable Web Debugging, so in the app go to Settings   Developer tools   Enable USB Web debugging.

Plug your Android device into your computer and launch Terminal in Aptana. Navigate to the Android SDK directory, which will usually be in ~/android-sdks/platform-tools/. Run the following command.

```
./adb forward tcp:9222 localabstract:chrome_devtools_remote
```

This is a port forward and will allow you to access the Chrome inspector from your computer's browser.

Open any web page in Chrome for Android and go to the following URL in your desktop's browser: localhost:9222. You will see a screen similar to Figure 8-8.

Figure 8-8. *Chrome page debugging selection*

Select the page that's highlighted and a screen similar to Figure 8-9 will appear.

Figure 8-9. *The debugging console*

If you now select or mouse over an element in the debugging console and look at your mobile device, the element should be highlighted. You can see the size and property of it, as shown in Figure 8-10. You can also double-click on the CSS rules to alter their values, and they will appear on the device.

Figure 8-10. *Highlighted element*

You can even bring up the JavaScript console and type JavaScript code that will directly affect the page on your phone, as shown in Figures 8-11 and 8-12.

Figure 8-11. *JavaScript console*

Figure 8-12. *Chrome alert*

It's an excellent tool to have. If you want to do rapid debugging or quickly test changes to your CSS, it's much quicker to tweak them directly in the browser instead of having to constantly have to save and reload your mobile web app.

> **NOTE:** As Chrome for Android is still in beta, the way you eventually debug may change. To get the most up-to-date instructions, head over to `https://developers.google.com/chrome/mobile/docs/debugging`.

Summary

This has been quite an in-depth chapter about what you can really achieve with JavaScript, outside the world of procedural language.

You should now have a real grasp of MVC and how you can use it to provide a solid framework from which to work. It's really important to take the principles behind it with you, as it will help you to further understand other JavaScript frameworks and design patterns that can make your life much easier.

This chapter has also taken you through how to group your code together in utility objects to reduce code repetition.

You should also have a greater understanding of JavaScript objects and scope, and how you can use this to your advantage.

Testing and Deploying Your Mobile Web App

Believe it or not, testing and deploying your mobile web application is one of the most important, yet overlooked, aspects of the development cycle.

The most basic testing and deployment method is to use an FTP (File Transfer Protocol) client to upload your mobile web application to a public-facing web server. Typically, you then test the uploaded application in your mobile's web browser by "playing" with it to make sure that everything is working as it should. If there are any issues, then you make the amends on your local machine, test it, and then reupload the changed files.

This works for small applications and extremely small teams; however, as your application and development team grows, it becomes very time consuming to test every aspect of functionality thoroughly, and to keep track of code changes.

The natural "quick-fix" progression is to begin using file-sharing software or services such as AFP (Apple File Sharing Protocol), Samba, or Dropbox to manage group code and to share projects across development teams. This eventually becomes cumbersome, as those who are familiar with this technique are well aware—file conflicts aren't unusual and resolving them is extremely hard and laborious. There is also no code ownership or method of blame. If a developer breaks a piece of functionality, there is no finger to point and the code takes longer to fix or roll back.

Continuous integration principles help to solve this. Continuous integration is comprised of SCM (Source Control Management) to manage code within a team, automated testing, environment testing, and automated deployment.

Some of these principles might seem alien, but will be fully covered in this chapter. No project or development team is too large or too small to make use of continuous integration.

This chapter begins by explaining what each of these continuous integration elements are. You will then be given a practical exercise to show you how to create unit tests, work with the SCM system Git, and finally deploy your application to a production server using Capistrano.

Source Control Management

Source control management is at the heart of continuous integration. To date, there are several SCM implementations, including the following:

- Git
- SVN (Apache Subversion)
- Mercurial

SCM provides a way to store versions of your source files. SCM does this by storing the original file on the initial commit/save. SCM then stores only the changes/differences between each file with every subsequent commit. This saves on disk space and bandwidth, as the entire file isn't saved for every commit, unless the file is new.

When you store projects using an SCM, they are still accessible from your computer, just like any other file. The difference is that, with an SCM-based project, you can commit any file changes (including images, videos, etc.) so that they can be versioned and reverted back to or compared if needed.

To commit changes using an SCM, you need an SCM client such as Git or SVN. SCM systems will also generally store additional files as part of your project. Having used both Git and SVN, Git is my preferred SCM, as it stores only a single `.git` folder in the root directory that can be deleted easily; in contrast, SVN will store `.svn` folders in every folder of your project, which can prove to be a pain to remove.

There are currently two types of SCM: centralized and distributed. Centralized systems store all of the code on a central server. When a developer makes a commit, the changes are merged on the server and not on the development machine.

SVN is a centralized SCM system. Distributed systems have no central server. Commits can be made on any developer's machine. If a developer wants to share his or her code, another developer can clone the repository to their machine, which will contain every change from the original repository.

Git is a distributed SCM system. More often than not, Git repositories will have one main remote repository where all developers will push and pull changes to and from. The advantage of systems such as Git is that you can work on a project without a network connection, but still commit changes to your local repository as you work on a project. Once you have network access, you can then pull and merge any changes, test them, and then push your merged changes up to the remote repository. This is particularly helpful if you have a central build system.

SCM also provides you with the ability to store comments with every commit so that as you go through a project commit history, you can see who committed changes to which files and the reason behind each commit. SCM systems such as Git require commit comments by default, whereas SVN does not. Git is very popular within the development community, which is why it will be the focus of this chapter.

Branching and Tagging

Most SCM systems follow a methodology of branching and tagging. The master branch in Git is the main code base; this is usually always production-ready and contains the most up-to-date version of the project's code. When a new feature needs to be added, a branch is usually created from the master branch. These are usually code-named; some development teams use names from popular cartoon shows such as Peter, Meg, or Stewie, and others use planet names such as Saturn, Jupiter, or Mars. You can use any naming convention you like, as long as each branch has a unique name. What's important is the comment you make when creating a branch. It must be clear what the branch is for and what it should contain.

The branch is simply a copy or snapshot of the master branch so that any new features do not interfere with the production-ready code. Usually, the master branch is periodically merged with the new branch. This is to ensure that any changes to the main codebase are compatible with changes to the features in the branch. After the features in the new branch have been implemented and tested, it is then merged with the master branch, ready for production.

A tag is simply a significant snapshot of your project's master branch that you would like to keep for future reference. These are usually significant versions of your project. This can be useful if other developers are constantly working on the main branch and you would like to make a working deployment.

Testing

Testing your mobile web application is one of the most overlooked aspects of the development cycle for new web developers. Most new mobile web developers will simply load their web site on a mobile device and then play with it to see whether it works. This can be laborious as you add more features, and you really don't know what's going on inside your code. As you begin to write more object-oriented code, you begin to see the complexity of your application grow (in an organized way). You can test each unit of code, based on what you put in and what you expect to get out.

For instance, in previous chapters, you touched upon creating models to store data within your application. The integrity of your presentation and the logic behind your application really relies on how these models accept and output data through getters, setters, and other model-based methods. You can write a suite of tests, based around each unit of code, with what you put in and what you expect to get back. This method of testing is known as unit testing. Unit testing allows you to test each method in your application. The more unit tests that you write for each aspect of your project, the more confident you should be that the application will work. This is known as code coverage. Keep in mind that unit tests will cover only a certain percentage of your code, and you should aim for at least 80 percent code coverage.

By creating unit tests, you can run a series of tests all at once, which target every target web browser. This should give you the confidence that your code is working as it should. This is especially helpful when a new browser or browser version is released, as you can ensure that your JavaScript code is compatible with the new browser by running the unit tests in it.

Deploying Your Application

Your application can be deployed in many ways. The most common method is to deploy it through FTP (File Transfer Protocol) or SFTP (Secure File Transfer Protocol). More often than not, you will have a production server where your production code sits, a development server where you test your latest integrated code, and a local development server. There are other environments that you might want to create, such as a preproduction server, which will mimic the exact configuration of the production server, and you might want to create a staging server where a client or testers will test your final code before it's put into production.

Managing all of these environments and their code base can be problematic, and manually deploying code changes with every commit to several environments can become laborious and prone to human error. You might also have to perform tasks for each environment, such as CSS precompiling, JavaScript and CSS minification and concatenation, and so on.

You can offload much of this to a deployment application such as Capistrano. Capistrano will allow you to write deployment scripts for each environment and deploy your application with a single command to any environment. Capistrano also allows you to roll back any changes to a previous working version, as with every deployment, Capistrano will store a copy of each version so that you can roll back at any time.

Continuous Integration Server

The glue that combines all of these applications and practices together is a good continuous integration environment. A continuous integration environment will detect changes in your application's code and automatically build and deploy it, as well as perform other tasks. This means that you can concentrate on producing a world-class web application and leave the repetitive deployment and testing tasks to the continuous integration server.

The continuous integration server of choice for this book is Atlassian's Bamboo. This product has been chosen because it's easy to install, has many plugins, it's easy to set up, and is compatible with Atlassian's other popular software development tools, such as JIRA, Crucible, and FishEye.

Your First Continuous Integration Project

Creating a continuous integration project for the first time can be quite laborious. You'll begin by first creating a new project in Aptana Studio 3. To do this, open Aptana Studio and go to **File ➤ New ➤ Web Project**. Name the project `ci`.

Create a new folder within the project called `js`. Inside this folder, create two folders called `app` and `tests`. In the `app` folder, create a new empty JavaScript file called `calculator.js` by going to **File ➤ New ➤ File**. You won't add anything to this yet. TDD (Test Driven Development) states that you must write your unit tests first, so that they fail before you write your code. This means that all of your expected outcomes are written in tests, so that your code satisfies them as you write your code. It's a good practice. As you write your logic rules in unit tests, it doesn't matter how you implement your final code, as long as the output satisfies the unit tests.

This method of working really helps you to write much cleaner code, as your code will now be written to satisfy only the expected output.

Writing Your First Unit Test

You can either choose to write your own unit-testing framework or use one that's readily available. The choice for this book is QUnit. It has been developed by the jQuery community and has regular updates. Not only this, but it can be run from the browser, or optionally, can be run from the command line using a program called PhantomJS.

To set up a QUnit unit test for the calculator, first create a new file called `calculator.html` in the `tests` folder containing the following HTML.

```html
<!DOCTYPE html>
<html>

    <head>

        <meta http-equiv="Content-type" content="text/html; charset=utf-8"/>
        <title>calculator unit tests</title>

        <meta name="viewport" content="width=device-width; initial-scale=1.0; maximum-scale=1.0; user-scalable=0; target-densitydpi=device-dpi;"/>

        <!-- Include the latest QUnit JavaScript file -->
        <script src="http://code.jquery.com/qunit/qunit-git.js"></script>

        <!-- Include calculator JavaScript file -->
        <script src="../app/calculator.js"></script>

        <!-- Include the latest QUnit CSS file -->
        <link href="http://code.jquery.com/qunit/qunit-git.css" rel="stylesheet" type="text/css" />

    </head>

    <body>

        <h1 id="qunit-header">calculator unit tests</h1>
        <h2 id="qunit-banner"></h2>
        <div id="qunit-testrunner-toolbar"></div>
        <h2 id="qunit-userAgent"></h2>
        <ol id="qunit-tests"></ol>
        <div id="qunit-fixture"><!-- If you have DOM that needs to be manipulated,
            this is where it should go --></div>
```

```
    </body>

</html> 1
```

This code represents the HTML required to run a basic, empty unit test in QUnit. As you can see, it does not contain any mobile-specific markup.

Within the body tag, you can see that there are several HTML elements with IDs. These are described in Table 9-1.

Table 9-1. *HTML Testing Elements*

Element	Description
qunit-header	Contains the header or title of the suite of unit tests
qunit-banner	Changes color depending on the state of the unit test (green for pass, red for fail)
qunit-testrunner-toolbar	Contains controls that allow you to show or hide tests
qunit-userAgent	Shows the browser information for the current test
qunit-tests	Contains a list of passed or failed tests after they have been run
qunit-fixture	Used if you have any DOM that needs to be manipulated as part of any test

You will need to run the tests in a mobile web browser. To do this, Aptana must first be configured so that its internal server binds to the computer's IP address instead of its local IP address of 127.0.0.1. To do this, go to **Aptana Studio 3 ➤ Preferences ➤ Aptana Studio ➤ Web Servers ➤ Built-in**. You will see a screen and drop-down menu that allows you to select what the IP address of the internal web server should bind to, as shown in Figure 9-1.

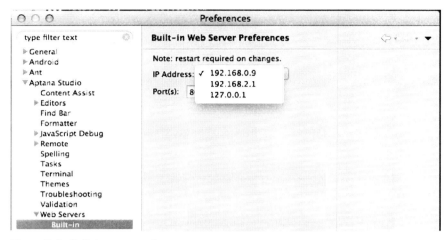

Figure 9-1. *Built-in server preferences*

Pick the one that matches your computer's IP address (usually the top one) click OK, quit Aptana Studio, and launch it again so that the changes apply.

After Aptana has finished launching, you can run the application in your web browser by right-clicking on `calculator.html` in the Aptana Studio App Explorer and selecting **Run As ➤ JavaScript Web Application**. This will launch Firefox. Type the URL from Firefox's address bar into your mobile device's default browser. You should see that the bar underneath the title bar is green, and that 0/0 tests have been run, as shown in Figure 9-2. Now it's time to start writing a few unit tests.

Figure 9-2. *Running QUnit tests in the browser*

Open `calculator.html` in Aptana Studio, if it isn't already. A unit test simply runs several assertions that check to see whether the outcome value for a method or property matches an expected value based on a predictable input. The calculator example in this chapter is simple in that it's easy to predict that 1+1 should always equal 2. There are no additional variables that should affect the expected outcome, so 2 should always be the expected result. When 2 isn't the result, you know that the application is broken somewhere.

In `calculator.html`, create a new `script` tag just before the closing body tag.

```
...
<div id="qunit-fixture"><!-- If you have DOM that needs to be manipulated,
    this is where it should go --></div>
<!-- This is your new script tag -->
<script>

</script>
</body>

</html>
```

Within the `script` tag, you can begin to write your first set of unit tests. Although the calculator code hasn't been written yet, you can begin to dictate what methods and properties should exist within the code, and how they should behave through the unit tests. A basic calculator should do the following:

- Add
- Subtract
- Divide
- Multiply

A calculator will usually take an initial value to perform these methods on and should return a result on each method. You should also be able to clear the calculator. On this basis, the following methods should be implemented:

- add
- subtract
- divide
- multiply
- clear
- getResult

You can then convert this description of the application into unit tests.

So to create the appropriate unit tests, end the following code and comments within the `<script />` tag for your first unit test on the constructor.

```
test('calculator constructor', function(){

    /**
     * Specify how many assertions this test will run
     * If assertions do not run for any reason, this
     * test will fail
     */
    expect(1);

    /**
     * You create a new calculator instance and set
     * initial value to 10
     */
    var calculator = new app.calculator(10);

    /**
     * You then assert that 10 is being held as the
     * current result
     */
    equal(calculator.getResult(), 10, 'the result should equal 10 with no
operation');

});
```

As you can see, the test method is part of QUnit, and accepts a description and callback function. When the test executes, the callback function is called and the test is executed. Within the test, you can see several methods. `expect()` specifies how many assertions will run within the test. You also instantiate the calculator class so that it can be used within the test. Any variables that are created per test are destroyed and cannot be used in another test. They can, however, be used within any assertions within the test. Finally, `equal()` is an assertion. An assertion simply takes a result and checks to see whether the resulting or returned value matches an expected value. In this instance, the `equal` assertion checks to see whether the new calculator has 10 as the initial result.

That's all there is to unit testing. There are a variety of assertions available. See Table 9-2 for a list of the important ones.

Table 9-2. *QUnit Assertions*

Assertion	Description
ok(*state, message*)	Checks to see whether a value (state) is true; if it is true, the assertion will pass.
equal(*actual, expected, message*)	Checks to see whether the actual value is equal to the expected value.
notEqual(*actual, expected, message*)	Checks to see whether the actual value is not equal to the expected value.
deepEqual(*actual, expected, message*)	Checks to see whether the actual value is equal to the expected value. This assertion is particularly useful when you would like to compare instantiated objects and their values.
notDeepEqual(*actual, expected, message*)	Checks to see whether the actual value is not equal to the expected value. This assertion is particularly useful when you would like to compare instantiated objects and their values.
strictEqual(*actual, expected, message*)	Checks to see whether the actual value is equal to the expected value. This is much stricter. For instance, if you set *actual* to "10" (with the quotation marks, this makes 10 a string), and the *expected* to 10 (a number), the assertion will fail.
strictNotEqual(*actual, expected, message*)	Checks to see whether the actual value is not equal to the expected value. This is much stricter. For instance, if you set *actual* to "10" (with the quotation marks, this makes 10 a string), and the *expected* to 10 (a number), the assertion will fail.
raises(*block, expected, message*)	Checks to see whether code executed within the block raises an exception, and whether that exception matches the expected value.

As you can see, assertions tend to follow the same pattern of having an actual value (which is usually the direct return value of a property or method), and an expected value (which you specify and a message to describe the assertion).

The assertion methods can change, so it's best to check out the QUnit documentation, which you can find at `http://docs.jquery.com/QUnit`.

If you now run the first test by refreshing the web page in your mobile browser, you can see that the green bar should now be red, as shown in Figure 9-3.

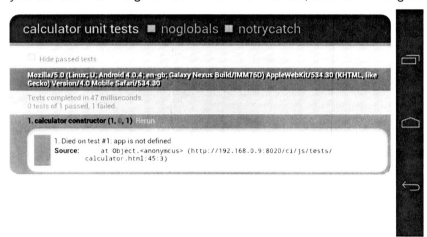

Figure 9-3. *Failed unit test*

As you can see, the failed test will also tell you where the test failed and why, which can be useful for debugging purposes.

With the first assertion, you can now follow with the code that comes next to complete the unit tests for the rest of the calculator.

```
<script>

    test('calculator constructor', function(){

        /**
         * Specify how many assertions this test will run.
         * If assertions do not run for any reason, this
         * test will fail
         */
        expect(1);

        /**
         * Create a new calculator instance and set the initial value to 10
```

```
     */
    var calculator = new app.calculator(10);

    /**
     * You then assert that 10 is being held as the current result
     */
    equal(calculator.getResult(), 10, 'the result should equal 10 with no
operation');

});

test('calculator add', function(){

    /**
     * Specify how many assertions this test will run.
     * If assertions do not run for any reason, this
     * test will fail
     */
    expect(2);

    /**
     * Create a new calculator instance and set the initial value to 10
     */
    var calculator = new app.calculator(10);

    /**
     * Assert that both the return value of the operation and the getResult
     * method both return 20
     */
    equal(calculator.add(10), 20, '10 + 10 should equal 20');
    equal(calculator.getResult(), 20, '10 + 10 should result in 20');

});

test('calculator subtract', function(){

    /**
     * Specify how many assertions this test will run.
     * If assertions do not run for any reason, this
     * test will fail
     */
    expect(2);

    /**
     * Create a new calculator instance and set the initial value to 10
     */
    var calculator = new app.calculator(10);

    /**
     * Assert that both the return value of the operation and the getResult
```

```
     * method both return 5
     */
    equal(calculator.subtract(5), 5, '10 - 5 should equal 5');
    equal(calculator.getResult(), 5, '10 - 5 should equal 5');

});

test('calculator divide', function(){

    /**
     * Specify how many assertions this test will run.
     * If assertions do not run for any reason, this
     * test will fail
     */
    expect(2);

    /**
     * Create a new calculator instance and set the initial value to 10
     */
    var calculator = new app.calculator(10);

    /**
     * Assert that both the return value of the operation and the getResult
     * method both return 5
     */
    equal(calculator.divide(2), 5, '10 / 2 should equal 5');
    equal(calculator.getResult(), 5, '10 / 2 should equal 5');

});

test('calculator multiply', function(){

    /**
     * Specify how many assertions this test will run.
     * If assertions do not run for any reason, this
     * test will fail
     */
    expect(2);

    /**
     * Create a new calculator instance and set the initial value to 10
     */
    var calculator = new app.calculator(10);

    /**
     * Assert that both the return value of the operation and the getResult
     * method both return 20
     */
    equal(calculator.multiply(2), 20, '10 * 2 should equal 20');
    equal(calculator.getResult(), 20, '10 * 2 should equal 20');
```

```
    });

</script>
```

As you can see, there are lots of assertions, but this is to ensure that every aspect of the application is covered. You can go into more depth within your unit tests, such as making sure that errors are thrown when invalid values such as letters are passed to the methods; this, however, won't be covered in this chapter.

With the unit tests complete, it's now time to write the code for the calculator. As this section is focused on creating the unit tests, the calculator JavaScript code won't be explained in great detail. The code comments should help to explain it a little.

```javascript
var app = app || {};

app.calculator = function(_initialValue){

    /**
     * The current result of the calculator
     */
    var _result = _initialValue;

    /**
     * Gets the current result of the calculator
     */
    this.getResult = function(){
        return _result;
    }

    /**
     * Adds a value to the current result and returns the new value
     */
    this.add = function(value){
        _result = _result + value;
        return _result;
    }

    /**
     * Subtracts a value from the current result and returns the new value
     */
    this.subtract = function(value){
        _result = _result - value;
        return _result;
    }

    /**
     * Multiplies a value from the current result and returns the new value
```

```
   */
   this.multiply = function(value){
     _result = _result * value;
     return _result;
   }

   /**
    * Divides a value from the current result and returns the new value
    */
   this.divide = function(value){
     _result = _result / value;
   return _result;
   }

}
```

Now when you run the unit tests in your mobile browser, the result bar should go green when you reload your mobile web browser, as shown in Figure 9-4.

You can tap on any of the unit test results to see the assertions that were run.

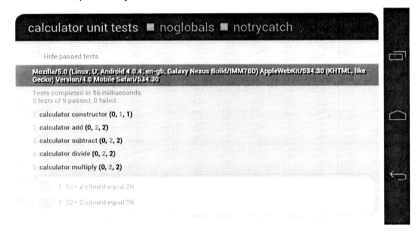

Figure 9-4. *Passed unit tests*

With the unit tests in place, it's now time to create a local Git repository for your calculator project.

Working with Git and GitHub

Now that you have a few files in your project, it's time to create a local repository. As mentioned earlier in the chapter, Git is a distributed SCM system. This allows you to commit to a local repository with no network connection and then push your changes to a remote repository, such as one hosted on github.com.

Creating a local repository is easy; simply click on the **Commands** icon just above the App Explorer in Aptana Studio and click on **Initialize Git Repository**. This will run the appropriate command, `git init`, in the background so that you can begin to check in files.

> **NOTE:** It's important to remember that Git, as a system, will not commit empty folders into a repository. If you have an empty folder that you need to check in as part of your project, you should create an empty file within it. Git will pick up the empty file and check the folder in.

Initializing the Git repository does not automatically check in any new files. To do this, click on the **Commands** icon again. Now that the Git repository has been initialized, you will see a few new commands within the drop-down menu. Scroll down to the **Commit** menu item and click on it. A new window will appear, as shown in Figure 9-5.

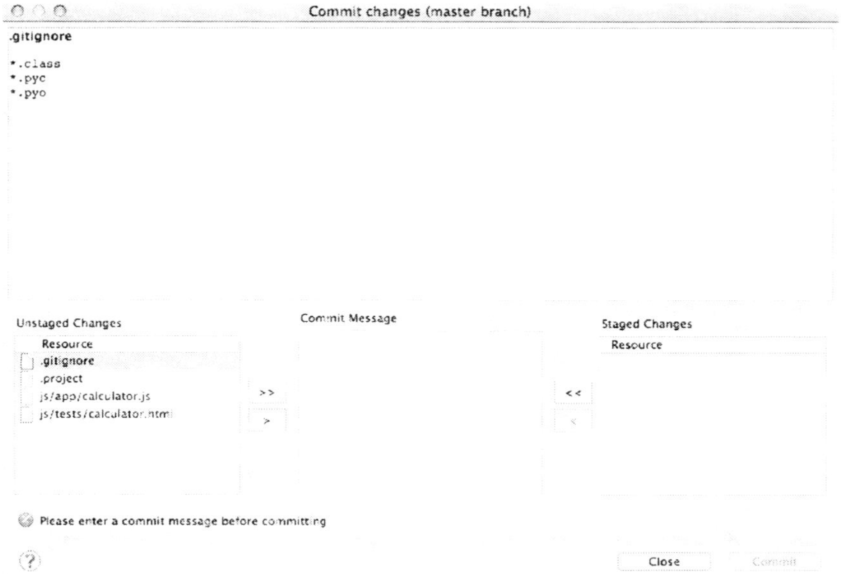

Figure 9-5. *Git commit window*

As you can see from Figure 9-5, there are four main boxes: the Commit changes box (top), the Unstaged Changes box (bottom left), the Commit Message box (bottom middle), and the Staged Changes box (bottom right). The Commit changes box shows the difference between the selected file in the Unstaged Changes box and the current version in the repository. The Unstaged Changes box shows all of the files that have changed since the last commit. The files have three states:

  White: New File

  Red: Deleted File

  Green: Changed File

The commit message box allows you to add a commit message; you need to add a commit message with every commit. The Staged Changes box shows all files that will be committed with the current commit. In order to commit files, you must move them from the Unstaged Changes box to the Staged Changes box. More often than not, you will want to commit all of your files. Click on the >> button next to the Unstaged Changes box. This will automatically move all files to the Staged Changes box. Enter a commit message and click on the **Commit** button. This will commit all of the changes to the local repository.

As you change files in Aptana Studio, you will see that their colors will change in the App Explorer, as shown in Figure 9-6.

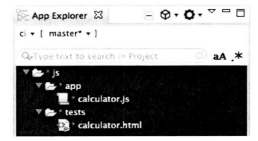

Figure 9-6. *Changed files in the App Explorer*

An asterisk (*) next to a file or folder indicates a change. Depending on your Aptana Studio theme, the file's background will also change color to indicate what the current state of the file is. If you would like to see what the colors mean for your specific theme, look into the Themes preferences in the Aptana Studio preferences pane and look for the Unstaged Files and Staged Files elements, as shown in Figure 9-7.

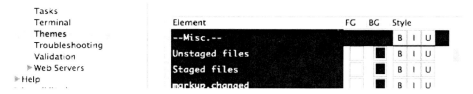

Figure 9-7. *Checking the color scheme for staged/unstaged files*

With your files now committed to the local repository, it's now time to push it to a remote repository.

It's always good to work with a remote repository, even if you are working on your own for a project. The main reason for this is that if something happens to your computer, you have a constant backup of not just your project, but all of your previous commits and changes.

The remote repository of choice for this book is GitHub. It is, without a doubt, one of the most popular repository services available today, offering free (but public) project source-code hosting space for hundreds and thousands of open source development projects.

First, head over to github.com and sign up for a free account and public repository called ci. Follow the instructions to set up your Git SSH keys for your local machine.

> Mac: http://help.github.com/mac-set-up-git/

> Windows: http://help.github.com/win-set-up-git/

> Linux: http://help.github.com/linux-set-up-git/

After you have set up the SSH keys and successfully tested them by attempting to log into github.com through terminal, go back to your project page on github.com. You should see something similar to Figure 9-8.

```
Global setup:
Set up git
   git config --global user.name "Gavin Williams"
   git config --global user.email gavin@fishrod.co.uk

Next steps:
   mkdir ci
   cd ci
   git init
   touch README
   git add README
   git commit -m 'first commit'
   git remote add origin git@github.com:gavinwilliams-fishrod/ci.git
   git push -u origin master

Existing Git Repo?
   cd existing_git_repo
   git remote add origin git@github.com:gavinwilliams-fishrod/ci.git
   git push -u origin master

Importing a Subversion Repo?
   Check out the guide for step by step instructions.

When you're done:
   Continue
```

Figure 9-8. *Default GitHub project page*

Instead of using the command line to push your project to GitHub, you can use Aptana Studio's built-in Git client. To do this, copy the project's GitHub remote URI. The address will look similar to git@github.com:gavinwilliams-fishrod/ci.git. It's the URI second from the bottom of the Next Steps section.

In Aptana Studio, go to **Commands ➤ More ➤ Add Remote…** as shown in Figure 9-9.

Figure 9-9. *Adding a remote repository*

A new dialog box will appear, as shown in Figure 9-10. Paste the GitHub remote URI into the Remote URI box and press the **OK** button.

Figure 9-10. *Add Git Remote dialog box*

Although Aptana Studio won't be very vocal about what it has just done, it has just added a remote repository to your project under the alias of origin. When you now open the **Commands** menu, there are a few new active items such as **Push** and **Pull**, as shown in Figure 9-11.

Figure 9-11. *New active remote commands*

Unfortunately, the Git client in Aptana Studio will not automatically push to the new remote repository. In order to get around this, you will need to make your first push through the Project Explorer. Go to **Window ➤ Show View ➤ Project Explorer**. Right click on the ci project in the Project Explorer and go to **Team ➤ Push to Remote ➤ Origin**. Your project should now be on GitHub and you can now use the **Push** and **Pull** commands from the **Commands** menu. It's important to commit as much as you can and push your changes at the end of your project's working day.

Head over to your project on github.com and you should see that your project has been pushed up to GitHub.

There's a lot you can do with Git and GitHub, so much so that there are many of articles and books about how to really take advantage of the system. You can find out more at http://help.github.com/.

Now that you understand the basics of working with GitHub, it's time to get to grips with Capistrano, the growing deployment platform of choice for web applications.

Getting to Grips with Capistrano

Capistrano is a deployment platform that helps to remove some of the repetitive deployment tasks. For a small mobile web application, Capistrano can be seen as using a sledgehammer to put a nail in a piece of wood. As your application grows and you eventually have more environments and details to configure within your application, Capistrano suddenly feels like a breath of fresh air.

In this section, you will focus on simply deploying your application to a production environment using Capistrano.

The preferred hosting provider for this book is theserve.com and the preferred server OS is CentOS 5; however, you're free to use any host of your choice that provides SSH access.

You should have Ruby installed after following the setup guide in Chapter 1. Capistrano is a Ruby gem. To install it, go to **Commands ➤ Open Terminal** from the App Explorer. A terminal window should open to the right of the window. Enter the following command to install Capistrano, Capistrano Rsync With Remote Cache, and Capistrano Multistage:

> Windows: `gem install capistrano`
> `capistrano_rsync_with_remote_cache capistrano-ext`

> Mac/Linux: `sudo gem install capistrano`
> `capistrano_rsync_with_remote_cache capistrano-ext`

After Capistrano and all of the required gems have been installed, you can now capify your project. Go back to the App Explorer and ensure that no items are selected/highlighted and then go to **Commands ➤ Open Terminal**. A terminal window will open, as shown in Figure 9-12.

Figure 9-12. *Terminal window*

This will ensure that any commands run will be run in the root of your project. To verify this, make sure that `ci` is shown somewhere in the command line, as shown in Figure 9-12.

In order to use Capistrano, you will need to create a set of configuration files. Capistrano can do this for you automatically through a command-line tool called `capify`. To capify your project, go to your terminal and run the command `capify`. You will see output similar to Figure 9-13.

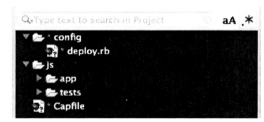

ci
FRMBPRO20100001:ci apress$ capify .
[add] making directory './config'
[add] writing './config/deploy.rb'
[add] writing './Capfile'
[done] capified!
FRMBPRO20100001:ci apress$

Figure 9-13. *Capify output*

As you can see, several files and folders have been created in your project. Refresh the App Explorer by clicking on it and pressing F5 on your keyboard to view the changes. The new files are shown in Figure 9-14.

Type text to search in Project
aA
config
deploy.rb
js
app
tests
Capfile

Figure 9-14. *New Capistrano files*

Before configuring capistrano, you should configure your production server so that you can deploy your capistrano project to it using a passwordless login. As part of this, you will need to use the public rsa key that you generated while setting up Git. This allows capistrano to run with no intervention. Copy the `id_rsa.pub` files contents to your clipboard, and log into your new production server using your server's SSH username and password. The command, shown in Figure 9-15, run from Aptana's terminal or Terminal on Mac OSX should facilitate this.

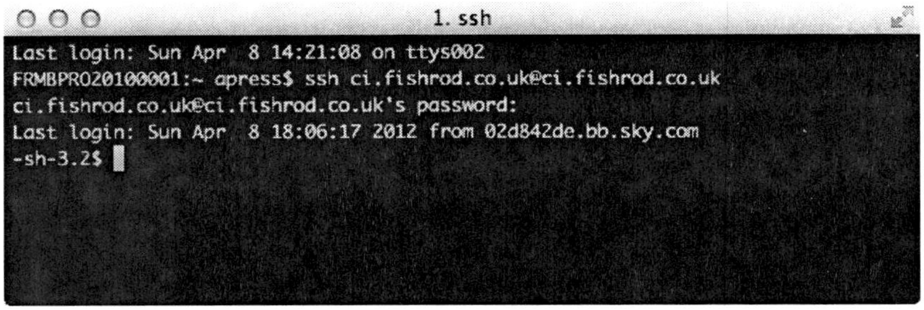

Figure 9-15. *Log into remote server using Terminal.app on a Mac*

If you are running Windows, you can use the PuTTy application (www.chiark.greenend.org.uk/~sgtatham/putty/) to log into your remote server.

You will need to change to the current user's home directory using the command cd ~/, as shown in Figure 9-16.

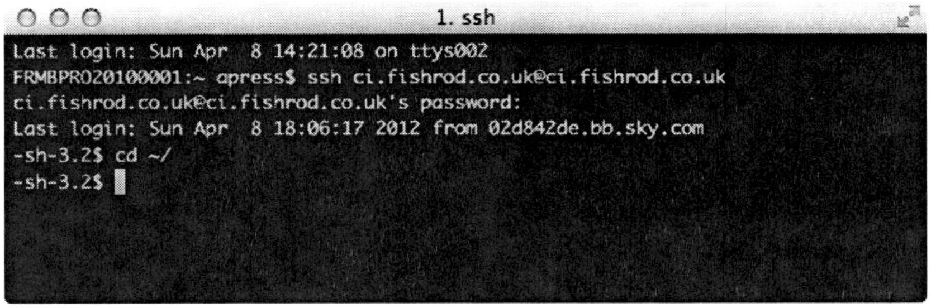

Figure 9-16. *Changing to the home directory*

There should be a folder called .ssh. You can check to see whether the folder exists by running the command ls. Go into that directory by using the command cd .ssh. If the folder doesn't exist, you will need to create the directory using the command mkdir .ssh, and then go into the directory by using cd .ssh, as shown in Figure 9-17.

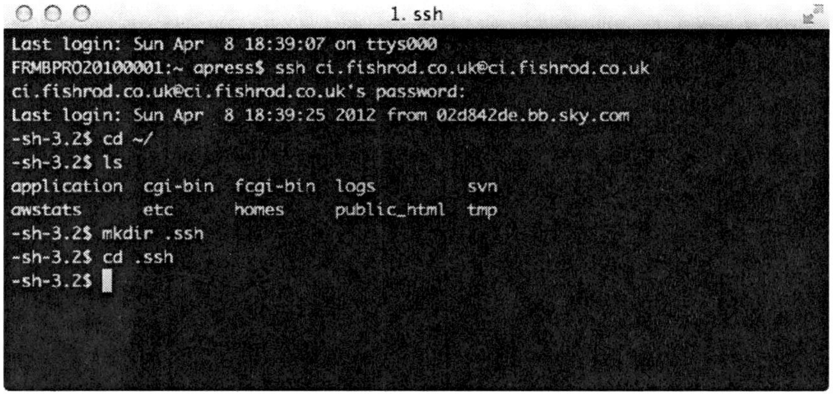

Figure 9-17. *Checking and creating the .ssh directory*

After you are in the directory, you will need to create a new file called authorized_keys if one doesn't already exist. Use the ls command to check whether the file already exists.

To create the authorized_keys file, if it does not exist, simply run the command touch authorized_keys. This will create an empty file, as shown in Figure 9-18.

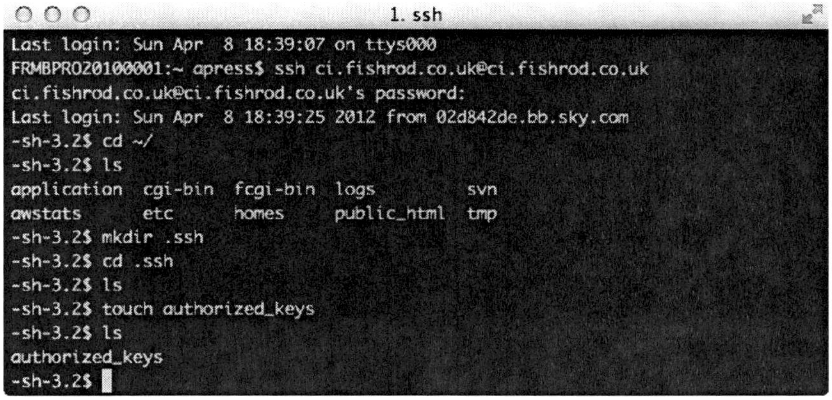

Figure 9-18. *Checking for and creating the authorized_keys file*

You will then need to add your computer's public key to the authorized_keys file. Edit the file using vi authorized_keys. If there is already content within the authorized_keys file, you will need to use the arrow key to go down to the bottom of it, and then hold down Shift + I (insert). Once at the bottom, paste the public key into the file, as shown in Figure 9-19.

Figure 9-19. *Adding the public key*

You now need to save the file. Press the Esc key on your keyboard and then hold down Shift + :. Then type wq (write quit), and press the Enter key on your keyboard. You should see something similar to what is shown in Figure 9-20.

Figure 9-20. *Writing a file in vi*

Finally, you will need to set the appropriate permissions for the new files. Move back to the home directory by using the command cd ../. The .ssh folder requires owner read/write/execute permissions. To do this, run the command chmod 0700 ./.ssh.

Next, the authorized_keys file requires owner read/write permissions. To do this, run the command chmod 0600 ./ssh/authorized_keys, as shown in Figure 9-21.

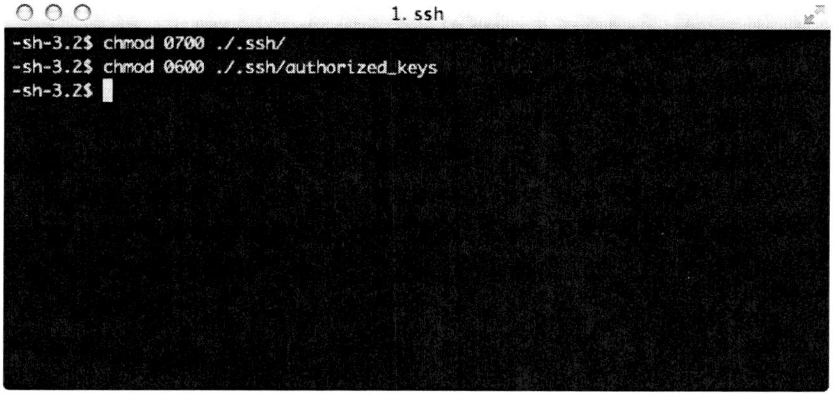

Figure 9-21. *Setting permissions on the .ssh folder*

Log out of your remote server by executing the exit command in the command line. You should now be able to log back in without a password, as shown in Figure 9-22.

Figure 9-22. *SSH without a password*

With passwordless SSH set up, it's now time to configure Capistrano to deploy to the production server.

Back in Aptana Studio, double-click on the new deploy.rb file in the config folder. This contains the deployment configurations for your project. It's written in Ruby, but you don't necessarily have to know much about Ruby in order to understand and configure it.

The default deploy.rb file has been set up specifically for Ruby projects, which isn't quite what you want to use. First, delete the contents of the file. The new first line in the deploy.rb file will be the application name. This can be configured using the following line of Ruby:

```
set :application, "continuousintegration" # The application name
```

This has no real functional use for now, but you can use this variable within your configuration tasks and options.

Next, you will need to include the multistaging and Capistrano-offroad gems using the following Ruby code:

```
require 'capistrano/ext/multistage'
require 'capistrano-offroad'
```

This will include the appropriate code to allow you to deploy and control multiple environments from a single command line. As well as providing a standard web-friendly deployment configuration, Capistrano-offroad allows you to use Capistrano outside of a Ruby project.

Next you will need to configure Capistrano multistage with the following lines of code:

```
set :stages, %w(production)
set :default_stage, "production"
```

The stages line dictates which environments you would like to deploy to. You can have as many environments as you want, as long as they are separated by spaces as shown next:

```
set :stages, %w(production staging development testing preprod)
```

The name of the stage environment should be used as the configuration file name, as shown a little bit further into this chapter, and you can name the environment anything you want as long as it only contains alpha characters and no spaces or special characters. The default_stage variable sets what the default stage environment will be, should you exclude the stage name from the cap command.

Next, you specify which offroad modules to use for the deployment. The offroad defaults module will override a lot of the default Capistrano hooks, such as creating shared file/folder definitions that capistrano will share between revisions instead of overwriting. This is usually handy for logs, configuration options, and user data. You can reimplement these hooks if needed, but for an application with no server side code, it doesn't make sense to include this.

```
offroad_modules 'defaults'
```

Now you have to configure Git. Capistrano will check out the latest specified branch from Git/GitHub so that it can be uploaded. The :repository variable is the project's GitHub URI that will be used to check out the latest code from GitHub.

```
set :repository,  "git@github.com:gavinwilliams-fishrod/ci.git" # The git repo URI
set :scm,         :git # Tells capistrano to use GIT
set :branch,      "master"  # Tells capistrano which branch to use
```

The `:scm` variable simply tells Capistrano that Git will be used as the SCM system.

You can specify which branch to use by amending the `:branch` configuration option. For instance, to use a branch named special, use the following setting:

```
set :branch,     "special" # Tells capistrano which branch to use
```

The next variable will tell Capistrano how to deploy the application. In this instance, `rsync_with_remote_cache` will be used. This will clone the Git repository and then deploy it to the production server using rsync. This can be handy if your server's firewall blocks incoming Git traffic.

```
set :deploy_via,  :rsync_with_remote_cache # Tells capistrano to deploy via rsync
```

Rsync is an application that will compare folders and synchronize them. You can also use rsync on remote folders on remote servers.

`rsync_with_remote_cache`, at the time of writing, has a bug that prevents you from synching from folders with spaces. To get around this, you need to specify an alternative temporary file location using the following configuration variable:

```
set :local_cache, '/tmp/ci/' # The directory where you want to store the rsync cache
```

Finally, the following Capistrano configuration options take variables from other configuration options:

```
role(:web) { domain }   # Your HTTP server, Apache/etc
role(:app)  { domain }  # This may be the same as your `Web` server
role(:db) { domain }    # This is where Rails migrations will run

set  :keep_releases,  5 # Tells capistrano how many releases to keep
```

Just to give you an overview, the complete configuration file should look something like the following:

```
set :application, "continuousintegration" # The application name

require 'capistrano/ext/multistage'
require 'capistrano-offroad'

set :stages, %w(production)
set :default_stage, "production"

offroad_modules 'defaults'

set :repository,  "git@github.com:gavinwilliams-fishrod/ci.git" # The location of the
git repo, this is the read-only url
set :scm,         :git # Tells capistrano to use GIT
set :branch,      "master"  # Tells capistrano which branch to use
set :deploy_via,  :rsync_with_remote_cache # Tells capistrano to deploy via rsync
```

```
# Or: `accurev`, `bzr`, `cvs`, `darcs`, `subversion`, `mercurial`, `perforce`,
`subversion` or `none`

set :local_cache, '/tmp/ci/' # Set this to a directory where you would like to store the
rsync cache

role(:web) { domain }    # Your HTTP server, Apache/etc
role(:app) { domain }    # This may be the same as your `Web` server
role(:db) { domain }     # This is where Rails migrations will run

set  :keep_releases,  5 # Tells capistrano how many releases to keep
```

As mentioned before, the Capistrano multistage gem is used to allow you to control and deploy to multiple environments from the command line. This configuration file is only set up for production. In Aptana Studio, go to the App Explorer and create a new folder called deploy within the config folder. Inside the deploy folder, create a new file called production.rb, as shown in Figure 9-23.

Figure 9-23. *Production stage configuration file*

Open the production.rb file in Aptana Studio and add the following configuration options:

```
set :domain,      "ci.fishrod.co.uk" # The domain name of the application
```

The previous line of code sets the domain name for the application, which will be used to log into the server.

```
set :deploy_to,   "~/application/" # The path to deploy the application
```

:deploy_to sets the path on the remote server where the application should be deployed to. As the web path for the SSH user in this instance lies in the users home directory, ~ is used. If your web path is somewhere else, you should use that path. For example, on most blank servers, it will exist under /var/www/application/. First, you will need to create the application folder on your server.

```
set :user,        "ci.fishrod.co.uk" # The SSH user for your website
set :deploy_group, "ci.fishrod.co.uk"
set :use_sudo,     false # Tells capistrano not to run commands as root
```

`:user` will set the user used to log into your remote server. `:deploy_group` will set which group Capistrano will set permissions for any uploaded files to. `:use_sudo` will stop Capistrano from uploading and changing files as a root user.

With Capistrano fully configured, it's now time to set up your production server for deployments.

In order to do this, log into your remote server again, and then go to the folder just above your web server's document root folder. For example, your root might be `/var/www/html`, so you should go to your `/var/www` directory. If you're on a shared host, you should go to `~/`, which will be your home directory.

Create a new directory called `application` in that directory, and remove your document root folder, as shown in Figure 9-24. Your document root folder may be called `htdocs`, `html`, or `public_html`; it will be referred to as `public_html` throughout this chapter.

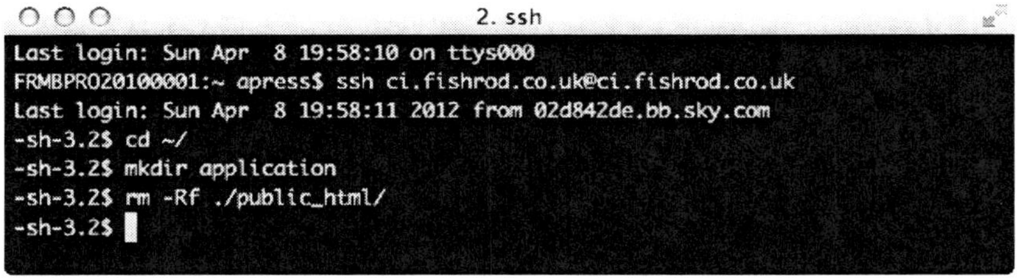

Figure 9-24. *Creating the application directory and deleting the document root directory*

You before finalizing the Capistrano configuration, you need to set up the Capistrano folders on the remote server. To do this, return to Aptana Studio and open the terminal view. Run the following command:

```
cap production deploy:setup
```

This will log in to your remote server and create the appropriate files and folders for you. You should see something similar to the output in Figure 9-25.

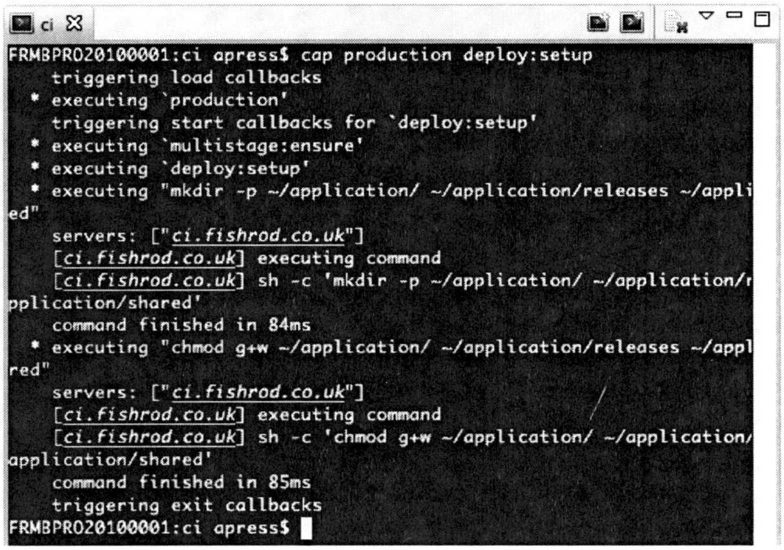

Figure 9-25. *Capistrano deploy:setup output*

Now you can deploy your application. Running the following command will do so:

```
cap production deploy
```

If all goes well, you will see a final output similar to that shown in Figure 9-26.

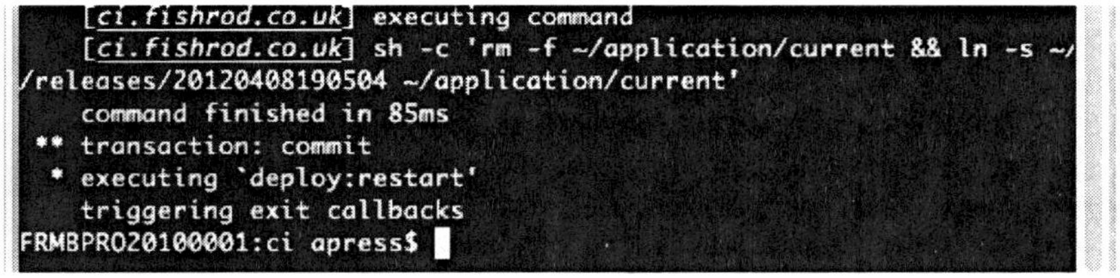

Figure 9-26. *Final Capistrano deploy output*

The final thing to do is to create a symbolic link between the web root directory and the current release. This allows you to keep revisions of your code on your server, and for Capistrano to roll back if anything fails during deployment.

To do this, return to the terminal window connected to your server (the one used to create the application folder and delete the `public_html` folder) and run the following command:

```
ln -s application/current/ public_html
```

Verify that the symbolic link has been created by running the command `ls`, as shown in Figure 9-27.

```
○ ○ ○                         2. ssh                          ⬚
Last login: Sun Apr  8 19:58:10 on ttys000
FRMBPRO20100001:~ apress$ ssh ci.fishrod.co.uk@ci.fishrod.co.uk
Last login: Sun Apr  8 19:58:11 2012 from 02d842de.bb.sky.com
-sh-3.2$ cd ~/
-sh-3.2$ mkdir application
-sh-3.2$ rm -Rf ./public_html/
-sh-3.2$ ln -s application/current/ public_html
-sh-3.2$ ls
application  cgi-bin  fcgi-bin  logs         svn
awstats      etc      homes     public_html  tmp
-sh-3.2$ █
```

Figure 9-27. *The new public_html symbolic link*

Now, navigate to your unit test on the remote server using the following URL, replacing *yourdomain* with your own domain, of course: `http://yourdomain/js/tests/calculator.html`.

As you can see, Capistrano can be a powerful tool. Not only can it be used to make deployments, but it can also be used to run commands on remote servers without having to log directly into them. This can be useful for recompiling SASS files or concatenating and minifying JavaScript files. What's even better about Capistrano, is that because it is run from the command line, it can be integrated into continuous integration servers such as Hudson or Bamboo.

Summary

From this chapter, you should have a basic understanding about continuous integration and how it affects how you test and deploy your application. Although this book does not cover how to implement a continuous integration server, it's a subject worth pursuing, even as a lone developer. When you have last-minute code changes, you can be confident that when you check in your code, once it reaches the production environment, it has been fully tested. You can also be confident in the fact that, due to the automation, if it successfully deployed the first time, it should deploy successfully again, and again, and again unless you have broken some element of your application. In such a case, your failed test will point out which piece of code does not work as expected.

Through this chapter alone, you should have a real foothold into how to create JavaScript unit tests using QUnit. There are other, more advanced testing products out there, such as Test Swarm (`https://github.com/jquery/testswarm`), Jasmine (`http://pivotal.github.com/jasmine/`), and Selenium (`http://seleniumhq.org` or `http://code.google.com/p/selenium/wiki/AndroidDriver`). It's important to remember that although TDD seems like a laborious task at first, it really allows you to think about your code and the way in which it is structured, which helps to produce cleaner, leaner JavaScript.

You should have a basic understanding as to how to use Git and GitHub through Aptana Studio, and the benefits that it has not just for you as a lone developer, but for others who eventually work with you.

Most important, you should now know how to set up Capistrano, a powerful deployment application that is primarily used to deploy rails applications. It is worth having a look at the Capistrano documentation to explore all of its capabilities. Find it at `https://github.com/capistrano/capistrano/wiki/`.

This book should have set you on the right path for mobile web development. Some of the topics might have seemed a bit advanced; however, I feel that it's always important to stay ahead of the curve and to challenge yourself as much as you can with development, as the industry moves so fast. Hopefully, some of the practices and principles that you have learned through this book have gotten you excited about the mobile web. You should now have all of the knowledge you need to build reasonably advanced mobile web applications for Android.

Appendix

Listing A-1

```
var app = app || {};

app.model = app.model || {};

/**
 * A movie model used for all movies within the application
 *
 * @alias app.model.movie
 * @constructor
 * @param {String} title
 * @param {String} rtid
 * @param {String} posterframe
 * @param {String} synopsis
 */
app.model.movie = function appModelMovie(title, rtid, posterframe, synopsis) {

    /**
     * The video's instance variables
     */
    var _title,
        _rtid,
        _posterframe,
        _synopsis,
        _releaseDate,
        _videos = [],
        _actors = [],
        _rating,
        _favorite = false,
        _self = this;
```

```
/**
 * Getters and setters
 */

this.init = function(){
   /**
    * Set the instance variables using the constructor's arguments
    */
   this.setTitle(title);
   this.setRtid(rtid);
   this.setPosterframe(posterframe);
   this.setSynopsis(synopsis);
}

/**
 * Returns the movie title
 * @return {String}
 */
this.getTitle = function(){
   return _title;
}

/**
 * Sets the movie title
 * @param {String} title
 */
this.setTitle = function(title){
   _title = title;
}

/**
 * Returns the Rotten Tomatoes reference ID
 * @return {String}
 */
this.getRtid = function(){
   return _rtid;
}

/**
 * Sets the Rotten Tomatoes reference ID
 * @param {String} rtid
 */
this.setRtid = function(rtid){
   _rtid = rtid;
}

/**
 * Gets the posterframe URL/Path
 * @return {String}
 */
```

```
this.getPosterframe = function(){
   return _posterframe;
}

/**
 * Sets the posterframe URN/Path
 * @param {String} posterframe
 */
this.setPosterframe = function(posterframe){
   _posterframe = posterframe;
}

/**
 * Gets the synopsis as a string with no HTML formatting
 * @return {String}
 */
this.getSynopsis = function(){
   return _synopsis;
}

/**
 * Sets the synopsis, a string with no HTML must be passed
 * @param {String} synopsis
 */
this.setSynopsis = function(synopsis){
   _synopsis = synopsis;
}

/**
 * Gets all videos associated with the movie
 * @return {Array}
 */
this.getVideos = function(){
   return _videos;
}

/**
 * Sets all videos associated with the movie
 * @param {Array}
 */
this.setVideos = function(videos){

   _videos.length = 0;

   /**
    * Rather than setting the videos all in one go,
    * you use the addVideo method, which can handle
    * any validation for each video before it's
    * added to the object
    */
```

```
      for(var i = 0; i < videos.length; i++){
         _self.addVideo(videos[i]);
      }
   }

   /**
    * Adds a video to the movie
    * @param {app.model.video} video
    */
   this.addVideo = function(video){
      /**
       * You can add any video validation here
       * before it's added to the movie
       */
      _videos.push(video);
   }

   /**
    * Gets all actors associated with the movie
    * @return {Array}
    */
   this.getActors = function(){
      return _actors;
   }

   /**
    * Gets an actor at a specific index
    * @param {Integer} index
    * @return {app.model.actor}
    */
   this.getActor = function(index){
      return _actors[index];
   }

   /**
    * Sets all actors associated with the movie
    * @param {Array}
    */
   this.setActors = function(actors){

      _actors.length = 0;

      /**
       * Rather than setting the actors all in one go,
       * you use the addActor method, which can handle
       * any validation for each actor before it's
       * added to the object
       */
      for(var i = 0; i < actors.length; i++){
         _self.addActor(actors[i]);
```

```
    }
}

/**
 * Adds an actor to the movie
 * @param {app.model.actor} actor
 */
this.addActor = function(actor){
    /**
      * You can add any actor validation here
      * before it's added to the movie
      */
    _actors.push(actor);
}

/**
 * Sets the release date
 */
this.setReleaseDate = function(releaseDate){
    _releaseDate = releaseDate;
}

/**
 * Gets the release date
 * @return {app.type.releaseDate}
 */
this.getReleaseDate = function(){
    return _releaseDate;
}

/**
 * Gets the movie rating
 * @return {String}
 */
this.getRating = function(){
    return _rating;
}

/**
 * Sets the movie rating
 * @param {String} rating
 */
this.setRating = function(rating){
    _rating = rating;
}

/**
 * Checks to see whether the movie
 * is in the user's favorites list
 * @return {Bool}
```

```
  */
 this.isFavorite = function(){
    return _favorite;
 }

 /**
  * Sets whether the movie is in the
  * user's favorites list
  * @param {Bool} value
  */
 this.setFavorite = function(value){
    _favorite = value;
 }

 this.init();

}
```

Listing A-2

```css
.footer {
   height: 40px;
   width: 100%;
   text-align: center;
   position: absolute;
   bottom: 0;

   .back {
      height: 100%;
      display: block;
      background: url('../img/back.png') no-repeat 10px 50%;
      text-indent: -10000px;
   }

}
```

Your final SASS file should look like the following code.

```css
body, html, #shoe, .deck {
   height: 100%;
   width: 100%;
   overflow: hidden;
   margin: 0px;
}

/**
 * Individual Card Styles
 */
```

```
#card-movie_search_results {
  z-index: 50;
}

/**
 * Deck styles
 */


.deck {

   position: relative;

   .card {
      height: 100%;
      width: 100%;
      left: -100%;
      position: absolute;
   }

   .card.active {
      left: 0px;
   }

}

/**
 * List styles
 */


/**
 * Standard list
 */

.list {

   margin: 0;
   padding: 0;

   li {

      padding: 10px;
      overflow: hidden;
      height: 82px;
      display: block;
      border-bottom: 1px solid #CCCCCC;

      .preview-image {
         float: left;
```

```
            width: 60px;
            height: 82px;
            text-align: center;
            margin-right: 10px;
        }

    }

}

/**
 * Movie list
 */

.movie-list {

    li {

        background: #A5CCEB;
        border-bottom-color: #FFFFFF;

        .more {

            display: block;
            height: 100%;
            overflow: hidden;
            text-decoration: none;

            h2 {
                margin: 0 0 10px;
                color: #BF2628;
            }

            p {
                margin: 0;
                color: #000000;
            }

        }

    }

    li:nth-child(odd) {
        background: #97B2D9;
    }

}

/**
```

```scss
 * Header taskbar styles
 */

.screenbar {
    @include gradient(#7D9DCE, #ABC1E1, 90deg);
}

header#taskbar {
    color: #FFFFFF;
    overflow: hidden;
    padding: 10px;
    border-bottom: 1px solid #BF2628;

    h1.branding {
        margin: 0px;
        float: left;
        width: 73px;
        height: 32px;
        text-indent: -10000px;
        overflow: hidden;
        background: url('../img/lowres/momemo.png') no-repeat top left;
    }

    .clear-search {
        float: right;
        width: 35px;
        height: 35px;
        display: none;
        overflow: hidden;
        text-indent: -10000px;
        background: url('../img/clear.png') 50% 50% no-repeat;
    }

}

header#taskbar.searchactive {

    .clear-search {
        display: block;
    }

    form#add-movie {
        margin-right: 40px;
    }

}

/**
 * Movie view
 */
```

```scss
/**
 * Animations for the poster header
 */
@keyframes posteranimation {
    0% { top: 0%; }
    100% { top: -80%; }
}

@-moz-keyframes posteranimation {
    0% { top: 0%; }
    100% { top: -80%; }
}

@-webkit-keyframes posteranimation {
    0% { top: 0%; }
    100% { top: -80%; }
}


.movie-header {

    position: relative;
    overflow: hidden;
    height: 20%;

    .poster {
        position: absolute;
        top: 0%;
        @include animation(posteranimation 10s ease 0 infinite alternate);
    }

    .movie-title {
        position: absolute;
        bottom: 0px;
        background: rgba(255, 255, 255, 0.75);
        padding: 5px;
        bottom: 0;
        left: 0;
        width: 100%;
        @include box-sizing(border-box);

        .btn-favorite {
            float: right;
            padding: 10px;
            color: #FFFFFF;
            background: #7D9DCE;
            font-weight: bold;
```

```scss
            border-radius: 5px;
            text-decoration: none;
            border: 1px solid #A5CCEB;
        }

        .movie-release-date {
            text-transform: uppercase;
            font-weight: bold;
        }


    }

}

.movie-content {
    height: 80%;
    width: 100%;
    padding-bottom: 40px;
    @include box-sizing(border-box);

    .block-container {

        width: 280%;
        height: 100%;

        .block {
            width: 33%;
            float: left;
            height: 100%;

            font-size: 1.3em;
            line-height: 2em;

            .content {
                @include box-sizing(border-box);
            }

            h3 {
                padding: 10px 10px 0 10px;
            }

            .content {
                padding: 10px;
            }

        }

    }
```

```
}

.footer {
    height: 40px;
    width: 100%;
    text-align: center;
    position: absolute;
    bottom: 0;

    .back {
        height: 100%;
        display: block;
        background: url('../img/back.png') no-repeat 10px 50%;
        text-indent: -10000px;
    }

}
```

Index

CPSIA information can be obtained at www.ICGtesting.com
Printed in the USA
LVOW110743101112

306747LV00005B/11/P